Praise for Bob Delaney and COVERT

"Delaney [is] a man of unquestionable integrity who once logged countless hours as an undercover trooper with the New Jersey State Police task force on organized crime. Delaney lived to tell his tale—and now write it, too—so while his anonymity will soon perish, that, for once, is a very good thing."

—ESPN

"A slam dunk, a bull's eye, and any other glowing mafia or basketball metaphor you can think of."

—*Kirkus*

"Like a character out of a Martin Scorsese movie. . . . An amazing story [by] a very good storyteller."

—Harry Smith, *The Early Show*

"[F]ascinating . . . a must-read. . . . Delaney captures perfectly the daily routine and perils of undercover work."

—*Publishers Weekly* (starred review)

"As an undercover operative in Project Alpha, Bob Delaney infiltrated organized crime rings in New Jersey, ultimately leading to the conviction of more than thirty Mafia criminals. Delaney's heroic performance during his perilous assignment represents the finest traditions of the New Jersey State Police. My father, the first superintendent of the New Jersey State Police Department, would have been proud of him."

—General H. Norman Schwarzkopf, U.S. Army (ret.)

"A great book. A fascinating read."

—Jim Rome, host of *The Jim Rome Show*

"NBA referee Bob Delaney and writer Dave Scheiber tell a riveting and unforgettable tale in *Covert: My Years Infiltrating the Mob*. This is a surprising and important story, rich in detail and beautifully told. Bob Delaney has lived a fascinating life, and this book captures it vividly."

—Christine Brennan, *USA Today* columnist, and author of *Best Seat in the House: A Father, a Daughter, a Journey Through Sports*

"*Covert* is a riveting, true-life story—a fascinating look into the sensual, seductive, and violent world of organized crime as seen through the eyes of a singularly brave and bright cop."

—Robert Leuci, the real-life Prince of the City and author of *All the Centurions*

"There have been other books about the world of the undercover operative, but none as beautifully written and intense as *Covert*. Delaney and Scheiber capture the emotion, adrenaline, and split-second decision-making that make the difference between life and death. Their account is raw, honest, and uncompromising, a must-read for anyone who wants to know what it's really like to live on the dark side. Delaney is a true American hero."

—John Haynes, retired detective Los Angeles County Sheriff's Department, and former writer/co-producer on *CSI: Miami*

"It sounds like a clone of *Donnie Brasco*, but this book is much more. . . . Delaney's street-smart, gutsy adventure is a quick, absorbing read."

—*The Tampa Tribune*

"Delaney and Scheiber mesmerize with this intriguing tale of life inside the Mob. Despite the rollercoaster of emotions and self-doubt, Delaney's moral courage and gutsy fortitude triumph. This book should be required reading for any decision-maker who desires to understand the risk and reward of uncompromising commitment."

—Jim Evans, Major League Baseball umpire, 1971-1999

"[A] brisk tale . . . of a fascinating life."

—Entertainment Weekly

"If you think Tony Soprano's fictional Jersey is chilling, come to the Jersey waterfront of Bobby Covert where a wrong word to the wrong guy can buy you a real bullet in your real brain. What Bob Delaney does here is show the value of a man's courage, what it cost him, and how it enriches all of us."

—Dave Kindred, *Sporting News* columnist and author of *Sound and Fury: Two Powerful Lives, One Fateful Friendship*

"At this time when a dark cloud hangs over professional sports, what a joy to read this story of courage and integrity. One of America's best sportswriters, Dave Scheiber, brings to life the incredible experience of Bob Delaney, a respected NBA referee, who spent years as an undercover State Police agent infiltrating the Mob. Not since baseball catcher Moe Berg became an American spy against the Nazis have we seen a story like this one. Read it—or be called for a two-shot foul."

—Roy Peter Clark, senior scholar at the Poynter Institute, and author of Writing *Tools: 50 Essential Strategies for Every Writer*

"Gripping . . . Fans of such undercover-themed books as *Donnie Brasco*, or organized-crime exposés like *The Valachi Papers*, will devour this one."

—Booklist

"From the mean streets to the hardwood, one undercover cop turned in his badge for a career as a different kind of enforcer. Bob Delaney has spent two careers as a whistleblower. Years before the referee ever stepped on an NBA court, he walked in these footsteps as an undercover New Jersey State Trooper, infiltrating the mob."

—CNN

"The only acting I ever see in the NBA is when players flop. But Bob Delaney isn't a player, he's a ref. And refs don't flop. So how was I to know that Bob was such a good actor? I learned it in *Covert*. Anything short of a convincing performance would have gotten him killed—which, frankly, is why I prefer show business. What other secrets are you keeping from me, Bob? It is Bob, isn't it? His years inside the Mob make for a riveting story, filled with incredible tension, surprising humor—and some great whistle blowing."

—Penny Marshall, Hollywood producer, director, actress, and NBA fan

"Bob Delaney is a quiet guy who looks at players on the court and says, 'Please, don't give me the prison stare. You're wasting your time, I've seen a lot worse.' In *Covert*, we get to know this man who as a cop worked undercover putting some very bad people away—people who without question would have put a bullet in his head if they knew who he really was. He doesn't flaunt it, but Delaney has a quiet power about him. He's a throwback to the kind of man men used to be."

—Bernard Goldberg, *HBO Real Sports* correspondent and author of *Bias*

"Here is a thriller, mystery, and sports lovers inside look at the life of an NBA official. Dave Scheiber's deft writing makes this a page turner. This book will change the way you see people at the heart of the game."

—Juan Williams, Senior Correspondent, NPR and FOX News

"Bob Delaney is one fine NBA referee. His successful 'street smart' approach to officiating relies heavily on the skills, techniques, and savvy approach he developed as an undercover agent bringing mobsters to justice. A thrilling read."

—Barry Mano, President, National Association of Sports Officials

"Bob Delaney takes you on a trip into the dark underworld of the New Jersey Mob. You will be with him every step of the way as he gets so deep into this heart of darkness that you fear he'll never make it out alive. That Bob now 'hides in plain sight' on national TV makes the whole wild ride even more incredible."

—Andy Hill, former President of CBS Productions, and co-author with legendary UCLA coach John Wooden of *Be Quick—But Don't Hurry!*

"It's a gripping tale. And the insight the book gives into the Mafia—and those who fight it—is like a real-life 'Sopranos' series that was way ahead of its time."

—*Dallas Morning News*

"Your testimony highlighted the importance and crucial aspects of the need for undercover procedures in investigations of the organized criminal element. You are to be commended for the innovative and thorough work you achieved while serving in an undercover capacity during Project Alpha."

—Senator Sam Nunn in a 1981 letter to Bob Delaney following his testimony before the Senate Subcommittee on Investigations into Organized Crime

"Bob chooses professions that require nerves of steel, and fortunately, that's what he's blessed with. When you've got to make calls that anger giant men on an adrenaline rush, you better make sure they respect you—and, with Bob, they do. In fact, we all do. Bob has raised the bar and has become the standard by which all other referees should be judged."

—Nick Bollettieri, professional tennis coach

"Bobby is one of the upper-echelon guys in the league, no doubt about it. He's a very passionate individual who gives 110% and always strives to be the best in any endeavor he undertakes. His desire and pursuit of excellence has made him one of the best at his craft. He has a special sense of pride and a great work ethic, which combined with his energy and enthusiasm are key factors in his success. He's highly respected and people are confident when he's blowing the whistle."

—Dick Vitale, ESPN college basketball analyst

Dan —
great working
with you —

COVERT: *all the Best*

My Years Infiltrating the Mob

Stay Safe!

By Bob Delaney, NBA Referee,
with Dave Scheiber

Foreword by Bill Walton

Bob Delaney

UNION SQUARE PRESS
New York

UNION SQUARE PRESS
New York

An Imprint of Sterling Publishing
387 Park Avenue South
New York, NY 10016

STERLING and the distinctive Sterling logo are registered trademarks
of Sterling Publishing Co., Inc.

© 2008 by Bob Delaney

ISBN 978-1-4027-6714-2

Library of Congress Cataloging-in-Publication Data

Delaney, Bob, 1951-
  Covert : my years infiltrating the Mob/ Bob Delaney, with Dave Scheiber ; foreword by
Bill Walton.
    p. cm.
  Includes index.
  ISBN-13: 978-1-4027-5443-2
  1. Organized crime investigation--New Jersey--Case studies. 2. Undercover operations--
New Jersey--Case studies. 3. Mafia--New Jersey--Case studies. 4. Delaney, Bob, 1951- I.
Scheiber, Dave. II. Title.
  HV8079.O73D45 2008
  364.1'06092--dc22
  [B]
                                    2007042585

Distributed in Canada by Sterling Publishing
c/o Canadian Manda Group, 165 Dufferin Street
Toronto, Ontario, Canada M6K 3H6
Distributed in the United Kingdom by GMC Distribution Services
Castle Place, 166 High Street, Lewes, East Sussex, England BN7 1XU
Distributed in Australia by Capricorn Link (Australia) Pty. Ltd.
P.O. Box 704, Windsor, NSW 2756, Australia

For information about custom editions, special sales, and premium and corporate purchases,
please contact Sterling Special Sales at 800-805-5489 or specialsales@sterlingpublishing.com.

Manufactured in the United States of America

10 9 8 7 6 5 4 3

www.sterlingpublishing.com

CONTENTS

DEDICATIONS

To my wife, Billie—your love, kindness, and support make life light, fun, and so good—any bumps along the way are easier because of you.

To my mom and dad—having my role models sitting across the dining room table is a gift from God. Thank you for teaching by example and loving with all your heart.

To my daughter, Shannon—the day you were born was the beginning of a new chapter in my life, one that has been filled with happiness and pride. You are my hero. I love you.

To my sister, Kath—my biggest fan—thanks for always being my friend.

To my four stepchildren, Danelle, Carter, Chase, and Summer—God put us together for a reason, and I am a better person because He did.

To my grandchildren, Austin, Landon, Michael, and Karli—love, laugh, and learn. That is what you do for me!

—BD

To my wonderful wife, Janie, for all her loving support, humor, and steadiness through the years; our sensational kids, Valerie, Laura, Mollie, Julia, Emma, and Davey, who are a constant source of joy and pride; and my parents, Barbara and Walter—always there to encourage and help, not to mention the best backup readers a writer could ever want.

—DS

Introduction to the Paperback Edition

There are moments in life that grab you by the collar. They make you stop and reflect on the road you've been so busy traveling—and shine a new light on the path that lies ahead. We've all experienced the feeling of a sudden revelation that disrupts our daily routines and gives us a new level of understanding. For me, such an instance occurred on June 7, 2008, when I clicked on one of the countless e-mails that hit my inbox every day.

It had been almost four months since the publication of *Covert: My Years Infiltrating the Mob*, a book about my life as an undercover New Jersey State Trooper. The ride in the days and weeks after the book launched was amazing and gratifying—a blur of national TV and radio interviews and a whirlwind book tour.

Sharing my story has always been personal therapy. Yet writing about Project Alpha, the landmark undercover mission that placed me in the midst of the Genovese and Bruno Crime Families, took it to another level. I wore a wire for three years in the ground-breaking State Police-FBI investigation. We arrested more than thirty members of organized crime and learned volumes about the inner workings of the Mob, laying the groundwork for large-scale operations that followed.

None of it would have been possible without the help of Patrick John Kelly, the Bruno consigliere-turned-Mob informant who opened so many doors for us with the wiseguys. Because of his unique mix of street smarts and people skills, Project Alpha realized the success it did. Pat died while in the Witness Protection Program and I'll always regret that he never had the chance to read this book.

Following the publication of *Covert*, I heard on almost a daily basis from people I'd known throughout my life—old friends from the close-knit Italian-Irish neighborhood in Paterson, New Jersey, my co-workers from the world of law enforcement, and colleagues past and present from the National Basketball Association, where I have been a referee since 1987. But one e-mail in particular—from a name I didn't recognize—heightened my senses, fixing all of my attention on the laptop screen. "Dear Mr. Delaney," it began:

> On Friday June 6th, 2008, my prayers were answered. It had nothing to do with the fact that my cherished Boston Celtics had defeated the LA Lakers in game one of the NBA Playoffs. My prayers were answered that day when I learned of your book, *Covert*.
>
> I knew Patrick John Kelly by a different name: I knew him as Pop! I knew him as a successful businessman, an avid sports fan, a devout Catholic, a loving father, and as my amazing grandfather.
>
> I was also aware that there was a part of him I would never know. For years after his unexpected death I wondered if I would ever learn of the chapters of his life he tried so hard to keep from us. I often prayed that we would find a journal or the beginnings of a book he had been writing. I had even considered contacting you to see if perhaps you could provide closure to the curiosity that plagued me. As the years went by, I began to lose hope.
>
> The purpose of this letter is to thank you on behalf of my cousins and the future generations of my family . . .

As I hurried through the words, scrambling to piece it all together, I realized that the letter's author was one of Pat Kelly's granddaughters.

I never would have had a chance to meet a guy like Pat if I hadn't become Bobby Covert. Our sides of the track couldn't have been further apart. But once Pat and I learned to trust each other—and believe me, it wasn't easy—we became a team that handled dangerous situations in the most difficult of conditions. We worked well together, but, perhaps more importantly, I grew to really like the guy. In 1981, we went our separate ways when we were finished testifying against the wiseguys. Pat entered Witness Protection, and I became a detective who coordinated a world-renowned program known as the Institute on Organized Criminal Groups, part of the Criminal Science Unit within the New Jersey State Police Training Center.

Years later, I met him entirely by chance, and that single meeting allowed us to develop a deeper friendship and a greater understanding about everything we had experienced together during our time inside organized crime.

I thought our encounter had given me some degree of closure, but this letter from Pat's granddaughter swung that door wide open again. I was moved reading about the generation of achievers Pat had left behind: ten grandsons and eight granddaughters, including an assistant district attorney, successful real estate agents, award-winning restaurant and hotel owners, members of the United States Air Force, Army, and Navy who have served in Iraq and Afghanistan, and others working to become psychologists. One was even in training to become an FBI agent. The chain of criminal behavior that Pat could have passed on to future generations had been broken.

With these thoughts running through my head, I went back to the letter:

> I am sure that you are well aware of the lives your work saved by infiltrating the New Jersey Mafia. But I want to be sure you are aware of the lives your work helped to create . . .

I'd never heard anyone describe the essence of law enforcement in that way.

Pat and I, and other members of the Project Alpha team, worked in highly charged, perilous situations. We learned to think fast when one wrong move could have ended the operation or gotten us killed. We faced long, grueling hours on the witness stand in state and federal courts to help convict the mobsters we had investigated. We had a mission: to wipe out crime. The concept of creating something through our work had never occurred to me.

I now use that e-mail from Pat's granddaughter in every presentation I give to law enforcement groups. I read that letter aloud and say, "This is what you do. You not only save lives, but you create lives." It's a powerful statement.

I thought when I wrote *Covert* that I was literally closing the book on a chapter of my life that had happened decades ago. I was a Jersey boy who had lived his dream, learned about life in the process, and then got the chance to write it all down. My undercover life started in 1975 and to this day I grow from that experience. It teaches me essential life lessons that I have to be on the lookout for—even when they arrive out of the blue in an e-mail from a stranger.

FOREWORD

Undercover cop fighting organized crime? New Jersey state trooper? NBA referee? What is going on here? And why does Bob Delaney keep taking ever-harder jobs?

Covert, the story of Delaney's amazing life, will take you deep inside the heart, soul, and mind of one of the most intriguing, colorful, and dynamic personalities I have ever met.

You are about to read a fascinating and gripping tale of one great American's fight for truth and justice. And you will find yourself right in the middle of so much more than just a game. Delaney's story is both courageous and inspirational. It just may rekindle your faith in the human spirit and prompt you to reevaluate your own life.

His life is one that reinforces the timeless notion that integrity and credibility are still the most important and valuable virtues that any of us could ever possess. I am proud to be a small part of his tireless efforts in seeking a more humane and sensible world.

And while I would love nothing more than to be on his team, if I can't, then Bob Delaney is most certainly the one guy I know who I'd want to be the judge and jury of my next fight. Hold on, you are about to embark on one heck of a journey.

> Bill Walton
> ESPN Basketball analyst
> Basketball Hall of Fame 1993
> Academic Hall of Fame

COVERT

CHAPTER ONE

A VOICE FROM THE DARK SIDE

Sunday night, April 18, 1999. The P.A. system is thumping out rock beats and blaring the usual pre-game NBA promotional announcements at the America West Arena in Phoenix. Spectators filling the endless sections of purple seats pay little attention to the man in the light gray referee shirt and dark blue pants standing at midcourt near the gaudy Suns logo, a big painted orange basketball blazing amid streaks of yellow and amber.

He appears short and anonymous, compared to the towering million-dollar players taking their warmup shots at each end of the court. But if you saw him on the street, he would stand out with his 6-foot-1, 190-pound frame, chiseled facial features and Kirk Douglas chin dimple, slicked-back, graying hair, and light blue eyes that can instantly shift from warm and affable to smoldering and tough.

Those eyes have seen a lot as an official in the National Basketball Association by 1999, his twelfth season in the league. But nothing, not even the most intimidating glare from a Shaquille O'Neal, Michael Jordan, or Phil Jackson, can compare to what they witnessed in another time and another life. What he experienced as a young man forever changed him, nearly made him unravel in the aftermath. He lost touch with the person he had been and grappled with the same kind of post-traumatic stress a soldier faces after years of combat. But he found his way back from the darkness—virtually willed his way back with the same strength it took to survive in it—and discovered a new path in the world. He is always aware that his life is in danger, yet he refuses to be ruled by fear or to change the way he wants to live.

Many of his closest friends, even family members, wonder why he would ever take the chance of being singled out in public, let alone an arena packed with twenty thousand people before a national TV audience.

They worry that some people from that other life, no matter how long ago, will never forget . . .

From the time I was twelve, an outgoing Irish kid growing up in Paterson, New Jersey, in the most tightly knit Italian neighborhood you can imagine, I loved the feeling of stepping onto a basketball court. It was a surge I felt even on the imaginary court in my back yard after, much to my disappointment, I got cut from my seventh-grade team. My dad, who was rising up the ranks of the New Jersey State Police, put up a hoop behind our house on Maitland Avenue. He knew how down I was about not making the team, even though it was the first time I'd picked up a basketball. I became obsessed. I'd shoot baskets for hours every night, even shoveling snow off the concrete if I had to. My game improved in a hurry, and the magic of stepping onto courts kept growing stronger—as an All-State forward who scored more than a thousand points at my all-boys Catholic high school, Blessed John Neumann Prep, or during my two years at Jersey City State College in the early 1970s.

And you know what? It's no different for me as a referee. When I'm changing out of my street clothes into my NBA ref's uniform, I get this overpowering sensation of wanting to get out of the locker room and onto the floor. It's a big adrenaline rush, with the same butterflies in the gut felt by any player in any sport—a charge that tells you it's game time. Of course, I can't be like a player, running and jumping up and down and screaming so I can release that adrenaline. I have to be in control. That's what a referee is to the sporting event: control.

It's a lot like life. To be your best, to do your best, you have to stay in charge of your emotions, stay constantly alert. In my world, I've had to be able to spot trouble in a heartbeat, recognizing the people who violate the rules and disrupt the orderly flow of things. Believe me, I know what it's like to be in control—and I also know what it feels like to almost lose it.

As an NBA ref, you have to remain focused in the most grueling of circumstances, like the three miles or so I run up and down the court in a single game. Not to mention the collisions with 7-foot, 300-pound centers that, in my case, have resulted in broken elbows, torn ligaments, and enough bruises and contusions for a lifetime. You have to keep your composure, with players and coaches getting in your face over calls they don't happen to agree with, and that lovely chorus of comments coming at you from the fans. You hear just about everything and, truthfully, you grow numb to it all pretty fast: "Hey, ref, get it right for once!"... "Hey, ref, your fly's open!" ... "Hey, ref, eat me!" ... "Hey, ref, you suck!" ... "Hey, ref, don't quit your day job!" ... and one I have to give points to for creativity: "Hey, Delaney, I've seen better referees at the Foot Locker!"

So the truth is that night in Phoenix in April 1999 was pretty much just like any other day at the office for me. I didn't expect anything that I hadn't experienced before. I was simply gearing up for another intense, high-pressure NBA game. We were on an abbreviated schedule at the time, thrilled to be back at work after a lockout had almost wiped out the 1998–99 season altogether. A new, shortened season had begun on February 5, 1999, and two and a half months later here I was in Phoenix, having officiated a Trail Blazers–Spurs game in San Antonio two nights before. The Seattle SuperSonics were visiting, trying to even their record at 20–20, and the Suns had just won two straight to *reach* 20–20, each team already with the playoffs on their minds.

As usual, while dressing in the locker room with my crew, Terry Durham and Kevin Fehr, I couldn't wait to get onto the floor. There was that same familiar rush when I got to midcourt, looking out at the packed arena. One of our responsibilities is to be out on the floor when the first team comes out, which is usually with about eighteen minutes left on the game clock prior to the opening tipoff. The players start going through their warmups, taking their three-point shots. Like clock-work, my thoughts zeroed in on the players I'd be dealing with this day, guys like 6-foot-10 forwards Danny Manning and Tom Gugliotta of Phoenix, along with 6-foot-4 playmaking guard Gary Payton and 6-foot-9 forward/center Detlef Schrempf of Seattle.

I watched the players at each end shoot and move, focusing my eyes on the flurry of action, making sure none of the players started hanging on the rims and that there was nothing unusual going on. I went through a routine of my own, looking at the pivot foot of the players and mentally reffing the little one-on-one games various guys on each team were playing. Contrary to the popular belief that we in the NBA don't make any traveling calls, we're constantly working on picking up pivot-foot violations. In the game of basketball, you're allowed to pivot your foot, but you can't pick that pivot foot up before you release the ball from your hand to either dribble or make a move. So as a ref, you're always keeping a sharp eye out for violations, even practicing that during warmups.

All the while, I acknowledged the players on the court but, as always, was careful not to act too friendly. You can't, because if you shake hands with a player from one team, the other team will be watching. Players have a built-in suspicion—a paranoia that an opponent may gain an advantage.

At ten minutes before game time, Fehr approached the scorer's table, making sure the game clocks were running correctly, while I fixed my gaze on the red light behind each backboard to ensure that they were in sync. Those were the "old days," before the 2002–2003 season. (Until then, so many last-second shots were taking place that it was difficult to determine if they were late or good. That prompted the league to install LED lights all around the backboard and along the scorer's table, so we could easily see when time ran out at the end of each period and the end of the game. In addition, instant replay was introduced—all to help us do a more effective job.)

Now the five-minute mark was approaching. We gathered the team captains for a quick meeting, and stood at midcourt waiting for the game to start. I could hear the usual stuff from some of the fans who were just getting warmed up like everyone else. "Be fair, ref, call 'em at both ends," and other lines with choice adjectives and nouns attached. As always, I refrained from looking at or acknowledging any of it, because that only adds fuel to the fire. I make it a practice not to get into banter with them or make eye contact. But then I heard something at my back, coming from the stands.

"Hey, Bob . . . hey, Bob . . . hey, Bob!"

The tone of the guy calling out my name didn't sound sarcastic or nasty. So I did a partial turn, giving a nod to be polite without really looking and then turning my eyes back to the court. Again, I was standing there going through the normal pre-game motions; and then all of a sudden this same voice I'm hearing yell "Bob," I hear yell something else.

"Alamo Trucking!"

Well, that changed the whole picture. When you hear a phrase that instantly jars you into the past, your mind momentarily freezes, the muscles in your body tense. In my case, the past was defined by danger and the constant threat of violence. My hair-trigger reflexes immediately seized on those words: *Alamo Trucking.* All I could think was: This person has more information than the average fan, and that might be a very bad thing for me. Slowly, out of the corner of my eye, trying as hard as I could not to give attention to the comment with any obvious movement, I began to turn in the direction of a voice that, while oddly calm, thundered inside my head and made my pulse start to race.

"Alamo!" I heard it again. I was fully turned toward the stands now, my heart beating hard, my eyes scouring the faces thirty or forty feet away trying to locate the voice that had yanked me so swiftly from my world of control and equilibrium.

Suddenly I was looking right at the man behind the voice, sitting just one row up from the mega-expensive courtside seats, and he's calling out *"Alamo! Alamo!"* He looked at me, and I stared right into his eyes, and it wasn't connecting. I had no idea who he was or why he was baiting me in public with a loaded reference to a time almost a quarter-century before and a place nearly three thousand miles away on the New Jersey waterfront.

"Bob . . . it's me . . . *Pat* from Alamo."

Like that, hearing the name, the picture snapped into focus. I absolutely couldn't believe it. It was Pat—Pat Kelly! I hadn't laid eyes on him in twenty years. In fact, the last time I had seen him, he had been in a federal court testifying against the Mob and about to enter the federal Witness Protection Program.

Now it's about four minutes away from when they're going to send the teams off the court to get set for the introductions. And I'm just looking at him. He's sitting there smiling. So I give him a smile and a nod. In the moment it takes to get my bearings, I can see the resemblance to the old Pat I knew—my old partner in crime, so to speak, Patrick John Kelly—the Mob consigliere for the DiNorscio Family. Think of a young Robert Duvall, as Tom Hagen, the Irish consigliere for the Corleone Family in *The Godfather*.

Pat had been overweight back then, but had covered it well with his dapper style of dressing—expensive suits, monogrammed shirts, silk ties, Italian leather shoes. I remembered him with neatly coiffed brown hair, baby-blue eyes, and a big, friendly grin that seemed to connect with everyone he met. Now he appeared to have trimmed down a bit. He was gray on top and was wearing a golf shirt—senior leisure lifestyle all the way. His engaging smile hadn't changed a bit, though, nor had his taste in women. I couldn't help but notice that he sat beside a well-tanned, attractive woman who appeared mildly curious about the spontaneous reunion occurring in her presence.

My mind was still spinning, like "I cannot believe this." I mean, this guy was in the Witness Relocation program and here he was sitting courtside. I called the ball boy over and said to him, "See that gentleman sitting over there? Tell him at halftime you're going to bring him a note." He went over and Pat nodded his head. Meanwhile, in the midst of everything that had just happened, the horn had sounded to start the pre-game introductions. It was all I could do to muster the concentration skills from my training and get my thoughts straight. Next thing I knew, the house lights were going down and the place was revving up like a rock concert—strobe lights flashing in the darkness, cheerleaders doing their moves, and the P.A. announcer booming out the names of the Suns players as they jogged onto the court.

"Who is that guy?" Durham whispered in my ear.

"Just an old friend I haven't seen in a while," I answered.

Then it was time for the National Anthem. Something felt different about it this time. While it was being sung, I looked directly across the court, past the honor guard holding the flag, right at Pat. A thought kept running through my mind during the whole song that what he and I had done—even though we came from totally different ends of the ethics spectrum, and for a good while distrusted each other intensely—was as patriotic as you could get. It gave me a chill as I thought back to my other career—the one as a New Jersey state trooper. And to the double life I had led, as an undercover agent who infiltrated the Mafia for three years as part of an FBI–State Police operation that overlapped—and even had me crossing paths with—the Mob investigation of *Donnie Brasco* fame.

It was called Project Alpha, one of the nation's first major undercover investigations of the Mob, and Pat and I had been smack in the middle of it all. I was a young trooper who wanted to take on the bad guys; he was a slick Mob associate who had a decision to make—go to jail or flip over to our side. Pat chose us. And there we were, dealing every day with what they call "capable" guys, meaning guys that are capable of putting a bullet in your head if you make one small slip.

The game started, and I focused on what I had to do. At halftime, I got a piece of paper and jotted down the name of the hotel NBA officials always stayed at when we did games in Phoenix, the Marriott Mountain Shadows. "See you in the bar after the game. Just let me know if you can go." The kid delivered the note to him, and, as we started the second half, Pat just nodded to me and I could make out the words "I'll see you there."

A couple of times during the game we made eye contact. At timeouts, I winked over at him. He was yelling things like "Good call, ref!" It ended up being a pretty good game. Phoenix won, 99–93. Afterward, I drove back to the hotel and walked into the lounge.

I spotted Pat right away with his lady friend, and pulled up a chair. "Pat, how you been?" I asked. Of course, I had to be cautious about what I said to him, because I wasn't sure what, if anything, he'd told people about himself. I mean, I had been with him through all the testifying and I knew that he now had a new identity and life in Witness Protection.

I had a quick image of the old Steve Martin movie *My Blue Heaven,* where all the old Mob guys wind up in the Witness Protection Program in Arizona. And here was Pat, in Phoenix! I figured he was about sixty-three now. It occurred to me that the last time I'd seen him, in 1979, we had been doing our best to slip unnoticed out of the Federal Court Building in Manhattan. I was helping U.S. Marshals get him safely on his way before some Mafia guy had a chance to shoot him. We made it look like Pat took off heading north in the first car, but he was actually lying down on the back seat of the car behind it. That one headed south, and the deception worked. Pat was gone.

Now, twenty years later, he and I had to talk cryptically, the way we always had when we were around the Mob guys. Finally, when his friend got up to go to the ladies' room, I said, "What the *hell* are you doing?" He started smiling. "I've been thinking of you, and following your NBA career," he said. "Ever since I've been with her, she has season tickets, so I've been going, hoping to see you."

"Does she *know*?" I asked.

"No, of *course* not, she doesn't know," he said. "I just told her you were a friend of mine back from the days I used to live in New Jersey. She only knows me by my Relocation name. I didn't tell her the whole thing."

"The whole thing." That phrase floated in my mind for a moment. I couldn't be sure of what the words meant to Pat, but I definitely knew what images they conjured up for me. How do you tell people so they understand the constant fear that wrenches your guts in spite of your cool, calm façade; how it feels to immerse yourself in a world filled with risks and peril so that you actually become a different person? How do you tell them about the ways the street pulls you in and changes you, so that many of the criminals you are investigating suddenly don't seem so very different from you after all? How do you tell people that you once contemplated crossing a line that should not be crossed, and then struggled to cross back over to the nice, neat world you had left behind?

Pat excused himself. When he returned alone, I asked where his friend was. "Sent her home in a cab," he answered. So we were free to talk, which we did for almost two hours, until the place had emptied out. When it was time to go, we hugged like two guys who have been to war together.

Only the two of us truly understood what we'd lived through.

Seeing Pat that day triggered a flood of memories and emotions from a time that changed the person I was and ultimately pushed me in a new direction in life. And I never saw it coming, certainly not on the day back in 1973 that was easily the proudest moment I'd ever experienced.

That was the day my dad, Robert D. Delaney, a lieutenant in the New Jersey State Police, gave me my badge. I was thrilled to become a link in the long chain of the state police's history dating back to 1921— the year it was founded by Colonel H. Norman Schwarzkopf, whose famous son and namesake went on to become a heralded U.S. Army general and hero of the 1991 Gulf War.

My father wore badge No. 978—a sequential number that equated to his overall seniority—and I would be No. 2853. It was a formal ceremony, the kind of thing you remember your whole life. In fact, a photo of that occasion hangs on my office wall to this day. I'd left college at Jersey City State a year early because I'd heard the troopers were looking for new recruits. That didn't happen every year, and I made the decision to go for it when there was a chance. And after sixteen weeks of intense West Point–type training, I was following in my father's footsteps and starting my own State Police career.

I got my uniform and was assigned to the rural areas of the state, since we provided police services in locales where there was no local police department. We patrolled the highways as well. I was stationed in Flemington, a prime State Police barracks that had been made famous as the center of the investigation of the Lindbergh baby kidnapping in 1932.

We had about six different townships for which we were responsible—handling domestic disputes, drunk drivers, barroom brawls, break-ins at homes—all kinds of police work.

I loved putting on the uniform—the blue-and-gold suit and military-type hat with my gold badge prominently displayed. Everyone in law enforcement feels that pride. You graduate from the academy and you hit the streets. And all of a sudden you think you're better looking because everybody's staring at you and wants to talk with you. You've got instant status and stature. It reminded me of how I had felt as a basketball player in the spotlight during high school and at Jersey City State. Only this was bigger, much bigger.

At night in the barracks, I was always cleaning my gun, boots, leather holster, and badge. I lifted weights to stay in shape, and I kept up basketball as much as I could. In my off hours, I played on the State Police basketball team and refereed games for some area fifth- and sixth-grade teams. When it came to socializing, I'd usually hit the local taverns to drink beer with other troopers, firemen, and everyday guys.

They teamed me up with a senior trooper, Bobby Scott, who was not just my partner but my mentor. He was a great uniformed cop and later became one of the best homicide detectives in the history of the New Jersey State Police. Bobby had just left turnpike duty and was also stationed at Flemington. He's told me that when we met, he liked that I was so energetic, a real go-getter. Bobby could tell I was just as fired up about law enforcement as he was, about protecting the world from the bad guys. He took me under his wing and tried to teach me as much as he could. We got along great.

Back in those days, we slept at the barracks, working fifteen days on, fifteen days off. Bobby joked that he spent as much time with me as he did with his wife. I wasn't married, except to my new job. The married guys would go home when they weren't on duty, but this was my full-time home, like an apartment. I'd go to my parents' home and my mom would wash my clothes, and then I'd go back. A lot of guys couldn't wait to get out of there, but on my days off, I wouldn't even leave.

I remember one night when I got back to the barracks after a late night out, having a few beers with some buddies. I was coming in to go to bed, and I saw this one drunk guy, about to be cuffed, who was beginning to give Bobby a hard time. I was bigger and younger than Bobby, so I grabbed the drunk by the collar and held him up against the wall and said, "Listen, don't be giving my friend any bullshit. Now be nice." It was just a little intimidation technique and it worked. He got quiet fast. So I sat him back down and went upstairs to bed. At the time, I was just trying to help a friend. It wasn't until years later that I realized that it had been the same kind of intimidation technique used by the Mafia, making me acutely aware of the fine line between the good guys and the bad guys.

I guess it was about three months into the job that I really came up against the brutal reality of criminals and their victims. Until then, I'd been handling accidents and Peeping-Tom kinds of law-breaking. But now I was about to get involved with my first major crime. It was the case of a girl named Debbie Margolis, a sixteen-year-old farm girl. Bobby and I went out to investigate. She'd been missing for ten hours and the search was on, with different law enforcement agency teams coming in. We found her body, a shocking and tragic thing. She had been horribly sexually mutilated before being killed. I was a twenty-one-year-old kid, and seeing that, all of a sudden, reality set in for me. For the first time, I truly grasped the victimology of crime—the suffering of innocent victims and the pain inflicted on their families and friends. My understanding of what it means to be bad, really bad, started at that point. We caught the guy who did it. His name was Frankie Miller. He had told her that one of her cows had gotten loose. She apparently got in his car and was never seen alive again.

I moved to my second station a few months later, in Newton. I was still getting an education, learning something every day. Just when you think you're starting to understand the job, a new challenge arises and makes you realize that you still have a long way to go.

I was out on my own one day and got a call to investigate a breaking-and-entry of a home. When I went in, the house was pretty well cleared out of jewelry, TVs, anything the burglars could fence. I did the preliminary investigation until the detectives got there. After about a day, I learned that I hadn't done a good enough job—I'd missed the most important clue. As a young kid, four or five months as a trooper, you may start to get cocky and think you know what you're doing, but I learned that I didn't really know that much.

What I missed, one of our senior detectives, Lieutenant Chuck Musselli found. He picked up some paint chips on the fencing in front of the house, left by a car that brushed past as it was exiting. It was an unforgettable lesson, reinforcing that I needed to pay greater attention to detail. It turned out that the house had been robbed days after the husband had been killed by a drunk driver.

The thing that really got to me was that the house still looked as if the family was about to have dinner. They never returned home after they learned the husband had been killed. Then, the obituary in the paper mentioned the time of the funeral, letting the bad guys know exactly when the family would be at the service. They just walked in and stripped the house of its belongings. But the paint chips from the getaway car—the crucial detail—eventually led to their capture.

After about a year on the job, I began to feel pretty good about things. I'd spent six months in Flemington, six in Newton, and now I was stationed in Somerville. I had my own apartment in Hawthorne, New Jersey, about forty-five minutes away. One day when I arrived at the barracks for work, I found a note in my box to call a Sergeant First Class Jack Liddy of Division Headquarters. I'd never met the guy, but of course I called him back. Everything is very military-style in the "Outfit," as we always refer to it, but on the phone he never addressed me as "Trooper." He just said, "Delaney, you workin' tomorrow?" I said, "Yes, sir." He said, "I'm gonna be up at the station. I need to talk to you."

We hung up. Talk about what? What the hell had I done? I asked some of the guys, "Who's Liddy?" Someone said to me, "He's in the criminal investigation section assigned to the organized crime bureau. Maybe you gave a ticket to a Mob guy and he wants to talk to you about it. Don't worry." But I kept wondering, what did I do wrong?

The next day, I told my sergeant, Gabe Simonetti, that I had to talk to a sergeant from division headquarters. He said no problem, just come in off patrol when he gets here. The next day, I got a "Signal 30" on the radio—which meant come back to the station. I drove around back where we had this big garage area and headed to the steps leading into the station. Right in the hall by the door, Jack Liddy was waiting for me. Jack was a big man, two or three inches taller than I am with meat hooks for hands. A thick, powerful guy, he was probably in his late forties or early fifties at the time. He wore a sport jacket and slacks—not a suit—with a tie that was always loose because he couldn't button the collar. He may have looked a little disheveled, but he had a quick mind and was all business.

When I came in the back door, he said to me, "I'm Liddy." We shook hands and he said, "Come on downstairs." We went down to the kitchen area, which was empty at that time of the day, and he didn't even sit down or anything. He said, "I need to talk to you. There's a job we're thinking about taking a look at you for, if you're interested. It's an undercover job. It'll be six months. We know your background. We know you're active in arrests. It seems like you might be a kid that would be good for this. Are you interested?"

My thoughts were reeling. Relieved that I wasn't in some kind of trouble, I was also thrilled to have the chance at a special assignment so early in my State Police career. But I didn't want to look too excited, so I kept my answer brief: "Yes, sir, from what you're telling me, I'm interested."

Then, totally matter-of-factly, he said, "You tell anybody that I talked to you about it, you're out of the running. It's got to be completely quiet. Now that I know you're interested, I'll get back to you."

As he turned to walk out, I remember asking, "Sarge, what is it, drugs?" All he said—without even turning his head to talk to me—was "I'll get back to you." It was as if he was already focused on the next thing, and then he was gone.

Just like that, I went from exhilaration to "what the hell is this?" He hadn't spent five minutes with me, and I didn't even know what he was talking about. I was thinking, "This isn't the way it's supposed to be. I'm supposed to be all happy and jumping up and down and high-fiving." Now I couldn't say a word, not even to my own sergeant.

It was three weeks before he contacted me again. The next meeting was at the Golden Star diner on Route 46 in Little Falls. We went to a back booth, and he laid it out a little bit more. What I learned was that the New Jersey State Police had joined forces with the FBI and were going to start an operation called Project Alpha. It would be funded by the elite Law Enforcement Assistance Administration (LEAA), a federal-government organization that only existed from 1968 to 1982. What's more, it was going to be a long-term, six-month investigation of corruption on the Jersey waterfront, focusing on organized crime's infiltration into legitimate businesses. Like the 1954 Marlon Brando movie *On the Waterfront;* times had hardly changed. The Mob guys were still running the docks. We'd investigate them with three undercover agents from the FBI and two from the State Police. One of them could be me.

I listened to it all over dinner, and Liddy set up another meeting with me. It began to look as if I had a good chance of being one of the two troopers selected. The suspense kept building, as I realized that this assignment was made for me. Finally, Jack told me that we had a noon meeting scheduled for the next day with Major Bill Baum, who was in charge of the Criminal Investigation Section in Trenton, where our headquarters was located. I couldn't wait. I pulled in around 11:30 a.m. and spotted Jack right away. He came up to me and said, "The major can't see you until about two o'clock. You want to go to lunch with me?"

We got to this restaurant, a nice place where businessmen, politicians, and higher-ranking cops would go. As soon as we walked in, he said, "What do you wanna do, kid, eat it or drink it?" "Whatever *you* do, boss," I answered. We sat down at the bar, and he put three beers in me. After almost two hours, we drove back to headquarters and he announced, "Okay, we'll go see the major."

I had a little buzz when we arrived at our rescheduled meeting at 2:00 p.m. with Major Baum. The major went through a couple of things and then told me, "One of the concerns we have is that your father is a lieutenant in the State Police and I don't want to catch heat from the union." To be honest, that really got my back up. I didn't get disrespectful, but I quickly responded, "Excuse me, sir, um, I've never asked for anything because my father was in the Outfit but I sure don't want to be held back because my father is a trooper. If that's the case, maybe you're telling me I need to go find another job."

Well, I got the undercover job. And I found out later that one of the reasons I got it was that I had had enough moxie to speak up. They liked that. And that noon meeting I was told to show up for? It had always been planned for 2:00 p.m. Jack had set me up, getting a few beers in me to see how I'd handle myself, because when you work undercover, you're going to be stuck in these situations. It was an ingenious plan—let's see how well the kid does when he's had a few and he's under pressure.

Things moved quickly after that. They decided I would be leaving the Somerville station on April 9, 1975, at around 10:00 p.m. Everybody else was out on patrol. I was called in by Sergeant Simonetti. When I got there, Jack Liddy was waiting for me on the same back step where we had talked at our first meeting. I was in full uniform, and he told me to go up to my room and leave all my gear. I went up, got into my civilian clothes, and put my uniform and gun on the bed. Then I went back downstairs as another trooper went inside the station and removed my uniform and all my stuff. Outside, it was just a typically cool April evening. I had a windbreaker and a pair of jeans on, and I climbed in my 1973 Cutlass Supreme, a two-tone car with a tan body and dark brown roof. All Liddy told me was "I'll be in touch with you tomorrow." I left for my apartment in Hawthorne, not knowing what lay ahead.

The very next day, a personnel order was issued stating that I had resigned from the New Jersey State Police. Instantly, the stories about what had happened to me started swirling—that I had gotten jammed up, smacked a woman around, had stolen drugs confiscated on busts, lost my temper and killed a man. It was amazing the things that were said about me. It was worst of all for my poor partner, Bobby Scott. He had been out of town for a week and came back to hear not only that I had resigned, but that I had gone to Miami with another trooper and got arrested for murder. Bobby knew I was the kind of kid who wouldn't take any shit from anybody, and he pictured some situation where that happened and just got terribly out of hand.

He took it really hard. Right away, my father told me, "You have to talk to Bob Scott. He's too good of a cop, and he's going to keep investigating. You're better off short-stopping him than letting him dig into what's going on." I said, "I *can't* talk to him." But my father set it up for Bobby to call my parents' house at 8:00 p.m. a week or two later when I would be there. The phone rang and my dad answered it, and he handed the receiver to me.

"Listen, I talked to your father and he's not telling me anything," Bobby blurted into the phone. "All I know is that something's not good in your life right now." And when I think of what he said next, I still get choked up. He told me he had talked to his wife, Fran, and they had decided to offer all their savings to help me out of whatever trouble I was in. Here was a guy with four young children; he didn't make much money on a trooper's salary; and he was offering me his life savings. His words came out steady and slow, sounding almost like an older brother. "Look, you're going to need it for lawyers," he said. "And I'll be a character witness for you at your trial."

It was an incredible gesture of friendship, because testifying in a criminal case on my behalf would very likely have gotten him fired for breaking State Police regulations. I responded by doing one of the hardest things I had ever done: nothing.

I said, "Bobby, thanks, but I'm okay."

"No, you're not okay," he snapped, the agitation returning to his voice. "I know that you need help and I want to help you."

All I could say was, "Okay, thanks. I'll see you." And I hung up. I put the phone down, feeling absolutely horrible. But in a way, it was my first undercover test. And I had passed—starting down a path of telling lies and convincing people that they were truths.

I knew it had hurt Bobby deeply; he had extended a helping hand and I'd shut the door in his face. But the fact was, I knew it would probably make him so mad at me that he'd never bother to investigate further. He didn't. And I never called him back. I couldn't, because doing anything like that might have jeopardized the operation. When I hung up the phone with him that night, there was no way I could tell him that I had tears in my eyes.

The whole thing was really hard on my parents, too, especially my mom. They'd go to State Police functions and hear all the whispering about me. Eventually they stopped going to them altogether.

Just like that, I was gone from the face of the earth, about to enter the dark side.

CHAPTER TWO

BOBBY COVERT, MEET BOB DELANEY

On a cool spring day in 1975, a tall, burly man in a rumpled sport jacket that appears one size too small walks briskly, virtually unnoticed, up the old gray concrete steps of the Newark City Hall building at 920 Broad Street. He strides between the two brass eagles perched with wings extended on tall, ornate towers, pulls open a heavy mahogany door, and disappears inside the massive granite landmark that presides over downtown Newark, its shimmering dome covered by sheets of 23-carat gold leaf.

Jack Liddy is not a man given to wasted motion or words. The planning for Project Alpha is moving swiftly and so is Liddy, striding purposefully across the faded marble lobby floor and entering Room 111, a place with which he has become quite familiar in recent weeks. Several minutes later, the sergeant first class in the New Jersey State Police's Criminal Investigation Section, assigned to the organized crime bureau, sits inside the Bureau of Vital Statistics, scrolling through microfilm records of the dead.

In particular, he is looking for names of males born in the state in the early 1950s but who died at birth or soon after. It is grim, tedious work, made all the more difficult because Liddy has to locate a poor, long-departed soul with the right birth year, a surname denoting Irish lineage, and—equally important—the first name of Robert.

If he's going to help unearth an effective undercover identity for the young trooper who'll be smack in the middle of this investigation, with his life on the line at all times, every detail will have to be just right on the birth certificate he finds. And that means the trooper, Bob Delaney, can't be assigned an alter ego with any other first name than the one his parents gave him. Answering to "Bobby" would be entirely natural, and eliminate any chance of a potentially fatal slip-up as he starts his new life and web of lies.

Suddenly the name "Covert, Robert Alan" appears on the screen. Liddy perks up. The birth year is in the right ballpark, and so is the Irish-sounding last name. At his next meeting with Delaney at the Tick Tock Diner on Route 3 in Clifton, with black-and-white photos of celebrities like Frank Sinatra and Dean Martin hanging on the wall behind the cash register, the sergeant runs the name past him. "Bobby Covert," Delaney says. He likes it just fine. There are no quips about the surname's double meaning, because "covert"—outside of the relatively recent Watergate investigation of the Nixon administration—isn't yet embedded in the American vernacular or in everyday law-enforcement terminology. At the time, undercover operations within the New Jersey State Police are short-term assignments that involve "narcs"—the long-haired, bearded guys busting drug dealers. Project Alpha would change all that. For now, this is still an era in which "undercover" evokes images of secret agents more than complex covert operations.

So Bobby Covert is reborn, and Bob Delaney gradually begins to fit into the skin of his new identity amid the gritty industrial strips along the Bayonne waterfront and the ever-tightening grip of the Mafia.

It's a world away from the endlessly curling ribbons of bustling neighborhood streets he grew up in. Yet this new life—anchored in deception and danger—is less than thirty miles from the friendly, working-class enclave of Paterson, New Jersey, where his true identity took root and blossomed.

The Veterans Apartments were seven boxlike buildings of seven floors each, a low-income complex of reddish-brown brick dwellings on the east side of Paterson, just on the outskirts of downtown. That is where I first lived and where I learned my first important lesson, one that would remain in my bloodstream all my life about the underlying bonds among all people, regardless of skin color or other differences. You had to be a veteran, or a family member of one, to live in those seven buildings. And my dad, Robert David Delaney, had served in the Navy, fought in New Guinea during World War II, and received medals he never spoke about—so common for members of his generation. He just came home and got on with his life.

My parents were born and raised in Paterson. They met for the first time at a skating rink when they were fifteen. As the story goes, my dad asked my mom, Mary, to fix him up with one of her friends, but my mom skated with him and fixed things for herself instead. They started going together at sixteen. When my dad turned seventeen, he enlisted and gave my mom a ring. Two years later, he returned home to the States and couldn't have wished for a better day to get discharged: St. Patrick's Day—March 17, 1946. The celebration party with his family and friends lasted well into the night at the Market Street Tavern.

One month later, Mom and Dad got married, honeymooning thirty minutes away in Newark at an old hotel called the Robert Treat. I came along five and a half years later on November 1, 1951, when my dad was a recruit in training at the State Police academy. My given name was Robert James Delaney—Robert to my mom and just Rob to my dad. After three more years, my sister Kathleen was born—almost everyone called her Kath—and there we were, a young, growing family on the sixth floor in Building No. 6 of the Veterans Apartments.

Those apartment buildings were segregated, like just about all of America then. Six of them were for white families. One—Building 7—was for blacks. As a young child, seven years old, I was afraid of that building. One of the women who lived there—a large lady who wore a scarf around her head—did our laundry and ironing, and my mom gave me the chore of taking our clothes over to her apartment. I was scared to death, but my mom forced me to go. I found out that this woman—I only knew her as Miss Rose—was welcoming and loving, always nice to me. She had lots of kids, boys my age and older, and gradually I started playing with them. There was a playground between our building and their building, but the unwritten rule was that it was really for the black kids. I'd go out there even though I wasn't supposed to. Not that it wasn't allowed, but in the late 1950s it wasn't the norm for white kids and black kids—we used the word "colored" back then—to be playing together.

That experience was my introduction to race relations. I learned that ignorance breeds fear. All I'd known was that the people in Building 7 were different, that they lived in a building by themselves. The very fact of separateness sent a message: Stay away. I was scared until we got to know each other. I didn't put my understanding into words then, but the human truth stayed with me, a natural part of my thinking and feeling. The kid who was afraid to enter a blacks-only building has become an adult who for the past twenty-plus years has worked in a predominantly African-American business. And one of my most rewarding moments in recent years was introducing Martin Luther King III at the 13th Avenue Community Center in Bradenton, Florida, where I serve as a board member for the facility benefiting at-risk African-American kids.

When I turned eight, my family moved across town to the west side of the city. Our new home was at 232 Maitland Avenue, a cozy brown wood-and-cinderblock house with well-trimmed shrubs out front and an American flag hanging by the front door. We lived in an Italian-American neighborhood, with families named DiLella, Luizi, and Picarelli who had simple two- and three-bedroom, one-car-garage houses just like ours.

There was a complete open-door policy. I'd run across the street and walk right into somebody else's house. We had this routine where you quick-knocked and just kept walking in. No doors were ever locked. When I addressed the parents of my best friend Jimmy DiLella, I didn't call them Mr. and Mrs. DiLella—it was Aunt Rita and Uncle Chris. Marty and Joey Luizi's folks were Uncle Marty and Aunt Mabel. I was the only Irish kid among all the kids I hung around with, and it never made a bit of difference to anyone.

At night in the summer, my parents would take their kitchen chairs out on a concrete slab where my dad had cleared away the shrubs in front of the house. Friends from across the street would come over and sit and talk and drink a beer. The next night, my parents would go across the street to sit and visit in the front yard of somebody else's house. Meanwhile, my friends and I would be playing stickball in the street or

Wiffle Ball in a little stadium we built in the woods behind Jimmy DiLella's back yard. Or we'd play touch football, which ended up being tackle football before it was over. The games always included Jimmy's brothers Chris, Al, and George, who became like my own brothers.

Our street was on an incline, great for sledding in the winter. At the top of the hill, past the intersection of Maitland and Chamberlain, was a patch of woods called St. Michael's Grove, a beautiful spot with stone chapels and shrines tied to St. Michael's Church downtown. Life-size statues of saints and the Blessed Mother stood amid the trees, along with picnic areas for visitors. Despite the ecclesiastical connection, it was also quite a popular make-out spot for teens. Once a year, the grove was the site for the Feast of St. Michael. Busloads of people, literally thousands of visitors from New York and all over the Northeast, descended on Paterson, parking miles away if they had to. The lucky ones found spots for their cars on our street and walked joyously up the hill to the grove. At the top, there was always one kid dressed up like St. Michael the Archangel. He would be suspended from a cable, swinging in the air fifteen feet off the ground. Even my friend Andy Picarelli, who was always the kid who got in trouble for something and was the *last* guy you'd ever think would be a saint, got to do it one year. He said when he looked down, all he could see was cheese, Italian bread, and bottles of wine.

All these things paid off for me down the road. Growing up in that atmosphere, I became familiar with many of the nuances of Italian culture, little things that you only know when you live inside a way of life. Many of the Mob guys I got involved with later had an Italian ancestry. It helped that I knew about a Christmas Eve meal called "The Vigil," a mind-boggling, multi-course dinner of seven fishes and seafoods— including grilled salmon, octopus, calamari, cod, steamed escarole with anchovies, and a full menu of DiLella family seafood delicacies and red sauce dishes that took two full days of cooking to prepare.

I knew what it was like to be in an Italian household on Easter, with the special prayers before the meal, the big plates of pasta, even Aunt

Rita's Easter tree tradition—she would put her Christmas tree out in the back yard after the holidays and bring it back inside when the Easter season arrived. By then, it was a sorry sight indeed—the green pine needles were long gone, and all that remained were brittle branches and twigs on a sun-baked trunk. She'd hollow out eggs, dye them all kinds of bright colors, and hang them on the branches. Suddenly, there it was—a magnificent Easter tree, a beautiful sight to behold. As a kid, the significance was lost on me, but years later I came to understand the religious symbolism of the Easter Sunday resurrection in that dead tree coming back to life.

I also became well acquainted with many customs dealing with Italian cuisine and Sunday meals, like the phrase "homemades." Everyone in an Italian family knows that that means one thing—homemade spaghetti and pasta. To be able to know and use such phrases and traditions—absorbing them by osmosis until they became second nature to me—became an invaluable asset later on. It's the kind of thing you can't fake.

But one thing I tell people to this day: "Organized crime" does not equal "Italian." It just happens that there is a segment of people of Italian ancestry who have been and are involved in the Mafia. I grew up on a street where there were no Mafia guys, but they were all Italians—cops, firemen, postal workers, health inspectors, working-class people who were all part of good, law-abiding families.

Paterson was a place with history—a silk-manufacturing city, as we were taught in school, and a hometown to such diverse names as comedian Lou Costello; American League black baseball pioneer Larry Doby; middleweight boxer Rubin "Hurricane" Carter, who was convicted of three 1966 murders in Paterson—though the charges were eventually dropped two decades later; Joe Clark, the hard-nosed principal of Eastside High portrayed by Morgan Freeman in the movie *Lean On Me*; poets William Carlos Williams and Allen Ginsberg; and, as I would later learn, undercover agent Joe Pistone, a.k.a. Donnie Brasco, whose life would one day intersect with my own.

My family's history was very much entwined with the town. I was surrounded by dozens of extended-family members. My grandfather on my father's side, Jack Delaney, owned a paint store in downtown Paterson, and my father's mom, Anne, worked at a clothing store called Meyer Brothers. They were considered upper middle class. He operated a successful business—anyone who was painting a house came to Delaney's. And he was also a political figure who once ran for mayor of Paterson and served as an alderman.

As young kids, one of the things we liked most was going to downtown Paterson. It was like making our way into the big city. Even though it was the inner city and we were young kids about nine or ten, Jimmy and I would just walk with our friends the four or five miles to get there, or sometimes take a bus if we had the money. Along the way, we'd usually hit a popular hot dog joint called Fall's View, and then gaze across the Passaic River toward the long walkway stretching above an amazing sight—the rushing water of Paterson's Great Falls, which was our own little Niagara Falls.

Main Street was all hustle and bustle, like a small-scale New York City. People would be dressed up to go shopping down there. The bus dropped you right off at Main, and you just started exploring. Roaming through those streets, I came to understand the underside of a city—I knew that there were bookmakers and people into things that were shady, not quite legal. Even though I lived in the safety and security of my neighborhood, I developed a strong sense of the complexities of urban life.

I often hung out at my grandfather's paint store. It was at the lower end of Main. There were all kinds of other shops nearby—fish markets with slabs of fresh-caught fish laid on ice; vegetable stores with all the freshest produce from Jersey farms; bakeries with amazing Italian sweets, from cannoli to zabagliones; and, one of my favorites, a shop run by Joe the Egg Man, a muscular Italian merchant who sold eggs and poultry. Joe and his men worked on sawdust-covered wooden floors, slitting the necks of live chickens, turning them upside down and letting the blood that wasn't absorbed by the sawdust run into the street. Joe even had a rabbi on hand who would slaughter poultry for customers who observed Kosher, the Jewish dietary code. The cops who walked the street knew everyone on the block. I always thought they were cool because of the way they'd twirl their batons, walking with confidence, receiving the respect of the neighborhood.

Looking back at my family tree, I can trace different traits in my personality. My gift of gab, I know, comes from Grandpa Delaney, a heavy-set man with salt-and-pepper hair parted down the middle. When I was seven or eight, I remember that I would go to his house—a huge, two-story structure with tan-and-brown wood siding—and he'd say to me, "You gonna come with me tonight?" I'd say, "Yeah, okay." And right away, he'd begin looking through the obituaries to find funerals of people he knew. He'd get all dressed up in a handsome vest with shirt and tie and take me with him. After the funeral service, we'd go to a diner, where he'd sit for hours talking to all his buddies over coffee. I was more interested in the dessert menu, with pictures of ice-cream sundaes and every kind of pie.

My grandfather—he and my grandmother Anne were third-generation Irish-Americans—pointed out a lesson from these forays. "You always should make time for people who are having hard times. It's easy to be there for the good times. But people remember you for being there when times are tough." He had an instinct for compassion, and may have given me my first sense of empathy for people who suffer hurt and pain—though I never could have envisioned the brutal depths of hurt and pain I would later see, working in law enforcement.

My mom's parents were born in Ireland. My grandfather, Patrick John Hamill, came to America first, looking for work. And my grandmother, Margaret, arrived months later, traveling on a ship for ten days by herself. I heard stories about how difficult it was for my grandfather to find a job. Time after time, he was greeted with a sign that read "No Irish Need Apply." It was devastating. Finally, he was hired by a company called Rustin's Express, hoisting machinery out of buildings and trucking it to different locations. He looked like a movie star from the pictures I saw of him, an Irish Joe DiMaggio. But his life was never easy. He died of cancer while still a young man, just forty-six.

My grandmother carried on without him. She was a tiny lady, but tough and unflappable in the face of heartbreak. She lost one of her six children—my mother's brother, Arthur—when he was only five years old: He walked behind a kid swinging a baseball bat and got hit in the head and died. The tragedy rippled through the family; I wasn't allowed to even own a bat until I was seven.

Other terrible losses lay in store for my grandmother. Two grown-up sons—my uncles Jimmy and Pat—belonged to the same union and had worked out a system for avoiding too many meetings. Members were required to attend twelve union meetings a year, but Pat would go to six and Jimmy to six and simply sign in for each other. One day when it was Pat's turn to go, he pleaded with his brother, "I've got a hot date, you gotta go to my meeting for me." Jimmy went. On the way home, he was killed by a drunk driver. The guilt was too much for Pat. He started to drink heavily and was never the same.

When I was young, I was embarrassed by the Irish in my grandmother's speech. She had a strong brogue, and I didn't want the other kids to hear her say things like "come here, wee boy." But as I got older, I tried my best to look after her. I'd go to her house and walk her to the store so she didn't have to go alone. Today, I like to think that gray-haired Irish granny passed along a piece of her toughness to me.

We had as close to a *Donna Reed Show–Father Knows Best* type of life as you can imagine. It was very structured: Sunday morning church, stop at the bakery for donuts, dinner at 3:00, and off to my grandparents' house after that. I was a straight-arrow kid who never got into any kind of trouble. My dad was making his way up the ranks of the State Police, and both my sister and I understood that we had to behave. My mother drilled that into us, telling us over and over that we had to adhere to a higher standard because of his line of work. And we did.

Of all the lessons that got imprinted on my young mind, the biggest was from my father. It wasn't something he told me or lectured me about; it was something I watched him do when I was ten years old. I was attending St. Mary's Grammar School, which stood right next door to St. Mary's High School and the convent—solid, beige-brick buildings that towered above Sherman Avenue. St. Mary's Church was two blocks away on Union Avenue. As a kid, my entire life unfolded within this two-block area. I was an altar boy, which made my parents very proud, then a lector. For a while, I even thought I wanted to become a priest, until I got older and *really* understood the whole celibacy thing.

Baseball at St. Mary's was a big deal. All the boys in the parish dreamed of making the St. Mary's Blues—the school's colors were blue and white, so "Blues" became the name of our baseball team. Everyone had a chance to try out, so there were thirty or forty would-be players to fill eighteen or twenty spots. One chilly spring night, we gathered in the school courtyard to hear the coaches' verdict. It was starting to get dark, and the coaches were reading names and handing out uniforms to the kids who made it. Coach Norm Leon called out my name, then that of my best friend, Jimmy DiLella. We were thrilled. But all around us were other kids who were going home heartbroken.

Then I heard my father's voice in the darkness. "Well, how about, you know, we start a second St. Mary's team and we'll call it the Whites?" Everyone was quiet. "These other kids can play on it, and I'll coach it." He nodded in the direction of his friend Chris DiLella. "I know Chris will help coach too."

The kids who hadn't made the team, and their parents, loved the idea. My dad already had his hands full with long, hard hours in the State Police. In the months ahead, he'd be going to my Blues games on one weeknight and coaching the Whites on another. He had no partic-ular connection to those kids, just his sense of fairness.

That core belief stayed with me, heightening my sensitivity to the less fortunate among us—victims of difficult circumstances or of the bullies of the world. That feeling fueled my resentment when I saw criminals take things from people—their savings, their property, their lives. The law isn't a cold, impersonal thing; it springs from that passion to respect every person equally, to establish fairness on life's playing field.

My mom was a big influence on me as well. She could be just as tough and feisty as her mother, always keeping me and Kath in line with our chores and responsibilities. But her big heart and generosity were always evident, especially when it came to St. Mary's baseball. My mom was constantly involved, not just cheering us on but organizing and running the bake sale to raise money for our uniforms and equipment. Her charitable nature—giving of her time to help others—is something that shaped the man I would become.

Back then, though, life was all about sports. I was a pretty strong baseball player from the start—a good all-around athlete—and that's why I was so shocked not to make the basketball team in seventh grade. When that happened, my parents handled it just right, asking me if I'd like to have a hoop put up in the back yard, so the decision would be *mine*. It was an easy one to make—I couldn't wait for my dad to attach that hoop, because I was determined to become a good player. After that, Jimmy and I were constantly playing basketball on school courts within walking distance. Sometimes, when the weather was too cold or rainy to play outdoors, the Brothers at Don Bosco Tech High School let us play on the indoor courts.

Jimmy and I were inseparable. We played CYO (Catholic Youth Organization) basketball and baseball. We both went to the all-boys Catholic school, Blessed John Neumann Prep, the new high school in Wayne, New Jersey, about fifteen miles away. To get there, we had to take two buses. Sometimes my dad dropped us off at school in his unmarked trooper car. It seemed like he was always on duty, and if somebody cut him off in traffic, he'd say, "Sit tight, boys, we're going for a ride." He'd get after the guy who did it, with no siren and no lights. He'd catch up and show him his badge and give him a chewing-out, maybe a ticket.

I'll never forget the evening in July 1967 when we saw live TV news reports of riots breaking out in Newark. You could see the intensity of what was going on at that very moment—the buildings on fire, the people running through the streets, fire departments and law enforcement rushing in. This was an era long before cable news transmitted scenes of violence into households around the clock, and this was something we'd never witnessed. Our knowing that the destruction was erupting only a few towns away made it hit home all the more.

My father was a sergeant at the time, and I remember him saying to himself, "This is not good—not good." About 2:00 a.m., the phone rang—and we all know the fear provoked by a call coming at that time of night. The next thing I knew, Dad was getting his gear and telling us he had to report to Newark. My mom, my sister, and I were all frightened as he walked out the front door, fully aware that he was headed directly into the chaos we had been watching on TV only a few hours earlier. I was a pretty confident sixteen-year-old kid at the time, but the only thing I could do was pray that he would be safe.

Two days went by before my father was finally able to call to tell us he was okay. It was a huge relief, because reports of people getting killed and injured had been growing, and there seemed to be no end in sight—with reports of rioting sweeping through Detroit, Washington, D.C., and other cities now. The uncertainty was the hardest part, not knowing what kind of danger my father was facing at any given instant.

Two days after his first call, we were glued to the TV—my mom and sister, Jimmy DiLella and his brothers, plus Aunt Rita and Uncle Chris. It was much like the experience of families across the country in times of war—Vietnam, Desert Storm, and Iraq—when your loved one is somewhere in the midst of battle and the television set becomes your connection to their lives.

"It's Dad!" I shouted as live footage filled the screen showing my father on the street, directing a unit that was making an arrest. We all watched, transfixed, until the camera panned to another shot of the rioting. "He's okay, he's okay," Jimmy said, trying to reassure everyone in the room. My pulse was racing, but at that moment it wasn't only fear that I felt; it was a sense of pride.

Jimmy and I went on to become three-sport lettermen at Neumann. I ran cross-country and played basketball and baseball. Jimmy played soccer, baseball, and basketball. There were only about forty kids in the class, so we both became leaders because of our athletic success. I readily admit that I wasn't much of a student. There were no girls to distract us, so sports dominated almost every waking moment.

I was already about six feet and could dunk the ball. Jimmy was 5-11 and our best defensive guy. We'd regularly get write-ups in the *Paterson Evening News* and *Newark Star-Ledger*. During summer evenings, to improve our play, we'd hop on a bus and go to Manhattan to find pickup games on inner-city playgrounds against some very talented black and Hispanic players. That helped hone my game quite a bit. During the day, we'd take on odd jobs, from caddying to working at a new company called Automatic Data Processing, long before it would revolutionize the business world. In fact, our fathers knew the guys who started it, Joe and Henry Taub, and had a chance to get in on the ground floor with a percentage of the partnership. Unfortunately, they didn't have the $12,500 each it would have taken to get them in the door, so they passed. Looking back, it's one of those what-if moments in life that every family seems to have: If my dad and Uncle Chris had become part of the company, they'd have been multi-millionaires and my life would have followed an entirely different course.

In my senior year, my class took a trip to Italy over the Easter vacation. It was a huge deal for us and a source of great excitement for our families. We had been saving money for the plane tickets and accommodations since our freshman year. The class went to Florence, Rome, and Capri, and I soaked up the Italian culture to which I had been exposed on Maitland Avenue—experiences I never dreamed would play a vital role in my life only a half dozen years later. That year, I started getting basketball scholarship offers and decided to accept one at a small college—Belknap—in New Hampshire.

Four months later, off I went to start a new chapter of my life at Belknap. My parents drove me up to the school, and I remember my mom crying when they dropped me off—she was saying good-bye to her boy for the first time. But before long, she was saying hello again. I was miserable at Belknap—I was trying to take it seriously, having come in on a scholarship, but this was 1969 and a lot of students were into drugs and I was troubled by an almost total lack of discipline. When the semester ended, I came back to Paterson, where I enrolled in Jersey City State College as a second-semester freshman. By my sophomore year, I was establishing a new identity on the basketball court—only six miles away from where I would establish my undercover identity barely four years later.

I made the team and played the role of sixth man, getting a lot of playing time because of my defensive skills as a guard. My coach, Larry Schiner, told me that he was relying on me to lead the team, and that's what I tried to do. I also found that I could play a key role with my communication skills. If my teammates had any problems, they came to me and I'd be their go-between with the coach. That's the reason the team voted me captain in my junior season, causing a dilemma for Coach Schiner because seniors traditionally served as captain. To avoid causing a rift with the seniors on the squad, his solution was to create a tri-captain situation: It would be me, along with two seniors who would alternate as my co-captain from game to game. I wasn't the best ballplayer around, but I made up for it with drive and determination.

My best moment came against Morgan State, the equivalent of a Division I team. My role was to cover a 6-10 freshman phenomenon named Marvin Webster, who was nicknamed "The Human Eraser" and who went on to play for the New York Knicks. I played the game of my life, staying on him wherever he went and totally disrupting his rhythm. We won the game in one of the school's biggest upsets in years.

I was planning to return to play as a senior, but, as I mentioned earlier, toward the end of my junior year I heard that the New Jersey State Police were conducting a series of tests for new recruits, something that hadn't been done for two years. One night, I asked my father if he would come downstairs to the basement to talk. My mom, I found out later, was listening on the top step. "What's up?" my dad asked. "What would you think if I wanted to go into the State Police?" I said. "Rob, it's up to you," was his answer.

He didn't want to pressure me in any way. I know my mom felt let down, because she was still holding out the hope that I would become a priest. But my dad helped her through it. He just said, "Mary, he's going to be serving in a different way."

CHAPTER THREE

LET'S END THIS THING OF THEIRS

*The ornate ranch-style mansion is shaded by the woods and lush green-
ery of a sprawling horse farm, an hour's drive and a universe away from
the seedy back streets and shadowy bars near Port Newark.*

*Here in the sparsely populated countryside of Bedminster, New
Jersey, not far from stables once owned by Jacqueline Kennedy Onassis,
the rich and famous live and play, away from the daily grind of city life.
But the owner of this particular home is a businessman whose travels
prevent him from spending much time at the million-dollar estate—one
of the man's three residences—hidden behind tall rows of hedges. So he
gives his good friend a set of keys and free run of the secluded house.
Once or twice a week in the spring of 1975, a handful of cars pulls
up the winding, private driveway and several casually attired men—
sometimes just two, sometimes a half dozen—step out. They enter the
pristine house and settle into the spacious rec room with its granite pool
table and massive stone fireplace. Unseen by the rest of the world, they
plunge for hours into their secretive planning.*

*It almost has the feel of the infamous Apalachin Meeting, when Mob
bosses from around the United States and beyond convened for a Mafia
summit in 1957 at the lavish country home of Joseph "The Barber"
Barbara in Apalachin, New York. That gathering ended in disaster for
the mobsters, with law enforcement raiding the wooded grounds and
making dozens of arrests.*

But this Bedminster meeting is staged by law enforcement itself.

*Unknown to the absentee owner, his country palace has been turned
into a classroom. And his friend, Jack Liddy of the New Jersey State
Police, is serving as instructor. He speaks to his students in calm,*

matter-of-fact tones, as if describing his investment portfolio. In fact, Liddy is carefully detailing the names of key members of major crime families in the Northeast suspected of having a grip on the New Jersey waterfront—in particular the Genovese, Bruno, Gambino, and DeCavalcante organizations. Liddy is a human encyclopedia, reciting suspected illegal activities, nicknames, ranks of crime family members, and all their known associates. Bob Delaney, one of five undercover agents recruited for the mission, mostly listens, itching to get the operation under way.

Delaney is getting a basic working knowledge of the life he will soon be living in Project Alpha, immersed in Mafia groups with deep roots in Sicily and long, bloody histories in the United States.

The Genoveses have evolved out of the Morellos, who were one of the first powerful Italian crime families in New York at the turn of the twentieth century. The lineage includes such legendary Mob names as Charles "Lucky" Luciano, Joey Adonis, Frank Costello, and Vito Genovese. Building his empire on narcotics trafficking in the 1950s and '60s, Genovese was convicted on a drug charge and sentenced to a fifteen-year prison term. He ruled from behind bars but died in prison in 1969. By the mid-1970s, the reigning boss of the family is Frank "Funzi" Tieri. His rise to power has been supported by close friend Carlo Gambino, widely regarded as the most powerful Mafia boss in the country and head of his own New York crime family, the Gambinos.

Tieri's top men in New Jersey are Tino Fiumara and John DiGilio, a.k.a. Johnny Dee—both considered cold-blooded crew leaders in the Genovese ranks—and both on Project Alpha's wish list. Then there is the Bruno Family, a Philadelphia organization run by Sicilian-born Angelo Bruno and also an ally of Gambino. Bruno has steered his crime family away from the illicit-drug business and focused instead on loan sharking and bookmaking. One Bruno-affiliated crew, the DiNorscios—run by father Dominick and his two sons, Jackie and Ralph—are known to have gained a foothold on the New Jersey waterfront, muscling their way into businesses through threats and physical intimidation.

The crime families may have had different agendas and tactics, but they have had the same collective impact: forcing legitimate merchants into the fold of organized crime if they want to survive. It is the way of La Cosa Nostra—a Sicilian phrase roughly translated as "This Thing of Ours."

The more Delaney learns from Liddy, the more he can't wait to help end "this thing of theirs." It is a feeling—a special sense of mission and confidence—shared by everyone involved at both the New Jersey State Police and the FBI. Project Alpha has a six-month federal grant to attract Mafiosi to a fake trucking company in Elizabeth, New Jersey—methodically building cases against them via hidden cameras and tape recorders, and thus cleaning up the waterfront. They are about to wage a swift, underground war. The trucking company will be the bait to lure a ruthless enemy.

There is only one problem: Despite all the months of meticulous planning and preparation by members of the law-enforcement team, despite all the ingenious, state-of-the-art electronics put in place for the investigation, no one has counted on one possibility.

What if the Mafia never bothers to show up?

After driving away from the State Police barracks, my heart pounded as I headed down the highway to my apartment an hour away in Hawthorne. My thoughts raced with images of the mobsters I would be seeking out and befriending and all the precarious situations that awaited me. I was ready to start the investigation right then and there.

Unfortunately, that wasn't what Liddy had in mind. Instead of going to work, I had to hang around my apartment while he finalized all the fake paperwork for my alias—right down to a phony social security card and driver's license. My days consisted of running small errands, buying this or that, and doing my best to avoid people. I was going absolutely stir-crazy. Finally, after a week, Liddy handed me my new identification. The transformation was official: Robert Alan Covert, whoever he had been a quarter-century earlier during his brief time on

Earth, had been brought back to life, reborn as an undercover persona, about to enter the unknown.

My first task was to get a new apartment. Just as I'd been stationed in the barracks at Flemington as a State Police recruit, now I was given a housing assignment by Liddy as an undercover recruit: Find a place to live in Bayonne. In short order, I located a simple one-bedroom, one-bath deal with a kitchenette on 21st Street between Broadway and Avenue C, and then I had to go out and buy furniture.

It's a funny thing. You picture yourself in the middle of this dangerous double-agent operation. But here you are pacing around a dark apartment, waiting for some guy from the power company to come turn on your electricity—and all you know is that he'll be showing up sometime between 8:00 a.m. and 5:00 p.m. Then you're waiting for days to get your phone hooked up so you don't have to keep searching for an unoccupied phone booth down the street. You're stuck doing all the mundane, boring things anybody does when moving into a new home. I mean, this was going to be the biggest investigation in the history of the New Jersey State Police, and I'm going around buying dishes.

With all that downtime, impatient for the lights to be turned on in my new life, my mind kept wandering to the not-so-distant past. I couldn't stop thinking about Bobby Scott. I hated the fact that I'd had to be so blunt and hurtful to my State Police mentor when he offered to help me. The memory ate away at me, especially as I tossed and turned at night, trying to fall asleep in the emptiness of my new surroundings. The conversation had taken place only a couple of weeks earlier, but it was starting to feel like a different lifetime.

Nothing about my new world was clear yet. I was now going to be working with four other undercover guys: A fellow trooper and one FBI agent were in a deep-cover role like me; the other two FBI men were in traditional undercover roles and continued to live in their own homes. Just so you understand—there are a variety of undercover levels. In buy/bust, a cop takes on an identity to buy drugs or stolen property, and the criminal is arrested immediately. The traditional undercover role has a law-enforcement officer take on an identity, allowing that agent an opportunity to pursue criminal cases or gather information while still living in his or her own home. The most complicated of all undercover roles is that of deep cover. This is what I was preparing to do. I took on a new name, became that person, detached myself from anything to do with my past, and lived this new life 24/7 for years on end.

For now, we were isolated from each other. The three of us in deep cover lived in different towns—Bayonne, Elizabeth, and Carteret—to make sure we'd get assimilated into our own areas and develop different contacts. The plan called for all five of us to be co-owners of Mid-Atlantic Air & Sea Transportation in Elizabeth, but we hadn't even begun to figure out how the setup would work. Right off the bat, we didn't want to identify any one of us as more important than the rest so no one would be stepping on any toes. Well, I've never seen a bus go down the road with five bus drivers. I knew in my gut that we were headed for problems.

Ralph Buono—undercover name Ralph Rascati—was the trooper, and he and I shared the same mindset. From the FBI was Richie Moyes, the other deep-cover agent carrying an alias of Richie Blake. Al Koehler would go by Al Denny, and Lenny Perreira as Lenny Perrone; they were also FBI agents. We were taking two law-enforcement agencies and blending them into a single unit. In those days, that kind of mix was unheard of—like insisting that Macy's and Gimbel's start working together, sharing all their secrets and getting along like one happy family. Back in the 1970s, it wasn't unusual for a surveillance to take place with the FBI on one corner and the State Police at the other, competing with one another to make a case. In fact, the FBI wasn't all that far removed from the white-shirt-and-tie days of J. Edgar Hoover. Bureau agents still carried themselves in a stiff, buttoned-down manner that didn't lend itself to the kind of street-savvy investigation we were trying to get under way.

It was no coincidence that our operation had been dubbed Project Alpha—the word "Alpha" symbolizing the first joint venture between the FBI and State Police in a waterfront investigation. You see, the Law Enforcement Assistance Administration was an arm of the federal government that provided money for local and state police departments that didn't have the budgets to conduct major investigations. The key was that the FBI could not get that money. When the New Jersey State Police requested LEAA funds for the project, the grant was written to include FBI participation, but the agency would work with us, not supervise us. Because the State Police was, in essence, holding the purse strings, we were also holding the upper hand in Project Alpha.

Despite the strained State Police–FBI pairing, I found myself more and more enthusiastic about getting this investigation into high gear. We were going to be taking on organized crime, busting up their operations, and we'd be done in six months. If I did my job well, I could tell everybody all the stories of what I'd been through, and I might even be looked upon as a hero. I mean, *Serpico* had been a huge movie just a year or two before, and Baretta was a big hit on TV. Hollywood was just starting to popularize tough-guy narcs and undercover agents, even though they always depicted them as wackos. But there was a definite mystique that the characters conveyed on screen, and I embraced it in real life—immediately starting to grow my conservative trooper-style hair long and trading my clean-shaven style for stubble that soon became an unkempt beard. I became like every other undercover agent—an armpit with eyes. I was ready for the role of a lifetime and I intended to look the part—at least the look I knew from film and TV. And it wouldn't be the last time I realized that life imitates art.

About three weeks into the assignment, I made time for one trip to my parents' house in Paterson. They had invited my grandparents over so that I could tell them in person what was going on. I parked around the corner and walked down to the house. My grandparents were there, waiting in the living room, along with my sister Kath, who already knew the whole story. When I entered, I could see that everyone was taken aback by my disheveled new look. I was wearing beat-up jeans and a faded T-shirt, not the kind of attire they were accustomed to seeing me in. I came right to the point.

"The reason I wanted you to be here is to tell you that you're going to hear some bad things about me—you may have heard them already. I'm actually working undercover. I'm still a state trooper and I'm involved in an investigation that not even the troopers know about."

My grandparents listened in stunned silence as I stressed how important it was for them not to talk to anyone else about my assignment. I explained that I'd only be gone for a few more months. Then, my mother's mom—Grandma Hamill—looked at me and smiled supportively. Grandpa Delaney, always the politician, started asking me questions. I tried to answer without really answering, doing my best not to appear impatient or anxious to wrap things up. But when I saw that my mom had made all kinds of hors d'oeuvres for the occasion, as if we were having a big family party, I knew I had to get out. It was too much to try to act normal or start socializing with my family. The truth was, I was so wrapped up in the allure of my present and future that I had no time for my past. I couldn't wait to get back to my new life.

Not that there was *that* much for me to get back to. It took about two months before we even opened Mid-Atlantic. First, I had to get an education in trucking. My teacher was a retired New Jersey State Trooper, Sam Cunninghame. He had actually worked with my father in the Outfit and retired in 1972 to go into the trucking business in north Jersey. So Sam was the perfect guy to show me the ropes. I went to work each day as Bobby Covert, loading trucks at a Seagram's bottling plant on Route 1 & 9 in Linden.

Sam gave me my Ph.D. in trucking, teaching me about safety, the inspection business, tariff issues, whether to lease equipment, whether to arrange for independent contracted drivers to operate your trucks or hire your own guys. Driving the trucks came easily, but I wasn't crazy about working at the bottling plant. The boxes of bottles came rolling down the conveyer belt, and you'd load them onto pallets and lift them onto the trucks. I'm thinking, I went undercover for *this*?

Sam's reputation as a former state trooper preceded him, with his mere presence making the employees uneasy. But when he wasn't around, they'd purposely crack bottles on the conveyer belt to slow down production for the day and avoid having to load so many trucks. In return for everything Sam did for me, all I could give him when I graduated with my informal "trucking degree" a month later were the names of a few workers who had sabotaged his operation by breaking bottles. I had to laugh. In this complex State Police–FBI undercover investigation, busting some bottle breakers had become my first big blow against the bad guys.

On a humid Jersey day in June 1975, we finally went to work at Mid-Atlantic. It was a gray concrete-block building with a chain-link fence on a bland industrial street—941 Fairmont Avenue in Elizabeth, to be exact. There were two loading bays in the front and three in the back, with some steps in the rear that led up to a small terminal office inside. The office was cramped and bare-bones, with two old metal desks—one against each wall—and a couple of file cabinets in between. But it looked great to me.

It was almost enough to make me forget about all the petty jealousies and mistrust that clouded the relationship Ralph and I had with the three FBI guys. My attitude was, "I'm listening to *Jack*—I'm not listening to an FBI agent tell me what to do. I don't work for them." They were thinking the same thing about Ralph and me—and Jack Liddy, too, I'm sure.

Despite my feelings, I had to hand it to the technical experts on the FBI's electronic surveillance unit. They had set things up so that when you went in or out of the office, you passed a big stereo speaker on the wall that concealed a camera. Anybody who walked past it had their picture taken. We even hung a clock and a Mid-Atlantic sign on the wall across from the speaker, so both the time and location would appear in every photo. In addition, an old Bell Telephone answering machine not only allowed us to tape phone calls, but also recorded conversations held in the room. Keep in mind that back then, telephone answering machines were nothing like they are today. They were big, bulky units that had to be turned on each time you left to go somewhere.

But our machine had an ingenious twist. If we flipped the switch to the "off" position, it actually turned the answering machine on and picked up the voices of anyone in the room. And no suspicions were ever aroused, because the machine appeared to be off. In addition, if you wanted to record a phone call, all you had to do was push down the button for line one or line two—whichever line the call came in on— and simultaneously push down a button for a line three that didn't really exist.

We thought of Mid-Atlantic as a giant operation—and it was, to law enforcement. But to the business world, it was just another small trucking company. Our fleet of trucks consisted of one 16-footer a lot smaller than an ordinary tractor-trailer, one van, and one station wagon. But we were excited about finally getting the show—and our vehicles—on the road.

Spreading the word about Mid-Atlantic was one of the first orders of business. After a typical workday, usually starting around 8:30 a.m. and ending around 5:00 p.m., I'd go home to my apartment, shower and change, then walk to any number of bars downtown and try to be seen and make contacts. When I would get back to my apartment, I'd turn on the TV and flip channels before falling asleep. One night in early October 1975, I stumbled upon a show that instantly caught my attention because the skits were so bizarre. It wasn't until the first commercial that I heard the words *Saturday Night Live*. In a strange way, the comical, crazy behavior in the *SNL* skits mirrored the behavior of characters I encountered on the street. The locals referred to Bayonne as the Beverly Hills of Hudson County, with fancy little shops, fine restaurants, clean streets, and nice suburban homes. Maybe that's why the bad guys liked living there, too. For me, it was the perfect place to hang my hat. There was even a port called the Military Ocean Bay Terminal, which meant I'd have the chance to create business opportunities for Mid-Atlantic.

Bayonne was John DiGilio's territory—a very closed community where newcomers such as myself tended to be conspicuous. Fortunately, I found a bar near my apartment that had opened only few weeks earlier—a good place for me to start showing up regularly, rather than a bar that had been around for thirty years where I would completely stick out. The joint was already a known Johnny Dee hangout, with what I thought of as a perfect name—the Sting Lounge. It was dark and smoky, with a catty-corner entranceway on the end of a block, like a lot of the bars and cozy neighborhood restaurants in the area. The place had quickly developed a reputation for loan sharking and gambling.

During the next month or so, I started to create a rapport with the Sting Lounge's owner, Tommy G., a DiGilio guy. Tommy was about 5-9, with a slight build, long brown hair, and a Fu Manchu moustache, looking to me like a dead ringer for Sonny Bono, only with no Cher by his side. I was one of the few people hanging around one Saturday afternoon when Tommy turned to me. "Hey, do me a favor and jump behind the stick," his way of asking me to work the tap for anyone wanting a beer, filling in as his bartender.

"I just need you to watch the place for a little while—I got a coupla things to do," he added.

"No problem," I said, feeling good that I had gained Tommy's trust so soon.

Actually, I was about to get a lesson in the ways of the Mob.

Over the course of the next hour, about six men came in. I recognized them immediately from Jack Liddy's organized crime classes. They were wiseguys: a goodfella with a bad toupee, beige leisure suit, and dark flower print shirt; a burly bouncer type wearing a white open-collared shirt revealing a thick gold necklace; a short, squat character who had to weigh more than three hundred pounds with a nose that looked as if it had been flattened in a bar fight decades before; a lanky guy all spiffed up in a dark sport jacket and slacks. It was quite a parade. And that's when it hit me—I'd been set up. Tommy must have been concerned because I'd been hanging around a lot, and he wondered if I was truly the trucking company owner I said I was. So he had arranged his very own lineup. Each of these mobsters—along with a guy I later learned was named George Weingartner, a close associate of John DiGilio—was looking me over to see if they recognized me as a lawman or informant. One minute I was feeling good about making headway with Tommy; the next I felt like a fool. Here I was thinking that I had the upper hand, but the upper hand belonged to Tommy G.

The very next day, I got stopped by a local cop. He tossed me pretty good—going through all my stuff, taking an extra long look at my driver's license and ID cards, asking questions like, "What was the year you were born? What day?" He was trying to catch me in a lie. Two days later, it happened again. Same cop, same routine. Obviously, this was no coincidence. I couldn't prove by this cop's actions that he was dirty, but in my gut I knew he was. Corruption doesn't have to involve a cash handoff; it happens on different levels. But what that cop was doing, whether he knew he was helping the wiseguys or not, was eroding the system of justice. If Tommy G. needed a favor, there were cops ready to comply.

One thing was certain: Tommy and all those mobsters had been doing their homework. They'd investigated me. And I'd passed. It was my first test as Bobby Covert. I had suddenly gained enhanced credibility with the people we needed to know.

Over the next few months, the Sting Lounge became one of my main stops each night after work. I quickly learned that it was a spot where payments were made on "shy" loans—loanshark loans that were overdue. It was not uncommon to find one of the boxing greats of the day sitting at a table in the Sting Lounge. When someone showed up who had a problem making good on payment day, Johnny Dee's guys indicated to the nervous loanee that he'd have to deal with that boxer. All the pugilist had to do was sit at the table or stand by the door, holding a drink the mobsters bought him. Johnny Dee's men would say, "See that guy over there? If you don't start paying, he'll kick your ass." They'd wave to the fighter and he'd raise his glass. The salute usually got the job done. I don't know if that boxer had any idea what was going on—but his mere presence was part of a weekly intimidation routine, and he was certainly effective.

For me, this early period was all about being seen, being around, and trying to make some breakthroughs for the operation. The truth was, however, that the Mafia types were not showing any interest in Mid-Atlantic. Mostly, we were drawing attention from low-level street criminals and guys who wished they were mobsters. So Jack Liddy came up with the idea of doing a "reverse sting" with a bar owner named Sam Smith who was connected to DiGilio. Sam ran a section of the Boardwalk, known as the poor man's Jersey Shore. I hung out in his club, the J.J. Tavern, for a while, got friendly and one night told him, "You know Sam, I might be able to help you out with stuff for down the Shore." Of course, that meant stolen stuff, at a price. He was interested, so our undercover team went to a warehouse and bought tons of ceramic owls, birds, all kinds of gaudy statuettes. We loaded them onto our truck, brought them to Sam, and acted as if the stuff was stolen. We sold it all to him for about 10 percent of what we'd paid. It was a way of ingratiating ourselves by making him believe we dealt in swag, the wiseguy's word for stolen property—a twist on the usual scenario in which undercover cops go out to buy the goods that have been ripped off.

It was a small triumph, but hardly what we had in mind when we'd started out several months earlier. You could feel the frustration beginning to build at the trucking company. We weren't making a dent in organized crime. On top of that, Ralph and I—the two state troopers in the operation—constantly had to iron out our difficulties with the three FBI guys. We disagreed on how to conduct the investigation, little things and big things. Finally, after some pretty heated arguments, we laid it all on the table, and the five of us arrived at this philosophy: We're not the State Police. We're not the FBI. We're our own little unit, and we'd better start acting like it. And we did.

I realized that we had to play to our strengths, and mine was out on the street, getting to know people. So I started branching out, having lunch at a restaurant called Zorba's, not far from Mid-Atlantic. It was run by George Mavrodes, an associate of two mobster brothers, Nicky and Joe Paterno—and no, not any relation whatsoever to the great Penn State football coach by the same name. They were lower-tier members of the Gambinos. George was a short, stocky man in his fifties with a dark, rugged complexion and a bushy moustache that he liked to twirl on the ends when mulling over deals. We told him there were some things we could do for him, trying to open up a few avenues for Mob business.

Not long after that, George and Nicky arrived at Mid-Atlantic with a startling offer for us. They had somehow scored about $500,000 in stolen New Jersey unemployment compensation checks and wanted to know if we would like to buy some. I couldn't believe our good fortune. *"Fuckin'-A,"* I said—a phrase that anybody from the Northeast Corridor, whether it's Jersey, New York, or Philly, understands as a definite "yes."

We set up a meeting in the terminal office, with the secret taping equipment set to record all the back-and-forth of our first big deal. As I sat in my chair listening to George and Nicky talk, I could feel the sweat beading on my neck and rolling down my back, but I stayed focused and projected an air of nonchalance as the negotiating began. In a matter of seconds, though, George and several of his guys went from negotiating in normal tones to yelling at us at the top of their lungs.

"What the fuck you mean we're askin' too much!!?" Nicky screamed. "We're offering you a gift, and you're fuckin' with us."

We yelled right back at them. Making matters worse, I was very conscious that everyone in the room had a gun on them, and I couldn't shake the feeling that I had a sign on my forehead proclaiming "I'm a cop!"

As the yelling intensified and we continued to counter-offer, it crossed my mind that this could quickly spin out of control and end in bullets flying. But at that instant, George raised his hand and his men grew quiet. Just like that, a broad smile crossed his face. He accepted our offer, and it was done as if tempers had never even flared. Then, to my utter surprise, he invited all of us to join his group for Chinese food.

We followed them to a Mob hangout in Bloomfield, had pepper steak and cashew chicken, and yukked it up with our new friends.

At around the same time, lowlifes began showing up at Mid-Atlantic trying to unload stolen bikes, clothing, electronics, just about anything, and we bought as much as we could without draining our budget for illicit transactions. But the big picture for us was a whole lot more important than buying stolen property from petty thieves. We wanted to understand how organized crime operated, how it infiltrated waterfront unions and strong-armed legitimate businesses. Still, there were some deals involving swag that we couldn't just walk away from. There were three street guys we got to know who said they could score "loads" from the Port—and that was of interest to us.

One day, they told us they could put together a tractor-trailer load of television sets. This sounded promising indeed. They let us know they'd bring the sets to the loading dock at about 2:00 a.m. We got there on time, and waited in the darkness. No sign of the load. At 3:00 a.m., still no sign. At 4:00 a.m., just as it seemed that a huge deal had gone south, the dead quiet of early morning was shattered by a God-awful screeching sound. We looked down the street, and here was a tractor-trailer crawling toward us. "You gotta be fuckin' kiddin' me," I said to no one in particular.

The idiots had no idea how to drive, and they had locked up the brakes on the trailer. They were literally *dragging* it to us from the port. The air was filled with the strong odor of burning rubber. I was thinking, "Great, we're all going to get arrested three months into the investigation, on our first major buy." Any rookie cop could easily have followed the trail from the port to our building.

"What the hell are you doing?!!" I yelled to the driver.

We made them drag the trailer to the back of our building as quickly as they could, and prepared to offload the TVs to our smaller trucks. Naturally, the three stooges had no idea that everything would wind up at division headquarters and be used as evidence against them. But it turned out that the joke was on us.

We opened up the back of the trailer and instead of TVs, they had these small four-foot refrigerators. "We can't do anything with these," I told the ringleader. "We got no outlet for little refrigerators. Are you fuckin' crazy?" Then they started arguing among themselves, with one of the guys screaming, "I told you we were supposed to take the other trailer!"

"Look, you guys are gonna have to figure it out—we have to get the hell outta here," I shouted.

"We ain't leaving without our money," the head thug shouted back.

"Fuck you—we ain't payin'," I yelled, suddenly sounding as stupid as the people I was dealing with. "We don't even know where we'd get rid of these!"

It was getting tense, but we had to stand our ground or we'd be seen as pushovers. The strategy worked. They backed down and eventually agreed to a reduced price. But the truth is, we were no better off than we'd been before the fiasco. We had just done business with the gang that couldn't shoot straight. Here we were, thinking we'd be making these big inroads into organized crime, and we had a bunch of bozos who didn't know what the hell they were doing. I'd gone from being an aggressive state trooper making frequent arrests to a rookie undercover agent who wasn't sure if *anything* was getting accomplished. We all thought we were going to wipe out organized crime in three weeks, and it just wasn't happening. We didn't even know if we were making any cases. It was completely frustrating.

Then, for me, the problems veered into personal territory.

I was having very little contact with my parents, with the exception of a short phone call here and there from pay phones to tell them I was fine. One afternoon I got a call from Jack Liddy, who told me to call my father. Something didn't feel right about it, so I hurried down to the corner outside the trucking office to the nearest pay phone. I was thinking, my dad knows I'm undercover; this has to be something serious. I felt a knot in my gut. My fear was that something had happened to my mother. I dialed the number, and my father picked up right away.

"What's up?" I asked. "Just *tell* me."

"Your grandmother died," he said quietly.

"Tell me the *truth*, don't tell me something just to get me there—is it Mom?" The words rushed out with the urgency I felt inside.

"It's your *grandmother*," he repeated slowly.

I felt momentary relief knowing it wasn't my mom. My dad told me the details—Mom's mother, my tough little Irish grandmother who I hadn't had enough time to talk to a few months earlier, had died of a heart attack. It was a short call, and I stood there tearing up. I felt terrible that I had rushed out of my parents' house that day. Now the chance to speak to her was gone forever, and I was left with waves of sadness and remorse. But I took a deep breath and pulled myself together. I went back into the trucking office and told my partners that I'd be gone for a day or two.

I attended my grandmother's funeral but mostly stayed to myself. There were dozens of troopers present, but they all kept their distance from me as well. I knew they had heard all the rumors about me, that I had gone bad and killed a guy in a fight or whatever other stories were getting passed along. They could see I looked scraggly and distracted, so people probably believed the worst. They'd glance at me and turn away. Even though I understood, it stung to see how easily my colleagues and friends had abandoned ship.

It was like being at my *own* funeral. I went straight home from the service to spend a little time with my parents and relatives, still grieving the loss of my beloved grandma. And then I was gone, back into the shadows of Bobby Covert's world.

I slipped into the role comfortably, but still we continued to spin our wheels, dealing with ripoff artists, bookmakers, and loan sharks. As the six-month cutoff for Project Alpha approached, we hadn't caught any big Mafia fish in our net. It wasn't a huge surprise when Sergeant Liddy notified us that our investigation would be extended another six months. We already had invested so much time and energy that it really didn't make sense to pull the plug. I think everybody—from the Washington, D.C., brass on down to us—realized that the undertaking was a lot more complicated than we had all imagined. We'd been naïve, thinking we could just show up on the waterfront and start busting up organized crime. We thought we'd created a large, attractive trucking company that made us appear like real players; well, it obviously didn't look that way to the Mob. Now the challenge was to build on the foundation we had created.

That was fine with me. I didn't have a wife and kids waiting for me at home, and my competitive juices made me want to push on and finish what we had set out to do. At that point, one of the three FBI guys, Lenny Perrone, who was older than the rest of us and had a family that needed him, requested to leave after the initial six-month grant from the LEAA ran out. Lenny was a pretty nervous guy—and therein lay the key to another breakthrough in my learning process.

I pretty much stumbled into this one. My partner Ralph and I had heard comments about Lenny's nervousness from George Mavrodes and Nicky Paterno. They'd talked about needing to be careful around nervous guys. That gave Ralph and me an idea for gaining some street credibility with our Mob-connected acquaintances.

It came about spontaneously when we went to Jersey City to have a bite at a little breakfast-lunch eatery owned by a bookie we knew, Danny Roche, a guy who took bets in his own restaurant. As soon as we were sure Danny was in earshot, we started talking about how we needed to whack Lenny because he'd gotten too jittery about things and we couldn't trust him. Well, old Danny boy was riding the Erie—a wiseguy term, short for riding the Erie Lackawanna, the famous railway line. In proper Mob lingo, Danny was riding the Erie Lackawanna on us, meaning he had his ear on our conversation, doing his best to eavesdrop on what we were saying.

The next time we came into his place, Danny pulled me off to the side and said he'd heard us talking. "I can help you," Danny said.

"Yeah, with what?" I asked.

"That thing you were talking about the other day. You got to get rid of something? I can get you the tools."

As he spoke, I had to do everything in my power not to reveal that I couldn't believe what I was hearing. All we'd done was lay out a line to explain why Lenny wouldn't be around any more. We definitely didn't intend to trigger a bookie, of all people, to provide us with the guns for the job.

But right there, we had just made another case.

"Okay," I said, drawing him out. "What are we talking about here?"

Danny quoted a price of $450 for two guns and told us to return the next day. I chuckled to myself: Where did they come up with these figures? How did two guns add up to $450, as in $225 per weapon—why not just make it an even $500? Hey, maybe I got lucky and this was Danny's blue plate special of the day. In any case, we did just what he asked and came back a day later, slipping him the $450. With a sly smile, he gave us a "to go" bag containing one automatic weapon and one .38 caliber pistol, both cleaned of serial numbers, and a pair of gloves to conceal the fingerprints.

This was another potential prosecution added to a list that was growing quickly, but we'd also just learned something our training didn't cover. In those days, if you were arrested for loan sharking, that's what we considered you, a loan shark, period. If we busted a guy for bookmaking, he was a bookie. Someone we nailed for stealing cars was, in our mind, only a car thief. Law enforcement had a tendency to take its paramilitary mindset and apply it to the street, putting neat little labels on all the organized-crime actors we encountered. We understood that everyone in our own ranks had a specific role, and the perception carried over to our view of the Mob's structure, simply because it made it easier for us to understand. But we were wrong. Here was an example of how willing and able these guys were to branch out into any illegal pursuit if they could make money from it. A friendly local bookie might, at the drop of a hat, turn into a not-so-friendly accessory to murder.

In the end, the Paterno brothers and George Mavrodes assumed we'd whacked poor Lenny—a step up in our credibility. George was starting to trust me. He even began to school me in his Mob methods. One night at the lounge inside a Holiday Inn, George pointed to someone. He told me he knew he was a cop.

"Get the fuck outta here," I said.

"I know because he has his back to the wall, watches everybody who comes in the door and looks them up and down," George replied. "And look at how he dresses—black lace-up shoes with jeans. He pays cash for his drinks. He doesn't run a tab. He orders beer and drinks it out of a bottle because he doesn't want to drink from the same glasses as us. His boss gave him $20 to do the surveillance in here—he'll only spend $5 and pocket the remaining $15 and go drink with his police buddies. He's a fuckin' cop, I'm tellin' ya."

Another time, George told me we couldn't go into that Chinese restaurant in Bloomfield because a car was backed into a spot. He explained it was something only cops did so they could make a quick move out of the police station, an old habit, hard to break even when they went undercover. George had a sharp eye but gave new meaning to the word paranoid. He was the kind of person who thought law enforcement could drop a microphone in the olive of a martini. He saw cops behind every tree.

Yet he showed no sign that he was suspicious of me. On the contrary, he continued to share stories of old crimes and ideas for new ones. I'll never forget his all-time classic caper—the tale of the tuna fish cans. It started with a couple of George's guys who were supposed to take down a load of tuna. They had outlets lined up with Mob-connected restaurants. But when they got around to breaking down the load, they opened one of the boxes and discovered it wasn't tuna; it was cat food. Somebody had screwed up big-time when they made their score.

George was pissed off, because the cans couldn't be delivered to the scheduled destinations and it looked like there was no way to make any money on the heist. But then he came up with an answer: He instructed his men to open all the boxes, put real tuna fish cans without wrappers on the top rows, and remove all the wrappers from the cat food cans underneath, making it appear that they too contained tuna. The re-packed boxes were then driven in vans and small trucks to diners and mom-and-pop grocery stores—meaning nonconnected Mob places—where they were sold as boxes of tuna that had fallen off the delivery truck.

The small food outlets eagerly paid the discount price Mavrodes's men offered, and, by accepting stolen goods, became participants. When they discovered they'd been ripped off, they couldn't report the scam to the police. George explained: "What are they gonna do? Run to the law and say 'We thought we were buying stolen tuna fish, and we ended up buying stolen cat food'?" So George got the money and got rid of the load.

He was always scheming. He asked me if I could buy a tow truck and paint it to look like an official Newark Police Department towing vehicle. His plan was to steal five or six cars by simply towing them away before the police caught on. He figured that with a $30,000 investment in the fake tow truck, we could make $100,000 in stolen cars. I acted impressed and interested, but made sure we *never* got around to helping him with that one. There were plenty of stories like this one—intelligence information that I would gather on a daily basis that were recorded in what I referred to as my daily reports. I would use a small Norelco recorder that I kept hidden in a wall behind the hamper in my apartment. It allowed me to document all of my activities on a daily basis. Once a week, those tapes would be turned over to Jack Liddy, and they were transcribed and brought back to me in writing for my approval and signature. Those daily reports were a documentation of my day-to-day activities throughout Project Alpha. They proved invaluable not only in the prosecutions, but years later in the writing of this book.

Then one day, completely out of the blue, George decided to see if he could trip me up. Right in the middle of a conversation we were having about the Yankees, he dropped in this line:

"I ran your license plate, Bobby. It comes back not on file."

I knew right away it was an attempt to rattle me, to see how I might react. In a deep cover situation, the confidence you portray comes from knowing you've covered every base, backstopped every possible situation that might blow your cover. In this case, I knew my car was registered to Robert Alan Covert. George had to be bluffing.

"George, my plate doesn't come back not on file," I said calmly, with a smile. "It comes back to my name. You want the registration? What kind of game you tryin' to play here?"

I put it right back in his face, careful to avoid seeming overly defensive or too riled up. It's essential for an undercover agent to know when and how to stand up for himself, not to overdo his reaction. If you go too far, you can actually look guilty as hell. That creates as much of a red flag as something like a plate coming back not on file.

The key was to project a steady, even-keeled demeanor while asserting myself. I looked George straight in the eye, moved in almost nose-to-nose, and said in a low, deliberate voice, "Why you testin' me?" Now George was on the defensive.

He began to laugh.

"Relax," he said, grinning. "We're going to be doing lots of work together now."

"Really? Why's that?" I replied, still trying to sound disgusted that he had some lingering doubts about me.

"Because I know you for more than six months," George said. "I marked on the calendar when we first met. It's been more than six months. And Johnny Law only writes grants for investigations for six months. So now I know for sure you're not a cop."

Project Alpha had begun making inroads into the Mafia; but after nearly ten months, ending this thing of theirs was nowhere in sight.

At least I was becoming a more convincing liar in a world that revolved around deceit and danger.

CHAPTER FOUR

THE CONSIGLIERE AND THE COP

In 1969, on a hot summer night along the Jersey Shore, Jackie DiNorscio and his cousin Anthony pick up two attractive young blondes on the boardwalk and head to a nearby diner to continue their come-ons and plans for some late-night fun. But as he heads for his favorite booth, Jackie Dee sees a mother and young daughter about to sit down there. He's been boozing it up, which makes him more belligerent than usual, and he shouts at them to get the hell out of the way—just as the woman's husband steps out of the restroom and sees the scene unfolding.

The man angrily confronts DiNorscio, only to be sucker-punched and pummeled to the floor in a vicious two-on-one beating delivered by the Mob cousins. As the man lies on the tile floor bloodied and unconscious, DiNorscio hurries off with his party—unaware that he has just assaulted an off-duty New Jersey state trooper.

When the local authorities show up, they learn that a law enforcement officer has been attacked and get the license plate number from an eyewitness. At 5:00 a.m., three State Police cars with two troopers in each descend on DiNorscio's north Jersey house. They drag him out of bed, leaving behind his boardwalk babe from the night before, and provide a return trip to the Jersey Shore—giving him a little taste of the treatment he inflicted on the trooper.

DiNorscio is booked at the State Police barracks in Laurelton. Later that day, to nobody's surprise, he is bailed out. But officials make a routine observation that will steadily take on a life of its own: The sullen, sore DiNorscio leaves the station house and drives off with a well-dressed, middle-aged man who has posted his bond for him: Patrick John Kelly.

He has not appeared on their radar before, and his presence hardly rates a blip compared to the busting of Dominick DiNorscio's 29-year-old thug son for attacking an off-duty trooper. But during the next two years, Kelly continues to show up with known mobsters at surveillance scenes and in photographs of Mafia gatherings. Gradually, he becomes a person of interest to the New Jersey State Police Intelligence Bureau and, later, to the FBI. The fact is, Kelly is far more important than either agency realizes.

He has made a killing in real estate and construction and other side ventures that tap his innate business acumen—and his gift for getting people to like him, to make new acquaintances feel as if they have known him for years and can trust him like an old friend.

Kelly is forty now, but learned years earlier that his gregarious, confident manner could open almost any door. He has a handsome Irish face—and a slightly pudgy 5-foot-10 frame that he squeezes into custom-tailored suits, an example of his voracious appetite for the finer things in life. But life has been fine, in no small measure because Kelly has started cutting financial corners and making more than a few Mob connections along the way that have increased his wealth. He is smart enough to make big money playing by the rules, but loses no sleep over breaking them if it will pad his bank account.

Kelly has become the inner-circle adviser—the consigliere—to the DiNorscios. Dominick and his two sons, Jackie and Ralph, have taken a strong liking to him. He not only keeps everyone in the crew laughing with his glib style, he keeps the money flowing steadily into the DiNorscio coffers. He is the epitome of what mobsters fondly refer to as an "earner"—a vaunted position in the hierarchy of organized crime. Earners who display continuing loyalty to their bosses are held in even higher esteem.

If he had been born Italian, Kelly would easily be on his way to becoming a "made man"—a full-fledged member of a crime family. Another term for it is "making your bones," which means you have killed somebody, buried somebody. That's what "made" guys were, under the Old World Mafia. You did have to kill somebody to become a made member. But in the Americanization of the Mob, there were made men who were big-time earners and able to produce boatloads of dollars to earn that title.

Yet even without that official standing, he receives the ultimate compliment one day from Dominick DiNorscio. He gives Kelly the "okay"—in wiseguy speak—to "sit" on his behalf and temporarily represent him in managing the criminal pursuits of the DiNorscios: everything from car theft to dealing stolen goods to narcotics trafficking, bookmaking, and extortion.

The old man needs someone to watch his criminal enterprise as he starts a two-to-three-year federal prison sentence at Lewisburg, Pennsylvania, for interstate transportation of stolen property. His son Jackie is now doing eight years at Rahway State Prison in New Jersey for bookmaking, though he remains convinced that the sentence was heavier because of his assault on the trooper; and Ralph, a drunk, isn't viewed as completely trustworthy by his father.

Kelly gladly accepts the responsibility, reveling in the adrenaline rush of working on the inside of a Mob operation, expanding his network of Mafia contacts with the Brunos and Genoveses and gaining added prestige in their eyes. But his enthusiasm is short-lived.

Two New Jersey State Police detectives greet him early one evening outside his home. They call his name and identify themselves, trying not to startle him. The detectives make their comments short and to the point. "We just want to let you know we've been watching you for a while and know you're active with the DiNorscios—we've seen you with Tino Fiumara and Michael Coppola and know more than you think," one of them says matter-of-factly.

They dole out fragments of information—all part of a bluff to get Kelly's attention. And then they calmly describe his possible future: face prosecution and the certainty of prison time—a choice they are sure he won't be able to stomach—or become an informant, cooperating with ongoing law-enforcement investigations of the Mafia. "I'd hate to see you wind up as Jackie DiNorscio's roommate at Rahway," the other detective remarks as they pull away.

Kelly is shaken and unsure of what to do. Two days later, he gets a similar visit from two FBI agents who have also had him under surveillance—unaware that the State Police had also approached him. They make him a similar offer. Kelly listens, the color draining from his face. "I'm sure Dominick DiNorscio would love some company at Lewisburg," one of the agents adds as they drive off.

Kelly panics at the thought of prison—but is equally unnerved by the notion of ratting on the Mob. During the next week, he barely sleeps, his ulcers act up, and he's smoking nonstop. Finally, Kelly seizes the one chance he has to retain a semblance of his old life: the five-star restaurants, the pretty women, the money. If it means he must do it while wearing a wire for the State Police and FBI, gathering evidence against the Mob, so be it.

The old Sicilian code of silence known as omerta—the absolute prohibition of cooperating with the authorities, under penalty of death—has been fading. With the gradual Americanization of the Mob in the sixties and seventies, the code has increasingly failed to deter arrested mobsters from giving up their colleagues. Bobby Kennedy's federal Witness Protection Program, created during his tenure as attorney general, has also made an impact, encouraging criminals to become informants in exchange for a new identity and secret Relocation.

Kelly, whose primary interest is above all else himself, has no intention of upholding some old code from a prison cell. So he flips—embracing a new challenge, new bosses, and new hazards, whatever it takes to keep the game going.

He is a prize catch, and both the State Police and the FBI—unbeknownst to each other—begin using him independently in their own investigations of organized crime in and around Newark starting in late 1973.

His true worth won't emerge until early 1976, although not because of any grand plan hatched by either law-enforcement agency. Project Alpha has been sputtering along for a year, hoping its undercover truck-

ing operation will catch a break. One cold winter afternoon—in an entirely flukish development—a jovial Pat Kelly, accompanied by two other men, shows up at Mid-Atlantic Air & Sea Transportation in Elizabeth.

His arrival will quickly change everything—for Project Alpha, and for Bobby Covert.

I'd rather be lucky than good, and we got really lucky when Pat Kelly walked into our lives. You'd like to be able to say it was all part of a brilliant plan by the State Police or the FBI, but really, the only brilliant part of the whole thing was Pat himself.

I had absolutely no idea what to expect when I first heard his name. All I knew—all *any* of us knew, for that matter—was that Project Alpha wasn't going the way we expected or wanted, and there was no clear road map for us to follow to the top Mafia guys we had our eyes on. One of the FBI agents in our operation, Al Koehler, was not in a deep cover role, and he still had some contact with his office. He found out about an undercover FBI agent, P. J. Jumonville, who was working the street as a lone ranger, with no operation or funding to back him. He was using an informant, a guy named Pat Kelly.

Kelly had set up a potential deal for Jumonville. He had a stolen portfolio of bearer bonds and stocks that he was trying to sell on behalf of one of the DiNorscios. But Jumonville didn't have any money to buy it, and his bosses hadn't even given him the go-ahead. That's when Kohler told him to bring the portfolio to us at Mid-Atlantic and we would see if a deal could be made.

One afternoon, we were all in our office and in walks P. J. Jumonville, along with a half-ass wiseguy carrying the stocks and bonds—Charlie Cannizzo, a heavyset grandfatherly type—and Kelly. We weren't overly enthusiastic. What were we going to do, become the freakin' clearinghouse for everybody else's jobs? In one way, we were happy about the prospect of making a case, especially against an attractive target like the DiNorscios. But some of us were not crazy about the idea of bringing a new FBI guy into the mix. I'd never heard of Jumonville, and had no idea who Kelly was, other than that he was an informant. Kelly knew he was dealing with undercover Jersey troopers and FBI agents, but Charlie Cannizzo had no clue. From the moment Kelly walked into the room, he stood out with his friendly, upbeat manner—big smile, big handshake for everybody. You'd think he'd just arrived at a family reunion. I have to admit, I was pulled right into his act, which is precisely what I eventually realized it was: a great con job. Still, it was hard not to like the guy.

Over the next month, Kelly showed up every once in a while with Jumonville and some different unsuspecting Mob guys, trying to sell us on this deal or that, just as they'd done with Uncle Charlie—the name we gave Charlie Cannizzo. One morning, Kelly and Jumonville came over with Ralph DiNorscio, wanting to know if we had outlets for stolen cars.

We immediately made plans to accompany Ralph—the bumbling "Fredo Corleone" of the DiNorscios—on a mission to steal a car. We had started out this night by meeting Ralph at the Alibi Lounge in Union, just off Route 22. Ralph wanted to go over his plan and it was another opportunity for him to sit at the bar and "get his balls up"— the term he used for mustering the courage to go out and commit a crime. It was close to 10:00 p.m. and we went over each step until almost 11. It all sounded good on paper, but turned into the most botched-up mess imaginable. I was driving my fellow undercover trooper, Ralph Rascati, who was supposed to be given the car at a diner and then pull away. It should have been a piece of cake. But when we got there, old Fredo Jr. and his sidekick told us they would steal the car on the right side of the diner and drop it off for *our* Ralph on the left side. A few minutes later, a gold Lincoln Town Car whipped around the left side of the diner as planned—and wiseguy Ralph jumped out of the driver's seat while undercover Ralph slid in. I was sitting in my car about twenty feet away watching, when I heard someone yell "Oh, shit!"

A police car had just pulled into the parking lot. Fredo and his boy scattered in between the parked cars. I was sure my Ralph was going to get busted on the spot, which could have seriously jeopardized our operation. But, luckily, the cops were just stopping by for coffee and didn't notice a thing. Ralph drove off, and we had a stolen car to log in at division headquarters.

It got even better. The very next day, Ralph DiNorscio came by to get paid for the stolen car. "You know, Ralph, I talked to Bobby about it and we can take this as a tax write-off if we pay you with a company check," Rascati said.

"Are you fuckin' nuts? I ain't takin' no fuckin' check," DiNorscio snapped.

But Rascati calmly explained to DiNorscio that he would accompany him to a bank in Elizabeth that would take care of everything. "We'll pay you with one of our checks—you just endorse it on the back, I'll endorse it, and I'll make sure you get the cash right there," Rascati said.

DiNorscio paused and said, "Okay, just make the check out to Ralph DeVita." In his mind, he had come up with a perfect way to protect himself—figuring the check couldn't be traced back to him if he used an alias. Of course, the bogus surname tactic made no difference at all—not with two undercover cops witnessing the whole thing.

The next day at 1:00 p.m., DiNorscio met Rascati and me at the bank, and we handed him a Mid-Atlantic check for $2,500; and, just as we'd hoped, he scrawled "Ralph DeVita" on the back. The genius had hand-delivered us direct evidence of a car he had stolen for an undercover operation.

That's the kind of case Pat Kelly was able to serve up on a silver platter.

The Pat & P. J. Show continued for a while. They'd come by to pitch deals and we'd listen. I didn't realize it then, but Kelly was playing a completely different angle.

When the opportunities arose, he made comments, almost as if he was trying to school us on what we could do better with Mid-Atlantic. He did it in a way that wasn't condescending. Instead, he'd smile and almost make us feel that we were the ones who'd had the idea.

"You know guys, nothin' is gonna happen with this company, 'cause it's too small to have an impact—but I can help ya," he said one day.

"Yeah, how's that?" I asked, taking the bait but totally unconvinced.

"I'm glad you asked, Bobby. I got ideas of how you could make this bigger. I could open doors. And I could help you make this into a trucking company that a lot of wiseguys would want to be around."

"How we gonna do that here?" I cut him off.

"Good point—exactly what I was thinkin'," Kelly answered. "You gotta move and get a bigger location. Believe me," he added, leaning in for emphasis, speaking quietly but firmly, "it can be done."

Then he wheeled around and headed out the door. As crazy as it sounded, Kelly had gotten our attention.

In the week or so that followed, we talked about him and his idea for expanding Mid-Atlantic. All of us were in agreement: The guy could deliver. Still, we weren't authorized to reach out and start utilizing him as part of our group. That decision would have to come from Jack Liddy and higher up. When the time was right, we went to Jack and urged him to bring Pat on board so he could help us start this larger trucking company.

Liddy listened without saying a whole lot, and then told us he'd think about it and get back to us. Of course, because Project Alpha was a joint operation with the FBI, he couldn't act unilaterally. He contacted his Bureau counterpart, George DeHardy, and they decided to speak directly to Kelly. A discreet, late-night meeting was set for Ralph Rascati's apartment in Elizabeth, where they talked with him for two hours.

Liddy and DeHardy were impressed by Kelly's knowledge and enthusiasm, and they contacted their own bosses to officially recommend adding Patrick John Kelly, Mob informant, to the operation. Eventually, the proposal had to be sent all the way up the ladder to Washington. It didn't take long for the approval to come back down.

Kelly—by now we were all calling him Pat—was elated. He had to be tired of getting dragged around by Jumonville from one small informant job to the next. A real trucking company—he could have fun with that. In fact, he went right to work scouting locations for a new building. In just over a day, he found one in Jersey City, a two-story structure at 231 Communipaw Avenue. It was a perfect Mafia magnet—twice the size of Mid-Atlantic, with a huge lot for trucks, right across the river from Lower Manhattan.

"How'd you find this place so fast?" I asked him as we stood outside the gray concrete building with Ralph, Al, and Richie.

"I'm a connected guy," he grinned, and we all knew exactly what kind of connections he meant.

We negotiated the lease immediately and started making plans for the new phase of Project Alpha. Moving to the building was just one aspect of the transition. A major change was in the works. And I soon found out that it involved me in a big way.

With Pat beginning to stir up the possibilities—ready to talk up a big new trucking venture to all his Mafia friends—Liddy realized that he needed more administrative help in overseeing the project. He went to his State Police supervisors and asked for an assistant. Looking back, it was one of those moments when a routine action—as simple as Jack Liddy asking for some help—triggered a chain of events that changed the course of people's lives forever.

It was October 1976 when the State Police assigned Sergeant Dirk Ottens to Liddy, to assist him in steering our move to Jersey City and building up a larger operation there. Ottens was a sharp young detective, part of the first wave of college-educated guys to become cops. We sat down with him—Pat included—mapping out strategies for the new corporation we were going to start. Dirk was adamant about one point. "We can't have five of you guys looking like you're all owners," he said. "It'll be a red flag to anybody who might want to do business with you.

"We've got to have one guy to take the role as president," he continued. "And you've *all* got to start playin' roles."

That meant putting our egos aside. Even though we were technically all equal at Mid-Atlantic, now we had to create a new structure, establish our own crew, and mimic *their* world—with one guy looking as if he was calling the shots. And that had the potential for stirring up old resentments, but Ottens had already thought it through. He saw an ideal match in Irish Bobby Delaney and Irish Pat Kelly as the key players in the new company. He perceived something in both of us, a similarity in our people skills. Listening to us talk, you could say we'd both kissed the Blarney Stone. We both had upbeat, energetic personalities and stayed cool under pressure. So the assignments were made: I became the quarterback—Bobby Covert, trucking company president—with Pat Kelly becoming the vice president and terminal manager.

Now we needed a name. It came from Liddy: the Alamo Transportation Company, complete with our own motto: "When it comes to trucking, remember the Alamo." From the start, we simply referred to it as "Alamo Trucking."

We also needed one other critically important item if we were going to start mingling with high-powered Mafia types on a daily basis: We had to embellish the back story that already existed for Bobby Covert. And it had to be completely believable, because the wiseguys would ask questions. Who was I? Where did I come from? How did a kid in his early twenties come into enough cash to open a trucking company?

We sat down one night in my Bayonne apartment—just Pat and me—to go over the details of Bobby Covert's life story, trying our best to forge a plausible tale.

"You think we should change the part where my dad's a lieutenant in the New Jersey State Police?" I quipped.

"Nah, that won't scare wiseguys off at all," Pat joked back.

"Okay, my parents were killed in a car crash and I inherited a ton of money from them," I said, thinking out loud.

"Good, good," Pat echoed. "Except, make it that you were awarded the money in a suit following their death; sounds more realistic."

I picked up on the thought. "The fact is, I always wanted to get into the trucking business, so the original investment for Alamo came from the settlement. I met you through an old friend of yours who happens to be my uncle. Well, not my real uncle, but a friend of the family who I call uncle—kind of like in my old neighborhood. You agreed to lend your expertise and connections, and here we are."

The story sounded convincing enough. And it was one I could tell and repeat without having to fall back on too many complicated details. I had another natural asset, too. Simply put, I was a Jersey guy through and through. I was continually aware that I had grown up only a short drive away from this new life and these wiseguys. I knew every inch of the Turnpike, the Garden State Parkway, and the back streets and towns in between. I could talk like they talked, exude the same Jersey attitude, and come across as real.

It was almost midnight. Pat decided it was time to toast our new partnership with a drink. We stepped outside into the sleepy Bayonne night. Moments later, we were driving in my government-provided undercover Chevy Malibu to the Holiday Inn lounge at the Newark Airport. "You gotta change your car, Bobby," Pat said with a grin. "Wiseguys don't drive Chevys. Tell Liddy you gotta get a Lincoln Town Car or a Caddy."

I liked the sound of that—even though he was telling me what to do. The new, improved Bobby Covert was going to drive in style, straight into Pat Kelly's world.

CHAPTER FIVE

IN THE SHADOW OF THE STATUE OF LIBERTY

The autumn sky is fading from pink and purple to a deep, ominous darkness above Liberty State Park. The grassy stretch of once-desolate shoreline had officially burst to life three months earlier as a tourist attraction—a gift from the state of New Jersey to the nation as part of the Bicentennial celebration of 1976. Booming fireworks flickered and fluttered to earth above New York Harbor and the Statue of Liberty, standing barely two thousand feet away from the tourists crowding the new park.

Now, an eerie late-October silence has settled in at nightfall, broken only by the drone of nearby traffic rushing along an elevated extension of the New Jersey Turnpike. The constellation of lights from Lower Manhattan and the Twin Towers of the World Trade Center, only six and four years old, glow across the Hudson River. But here at the edge of the park, virtually beneath the Turnpike, a solitary light shines on the second floor of a bland concrete structure. Like the park itself, the box-like building on Communipaw Avenue has suddenly sprung to life in the shadow of the Statue of Liberty.

Inside, the two new bosses of Alamo Trucking—Bobby Covert and Pat Kelly—sit at their wooden desks in an otherwise empty, undecorated office. They discuss plans to get the business up and running and the best ways to entice big-time mobsters onto the premises.

The place sits on a barren strip of land that runs parallel to the old Central Railroad of New Jersey—tracks that once transported countless European immigrants, shortly after their passage through Ellis Island, on trains bound for new hopes and dreams in America.

The entire area bordering Liberty State Park is a dimly lit dead-end. The only other business nearby is an impound lot, where stolen and towed cars are locked away. A person could disappear in the middle of the night from this decaying, industrial patch of swampy ground by the waterfront and nobody would ever know.

"Hey, anybody here?" a man bellows from the outside entrance below, pushing the buzzer repeatedly and pounding on the door.

Covert tenses at the sound of the unexpected voice. He notices Kelly grinning at his concerned reaction, and suppresses a mild sensation of aggravation—as if he's been left out of some joke.

"Relax, Bobby, I got somebody comin' over."

Kelly bounds down the stairs and moments later returns with a young wiseguy type who appears to have stepped right off a Hollywood set—a pudgy man with oily black hair and a moustache, wearing a black leather jacket, an open-collar flowered shirt, and a scowl. "Bobby Covert, say hello to Anthony Pacilio," Kelly says, smiling. The two men nod, but say little. "I'm gonna take a look around," Pacilio states in a nasal Jersey accent. "Be my guest," Covert responds, not trying to mask his sarcasm.

Kelly proceeds to give Pacilio the grand tour, upstairs and down and outside in the open truck yard, while Covert paces around the room, sits at his desk, then paces some more. The longer Kelly and his guest are gone—five minutes, ten minutes—the more perturbed he becomes. His new partner hasn't clued him in to this visit, hasn't even invited him to come along on the tour of his own company.

Finally, after twenty minutes that feel to Covert more like an hour, Kelly climbs back up the stairs and strides into the room with a pronouncement. "Bobby, this is big. That was Fat Anthony—one of Johnny Dee's boys!" he says. Pacilio is a direct link to the big Mafia players Project Alpha covets, and Kelly, clearly proud of his efforts, has arranged the whole thing. Then he delivers the kicker: Pacilio will be on the Alamo payroll, but all he'll have to do is collect a paycheck. "He'll be Johnny's guy here," Kelly explains.

"Pat, what the hell are you doing?" Covert says.

"Bobby, trust me, it's the way it's done, it's all part of the game," Kelly replies with a wink.

Covert starts to say something, but fights the urge to be confronta-tional. He simply stares at Kelly and thinks to himself, "I can play any game, as long as YOU don't make up the rules as we go along."

Those first few weeks in our new building were like starting over with an entirely new life. The challenge was exciting, but it was also filled with constant adjustments and headaches. For more than a year, I had played the part of a co-owner with four—and later three—other under-cover guys at Mid-Atlantic. We had finally learned to work as a team, play off of each other's strengths, and get a few things accomplished with our less than awe-inspiring fleet—that old 16-foot truck, van, and station wagon. Now, here I was as the main man. I was the president of a company with plans for twenty-five trucks, a payroll of thirty-two employees, and every resource we needed to operate as a genuine trans-portation business—doing short hauls around north Jersey or long hauls hundreds of miles away.

But the biggest change of all was the guy sitting at the desk a few feet away from me, Mister Charmer, Patrick John Kelly. Things had moved quickly. One minute my safety and well-being—and the success of our operation—was linked to a fellow trooper and a handful of FBI agents; the next it was tied to a smooth-talking Mob associate looking at prison if he hadn't chosen Project Alpha as his meal ticket. Not that I wasn't happy to have Pat in the fold. Hey, I had lobbied to make it happen. He had so much energy, so much enthusiasm, and so many contacts that we could never have dreamed of making ourselves.

The problem was that Pat had this tendency of acting without ask-ing. He knew all the steps we needed to take to get the right kind of Mafioso to walk through our front doors, and he didn't feel the need to ask my permission, even though his title read vice president. I over-looked it as best I could. The fact was, Pat knew he was the MVP of this team and played it for all it was worth.

I had a lot of important things going on now with Alamo Trucking, and I didn't have the time to worry about Pat's impulsiveness and his lack of regard for the chain of command. The actual chain originated now at 744 Broad Street in Newark, a massive stone building with gold doors that led to a spacious lobby. This was the place that housed Hanlon & Associates, a construction firm that my supposed Uncle Jack ran and that I had partial ownership of. Except for one thing: Hanlon & Associates was actually a cover name for the State Police and FBI headquarters overseeing Project Alpha, and my Uncle Jack was really Jack Liddy, who took on the undercover name John Ashford. That way, if I was seen in Newark going into that building, it created an instant alibi for me. Or if I needed an excuse to leave my Alamo office without arousing any suspicions, I'd just say I had to visit my Uncle Jack at his construction company. That was all Liddy's idea, and it came in handy on many occasions.

Hanlon & Associates was command central, and Liddy immediately brought in more detectives—Bob Mackin, John Schroth, Gary McWhorter, Barry Lardiere, and Al Duranik—to monitor the equipment being installed by the State Police Electronic Surveillance Unit (ESU). Their job was to listen to the recordings, evaluate intelligence information, and prepare criminal cases, with Duranik soon becoming the custodian of evidence. He was in charge of logging in all the material we gathered before it was sent to State Police HQ. Every tape had to follow strict guidelines for the chain of evidence, so that it could later be used in court. I handed each recording directly to Duranik, but it first had to be secured by evidence tape that wrapped around the envelope, over a seal that contained our initials. Anyone who broke the seal was required to initial it, ensuring the sanctity of those tapes.

The increase in manpower was a sign that Project Alpha had moved to a new level. But from an undercover standpoint, adding new people to the operation also caused concern. Liddy had hammered into all of us that everything in the operation was on a need-to-know basis. Each new person who knew what was going on created an extra layer of risk. You couldn't predict what might happen in a social setting, whether somebody might tell secrets to a best friend in the police department or go home at night and share information with his wife or girlfriend. Before, we had only been dealing with the three or four other undercover guys. After that, I had to worry about Pat. Now these other detectives were coming in. It added to the tension I lived with on a daily—sometimes hourly—basis.

Alamo had to be completely wired before these new detectives could monitor any evidence, of course. The State Police's Electronic Surveillance Unit, headed by Joe Saia, came in at night, looking like any construction company doing some interior renovations for the new trucking operation. With quiet efficiency, the guys took down the existing paneling in the upstairs office I shared with Pat. They installed tiny cameras in the corners of the room—pulling the molding strips along the ceiling to the side just a little bit and sliding in the cameras. Tape recording devices were also built into the walls to capture everything taking place in the room.

One time, I had to bring in an ESU tech during the day. He dressed as a trucker, in case any Mob guys might stop by unannounced. There was only one problem—I noticed just as we were leaving Hanlon & Associates that he was still wearing his New Jersey State Police belt buckle. "That really wouldn't impress my new friends," I said, giving him a look. It was the kind of mistake that could cause a major problem.

That incident aside, I was completely amazed by what ESU accomplished. One particularly ingenious innovation worked this way: I could stop in any pay phone and dial a certain phone number. The message I'd hear stated that I'd reached a nonworking number and instructed me to hang up and call again. But if I held on for thirty seconds and punched in a coded number, I could activate the recording equipment in the Alamo office so that it would already be on when I walked into my office. For added security, the code was changed periodically. One week, it was my badge number, 2853; another week it might be Jack's badge number, 1539. As soon as that number was coded in, it turned on the recording device, allowing me to tape myself in conversation with wiseguys as I walked through the door.

There are two types of recordings, legally speaking: consensual, and court-authorized. This was a sophisticated consensual recording device. As an undercover agent, if I was party to a conversation, I could record it. But I couldn't turn it on and walk away and not be in that room when the recording was being made. If that happened, the recording had to be court-authorized. Getting a court order meant involving more people in the process, and, once again, the more people who knew what we were doing, the less secure we were. John DiGilio was known to have had a secretary in the FBI on his payroll, so anything was possible. I always worked on the premise that the Mob guys had access to as much information as I did—all they needed was one dirty cop.

There was a special benefit for me in the coded phone system. It meant I didn't have to strap a wire on my body all the time in order to get conversations on tape. You have to remember: This was back in the 1970s—it was truly James Bond stuff for that era. I could turn the equipment on as I was driving down the street. I just had to stop at a phone—not unusual back in the days before cell phones, when everybody was *always* stepping in and out of phone booths.

The nice thing about our location was its proximity to Port Newark—only about eight miles away. And now we had plenty of space—room for administrative offices, a truck depot, a huge outside storage yard in the back, and a fully operational garage. The property, which was enclosed by a chainlink fence, included a wide-open dirt-and-grass lot. I didn't give any thought to that lot, but the gears in Pat's brain were already turning with a way to put the empty land to use. He'd told me he was having trouble making payments on a farm he owned in Bedminster, and working as an informant for us hadn't helped his financial outlook. I was still naïve enough to think that Pat wasn't going to take advantage of every situation he possibly could, but one afternoon, I drove up to Alamo and did a double take: There was Pat, standing beside two horses grazing in the fenced-in field adjoining our building.

"Bobby, aren't they beautiful?" he said with the usual Pat Kelly grin.

"Two horses . . . in a trucking yard . . . in Jersey City—yeah, that's absolutely beautiful," I said in the most dismissive tone I could muster.

"I had to sell the farm, and they needed a new home," Pat protested. "Hey, I'll even teach you to ride."

The thought didn't thrill me, considering that a merry-go-round pony was the only horse I'd ever ridden, and I wasn't crazy about Pat's pattern of forcing his ideas on me.

"Pat, you gotta tell me these things," I said.

"Bobby, this will be very good for business, you know—Mob guys and their kids will come down here on weekends for pony rides," he interjected. "Plus, riding is a great way to clear your head. I need it. And it'll be good for you too."

I wasn't biting, so Pat paused, then threw in one more enticement.

"I have these old Western-style saddlebags—just like the real deal from the Wild West—and we can ride down to the river when you have to take the tapes off me and just dump 'em in the bags. Nobody will suspect a thing. C'mon, Bobby, give it a chance."

I couldn't even respond, because my mind was preoccupied with the thought, "What the hell is this, Wyatt Earp and Jesse James teaming up to end crime in 1876? This is 1976. And stop telling me what to do."

It was vintage Pat. He always had a reason that made perfect sense and a quick response to anything—always trying to make you believe what he hoped would happen, not what he thought would happen. So now we had a trucking company and the beginnings of a wiseguy petting zoo. "Just ask next time," I reiterated, and then walked away.

Two days later, I showed up at work and shook my head in disbelief: Pat had gotten his hands on an old trailer on the property and had it cut in half to create a pair of horse stalls. I let it slide. After all, maybe his idea would work and we'd have mobsters lining up with their kids on Saturdays. If horses helped our cause, who was I to argue?

Except that Pat still wasn't getting it. Shortly after Fat Anthony's visit, he and I were looking over some of the new trucks in our fleet and another visitor arrived. "Ray, how ya doin'?" Pat called out. "Bobby Covert—meet Anthony Ray." I nodded politely and shot a glance toward Pat, but he was already motioning for our guest to follow him inside for the official tour. This was getting a little old. I was going to have to talk to Pat about who was president of Alamo Trucking and who was second in command. But as much as this new snub made my jaw stiffen, I didn't want to say or do anything that would scare people away or suggest we didn't have our act together at Alamo. Fifteen minutes later, Ray drove off in a black El Dorado and Pat turned to me with his all-too-familiar smirk.

"Bingo—Anthony Ray's one of Tino Fiumara's guys," he said.

"Let me guess—he'll be on our payroll but all he has to do is collect a paycheck so he can keep an eye on what we're doing," I said in a mildly irritated tone that Pat picked up on.

"Listen, Bobby—if we want to move up the ladder, there's only one way to bring them in here, and you have to give me a free hand to get it done the right way—or we'll get nowhere at all," he said.

Pat was smiling, but his usually cordial blue eyes had a steely, serious look that I hadn't seen before.

"I don't mind you doing what needs to be done—what doesn't sit right with me is you not *telling* me before you do it," I said, locking my eyes on his.

The tension couldn't have lasted more than a second before Pat suddenly broke into a laugh and reached over with his hand to give my shoulder a playful slap.

"Bobby, Bobby, Bobby—what are we doin' here? It's all gonna be perfect. We got Fat Anthony. We got Ray. Things are startin' to roll."

True enough. Maybe I was being a little oversensitive in allowing personal feelings to get in the way of the two roles I was playing—one as trucker Bobby Covert, the other as Trooper Bob Delaney. I was getting worked up just because he had left me out of the loop a few times. What mattered was that we'd barely set up the company and moved into our building, and already we had established a direct line to the upper echelon of organized crime—something we hadn't been able to do in more than a year with Mid-Atlantic Trucking.

What struck me was how everybody in the Mob seemed to be assigned to keep an eye on somebody else—a prime example of the paranoia and mistrust that defined the wiseguy world. Here we had Anthony Pacilio and Anthony Ray getting ready to watch us, so they could report back to their bosses about our finances, profits, and kickbacks. I was coming to learn first-hand that organized crime families were just like any other dysfunctional family: Nobody trusted *anybody*—even Pat was always looking over his shoulder.

As consigliere of the DiNorscio crew, he commanded a great deal of respect in Bruno Crime Family circles. Still, before Dominick DiNorscio had entered federal prison in Lewisburg, he had ordered Pat to report regularly on the DiNorscio operations to a Bruno captain—or "capo"—named Johnny Simone, a.k.a. Johnny Keyes. He was an important player in the scheme of things—working directly under the head of the family, Angelo Bruno. But Keyes had a logistics problem when it came to looking after Pat Kelly and making sure he was handling the DiNorscios' affairs adequately: Keyes lived in Hollywood, Florida, and was in charge of running Bruno's criminal pursuits in the Fort Lauderdale–Miami area.

He needed somebody in Jersey to track what Pat was doing. You'd think he would have tapped a member of the Bruno organization for the job, since the DiNorscios were with them. But we were sitting directly in the Genoveses's back yard, and Pat had already gained inroads with them. So to keep things sailing along, Keyes reached out to a highly regarded figure in the Genovese Family—a mobster seen as a rising star in the underworld ranks with a reputation as a cold, calculating killer. It was none other than Tino Fiumara, a gangster I knew plenty about from those early sessions with Jack Liddy. In Johnny Keyes's mind, Fiumara had such a stellar record as a money-maker for the Genoveses that it made more sense to form an alliance with him than to compete against him for business.

Keyes asked Fiumara if he would "mind the store"—wiseguy terminology meaning that, in this case, a made guy had to be able to represent Kelly in any sitdown or any other problem that might arise. Translation: It would allow Tino to have a piece of Kelly's earnings. And Fiumara—seeing a potential for more money—readily accepted. From a wiseguy's standpoint, it was better to have half a loaf of bread than none at all.

It again went against everything law enforcement had assumed up to that point—that Mafia organizations adhered to strict jurisdictional lines and family allegiances. But as we would continue to learn, if there was a chance to increase profits through new forms of illicit pursuits, family lines often blurred. As a result, it was only a matter of time before Tino Fiumara—reputed to have strangled a rival with piano wire in Paterson—became a dark and constant presence in our lives.

Pat and I had other things on our minds after we officially opened for business in December 1976. We started out with a workforce of four drivers and a handful of executives that included my fellow undercover operatives Ralph Rascati, Richie Moyes, and Al Denny. In short order, we began hiring more employees. Interestingly enough, everybody who showed up for an interview was, somehow or another, connected to a wiseguy. The mechanic we hired was a friend of a mobster; the drivers were cousins or brothers-in-law of another. It wasn't your typical applicant pool. They were all connected. And we had to hire every one of them.

Pat continued to exploit his underworld ties. Whatever he did worked. In a matter of weeks, we had our first big Mob contract, with a firm that the mob had dug its claws into on Henderson Street in Jersey City—just a few miles north of us—called Frigid Express. But the deal wasn't with Tino; it was with the other member of the Genovese Family we were linked to—John DiGilio.

The agreement Pat worked out made Alamo the "house" trucker for Frigid. That meant we would provide most of the transportation for Frigid's line of frozen seafood and frog-leg delicacies. Frigid was under the control of a senior Genovese member named Pasquale Macciarole, who used the nickname Patty Mack. Patty was a very powerful man, the underboss to the head of the entire Genovese operation, Funzi Tieri. That meant that both Tino Fiumara and John DiGilio—made guys and bosses to everyone else—had to report to the capos who answered directly to Patty Mack.

I practically needed a scorecard to keep track of the Mafia players coming in and out of Pat Kelly's game.

Over the next few months, we did work on a steady basis for Patty's Frigid line, and that enabled us to increase Alamo's truck fleet and workforce. As expected, the profits flowed right back to DiGilio, Tino, and even Jackie DiNorscio, who was still serving his eight-year sentence at Rahway.

In return for our doing business with them, they got to split a kickback that totaled 25 percent of Alamo's profits on a weekly basis—about $2,500 in decent weeks, sometimes even as much $3,500.

To complicate matters, Richie Moyes had to spend hours each day keeping meticulous records, in case any wiseguys demanded to see our books so they could make sure we were really kicking back 25 percent of our profits. On top of that, we had to keep a separate record of all the money we were spending from our government grant. Liddy realized he needed to bring in an additional guy to handle that job, so in came Detective Sergeant First Class Vince Matis. I was spending hours trying to keep track of the money and making sure Pat didn't keep spending as if we had no budget at all. The fact was, Pat marched to the beat of his own drum—setting up this deal or that—and continued to act like he was running the operation.

It was aggravating me more and more. But what made Pat's behavior the most troubling was that I had no idea if he really had my back. I mean, I knew that he wanted to stay out of prison, so it wasn't as if he was going to do anything to put himself in jeopardy. But what would happen to me if push came to shove? How did I know what was actually going on in his head? All I could tell for sure was that Pat was constantly scheming and working the angles in ways that usually benefited him. It left me with an increasingly uneasy feeling. Every time Pat abruptly got up from his desk to meet one of his wiseguy connections—or made calls that dealt with Alamo business—I wondered how safe and secure our top-secret operation really was, not to mention how safe I was.

One afternoon, Pat hung up the phone after talking in a soft voice, almost as if he didn't want me to hear what he was saying. He could have been talking to his girlfriend for all I knew, but the point was, I had no idea what was going on in his conversation, and my antennae were up. I imagined scenarios with Pat double-dealing—playing both ends against the middle, cutting deals where he would make money from the wiseguys while working for law enforcement. Just thinking about it caused my blood to boil.

Without realizing it, I had started to change. I was thinking like a real Mob guy, seeing everything through a prism of paranoia. The fact is, paranoia is a way of life in their world, and now that's the way I was processing information. But it was even more complicated than that, because I was living two lives: I wasn't really a Mob guy—I was a state trooper working undercover *among* Mob guys, and that was adding a whole extra layer of paranoia to how I reacted to the people around me.

As crazy as it sounded, deep in the back of my mind, I thought, "He may be setting me up." Our whole partnership hinged on conveying a sense of mutual trust to the wiseguys we were courting, and every movement we made had to reinforce that relationship. But bottom line: I didn't trust this guy.

I walked over to Pat's desk, placed my hands palms-down on the mahogany surface, and leaned forward, almost face to face. "I'm only gonna say this once—if I ever think you're giving me up, I'll give you up in a heartbeat, so we both end up with bullets in our heads."

It's not that I necessarily believed Pat would sell me out. I was just trying to get a message to him. But he looked at me as if I'd insulted his mother. He folded his arms across his chest and rocked back in his chair. Suddenly, I had the feeling that maybe I'd come in swinging a two-by-four when a slap on the wrist with a ruler would have sufficed.

"Bobby," he said quietly, sounding like a guy who had just lost his best friend, "all I'm trying to do here is bring in the right kind of business. I'm working my ass off—and I'm putting my life on the line with people who *trust* me—to help you guys."

An awkward silence hung in the air as I pondered how to respond, wishing now that I hadn't turned this into a showdown. I knew that in Pat's mind he felt he was doing the right thing, but he seemed to be addicted to the rush of manipulating everything and everybody around him to suit his own needs.

Outside, I could hear the sound of trucks rumbling in and out of our yard, suddenly conscious of them in the dead quiet of our office. It was like a kids' game—neither one of us wanted to be the one who blinked first. But Pat eventually gave in.

"So, Bobby," he said, forcing a smile, "we okay here?"

"Yeah, we're okay," I answered. And I hoped we were. Whatever lay ahead, the future of Project Alpha was going to hinge on Pat and me—the consigliere and the cop—and our ability to work together, to protect each other in the most dangerous of surroundings. Any lingering lack of trust could ruin everything. I needed to check on a truck shipment outside and turned to walk toward the door, when Pat called out to me.

"One other thing, Bobby," he said. "You gotta lose that beard. And you need a decent haircut. You're lookin' like a trucker, not a company president. You gotta start looking the part."

Before long, I had shaved my beard into a Fu Manchu—similar to how I remember Tommy G. and his Sonny Bono look, and I got my increasingly long, wavy brown hair cut into a short, stylish coif that made me appear more like a wiseguy. Fortunately, Liddy agreed with Pat's idea that I should drive a better car, so my Malibu was gone, replaced by a sleek white Lincoln Mark V. When Pat and I hit the bars at night, he broke me of my habit of ordering beers. Instead, Scotch and water became my preferred drink, much more in line with the company I would be keeping. I also upgraded my closet—leaving behind my jeans and T-shirts in favor of expensive European three-piece suits with no tie, just an open-collar shirt. But no wingtip shoes, Pat cautioned—only FBI agents wore them.

My new wardrobe, complete with matching vests, served a purpose beyond just helping me assimilate with the wiseguys: I also felt that the vest gave me a little more coverage on the recording device I wore inside my jock strap—and the wires that ran up the sides of my body—in meetings or at dinners. The recording device we used was called a Nagra, and it was a small, self-contained reel-to-reel machine, a little bit less than the width of two checkbooks stacked on top of each other. That might seem large and unwieldy by today's high-tech, microchip standards, but back in the seventies it was state of the art, capable of recording about two hours of conversation. Prior to that, law enforcement used R-/F transmitters that required a surveillance team, because the conversation being recorded would be sent over the airwaves to the recording location. That created problems. There were stories of undercover cops walking in a room and the TV channels changing. Or the wires burning against the skin of the undercover cop. And it also gave the bad guys an opportunity to utilize a device that I saw Anthony Pacilio use one day in one of our offices. It looked like an old-time walkie-talkie with an antenna coming off the top, checking to see if R-/F frequencies were being transmitted. Our system allowed us to fly under Fat Anthony's radar.

Fortunately, because I had been accepted in the Mob's inner circle, there wasn't much risk that I'd get patted down for a wire. In their subculture, that represented a major breach of etiquette—basically everyone in the room would be on notice that I was suspected as an informant. That would be viewed as an accusation—compromising my ability to make money—and from this would flow serious repercussions. Now, that didn't mean the wiseguys weren't thinking about it. It was common practice for a mobster to pat someone on the stomach with a friendly "Hey, putting on a little weight there"—or an overexaggerated pat on the back. This was one way of checking for a wire.

In this world of hidden recordings, I was the one who had to teach Pat. By strict rules governing our investigation—aimed at keeping our case airtight when it came to trial—he wasn't allowed to handle evidence directly. So the tape could only be taken out of the Nagra by me or one of the other undercover agents. Pat wore his wire in his belly button, and the whole thing made him nervous. His Mafia cronies thought of him as one of their own now, but if they discovered that he was wearing a wire, they'd bury him in concrete without giving it a second thought.

Little by little, we got used to the presence of the wires and the hidden recording devices all around us. And more people began to show up at Alamo. Fat Anthony and Ray were always there, of course, lounging around in our office, where we had a TV on much of the time. They'd watch *Let's Make a Deal, The Price Is Right,* one TV game show after another. Conversation was no different from that around any office watercooler—complaints about the Yankees, the Mets, the Jets, the weather, traffic. Harmless as that seemed, Pat and I could never let our guard down in their presence, aware that if we became too relaxed—especially if we'd had a few drinks with them at lunch or dinner—we might casually slip out of character. Anybody who's ever had to keep a secret just for a surprise party knows how easily you can reveal a crucial detail without meaning to; only, in our case, a slip could get us killed.

We hadn't yet been paid a visit by the two Genovese crew leaders, John DiGilio or Tino Fiumara. But we knew of their deepening interest in our business from the potential deals that were conveyed to us by their underlings. Pat and I, along with the other undercover agents, became increasingly aware of competition for our company's business—along with the demands for preferential treatment we were receiving from Jackie DiNorscio, even though he was locked up twenty miles away.

Early in 1977, Anthony Pacilio approached me on behalf of Johnny Dee, who, like all high-ranking Mafia members, preferred to insulate himself from direct dealings with businessmen such as myself. Anthony made the pitch, encouraging me to see the benefits of aligning Alamo with the DiGilio camp. It was an initial glimpse into the way of the wiseguy. Here we had three criminal factions making money off of us in the form of weekly kickbacks, but it was only a matter of time before each group would want more, want it all. They might have been willing to share some of our profits and assets in the early going, but I was learning that the greed of the beast was insatiable, and the desire to control us exclusively was inevitable. The first move was made by the DiGilio crew.

Pacilio explained that he had recently had a meeting with a well-placed official within the ILA—the International Longshoremen's Association—and had been assured that certain highly favorable contracts would be given to Alamo should we go with DiGilio. In short, it was a promise of lucrative trucking business—with no interference from the union. Pat got wired up and went to meet with DiGilio and Anthony Pacilio and a member of the union in February 1977. When he came back, Pat handed me the recorder, without touching the tape, and we later listened to it. "I want you to get 'em some work; I don't want no lip service," DiGilio said to the union boss.

"Where you located?" the boss asked.

Pacilio jumped in. "We're at 231 Communipaw Avenue."

"This Irishman can bullshit the ears off a monkey, so send them in," DiGilio said of Kelly. "I want this done. This is a fuckin' must."

Then DiGilio started turning up the pressure on Pat to accept. "Between me and Tino, me over here and Tino over there, you know, you fuckin' guys can *fuhgettaboutit*. I can only give you my strength. I wish somebody opened doors like that for me."

Everyone connected with Project Alpha was delighted about the recording. Here we had, on tape, known organized crime figures directing union bosses to open doors for our trucking company. What a difference a year made—or, more accurately, a Pat Kelly made. It was becoming very clear to everyone in the investigation: Without Pat, there was no investigation.

We listened to the overtures but, at Liddy's instructions, made no commitments. The idea was to create as wide a net as possible; going with one group would probably alienate and drive away the others.

When Fat Anthony's cousin, Neil Pacilio, was released from prison on a furlough, Anthony ordered Alamo to rent him a luxury car—at our expense, $320 a week to be exact—so he could drive in style during his week out of the slammer. Patty Mack issued his own directive to us: Alamo would have to pay $15 to his Frigid Express line for every Frigid load we carried. That might seem like chump change, but not when you consider that we were already kicking back 25 percent of our company profits. And now we had had an additional expense to Patty Mack for the twenty loads a week for Frigid. When you added that up, it came to $300 a week, $1,200+ a month, $15,600 a year. It turned out that this money wasn't even for Patty; it was delivered to employees of Frigid as a way of cementing their allegiance to him. But you have to understand—Patty was already getting a portion of our 25-percent kickback, because Johnny and Tino had to give him a piece of everything they were involved in each week, including what came their way from Alamo.

Monday mornings were especially annoying, when at least one or two ladies would show up for office jobs they'd been promised by some wiseguy they met at a club on Friday or Saturday night. These same wiseguys had turned Alamo into their own satellite office. Not long after opening our doors, dozens of mid- to upper-level soldiers in the Genovese and Bruno organizations were hanging out at Communipaw Avenue, arriving and leaving as frequently as our trucks loaded and unloaded stolen goods or Mob-connected food shipments.

Michael Coppola, Tino's lieutenant, was a frequent presence, representing Tino's interest in Alamo. We even installed a bar in a second room upstairs, designed for socializing, to make them all comfortable— and to create more opportunities to videotape and record our visitors. They were always making calls to who-knows-where—wives, girl- friends, bookies, setting up deals—and our phone bills were off the charts, though the cost was well worth the intelligence we gathered.

At the same time, I began to observe something interesting: The time we were all spending together, hanging around Alamo, led to conversations that were no different than the b.s. sessions I had encountered at the State Police barracks. I always imagined that the bad guys were an entirely different breed—just a bunch of lowlifes with no redeeming qualities. But all the hours I spent listening and talking to them were making me realize that everybody has the same problems in life; people are people, and they talk about the same stuff, whether it's a crowded barbershop on a Saturday morning, a warehouse break-room during lunchtime, or a roomful of Mob guys in a trucking company office.

They were all working to put money in their pockets and food on their tables—the only difference here was how they went about it. Half of them were guys with wives and children, and with parents who got mad at them if they didn't come over enough to visit. One of them was Charlie "Cup of Coffee"—I guess the wiseguy nickname machine must have been stuck on "literal" that day, giving old Charlie a moniker that was inspired by the constant sight of him sipping java. Charlie had a little boy about six who was mentally challenged. He talked about how he and his wife were really worried about their son and how he was going to fit in with other kids. Charlie was preoccupied with it, and I really felt bad for him.

I'd been told by my old State Police partner Bobby Scott, when I first became a trooper, that you never let things get personal because you can't be objective in an investigation if you let that happen. But the problem is, when you go undercover, that's what you're *trying* to do: You're trying to get personal. You're dropped in behind the lines, and you're going to become just like them. That's your job. And you learn things about people's families, like Charlie's kid. The logical extension of Bobby Scott's caution was impossible to avoid: This was going to get sloppy.

I was already getting to like Charlie and some of the other mobsters who spent time with us. And just as Pat had envisioned, the "Jersey City Horses" act was a huge hit: The wiseguys we did business with started bringing their kids out on weekends to get their pony rides, giving their wives—just like any wives married to regular working guys—some time to themselves away from the kids to go shopping, get their hair done, whatever. Against my better judgment, I started learning to ride, too—mostly so we could do the tape handoffs exactly as Pat had described. During the week, when our upstairs office and social room were filled with wiseguys, Pat and I would go outside and saddle up for a horse ride down to the water and the swampy area a mile or so away.

One afternoon around five o'clock, we were going to do our tape routine. As we got closer to the banks of the Hudson, I turned the horse back toward Alamo—but unbeknownst to me, when horses sense they're headed back to the barn, that means only one thing: It's feeding time. They're just going to run hell-bent for leather to get back to eat. The horse I was riding suddenly went from a gentle trot to a full-out gallop. I had my arms wrapped around his neck and didn't know how to stop him. Pat couldn't keep up with me, and I was thinking, "Do I jump off now, or what? I mean, is this the way I'm gonna die as an undercover guy? Falling off a freakin' horse?" Finally we got back to the stalls and the horse slowed down. I was so pissed off. Pat rode in behind me, laughing so hard that he almost fell off his own horse. It was the last time Secretariat and I went out for a ride before feeding time.

With business flourishing, Liddy decided that Pat and I should move into an upgraded apartment that had been wired to make a whole new round of recordings that would augment what we were getting at Alamo. Now we weren't just business partners; we were roommates at the Water's Ebb Apartments in Edgewater, a community that overlooked the Hudson River. The blunt exchange we'd had weeks earlier seemed to have improved our relationship, though Pat—sensing his immense value to us—had fallen back into his old habits of setting up meetings without telling me and making decisions without my approval. I hadn't gotten around to saying anything about it, mostly because we were working twelve-hour days at Alamo and getting visits at our new apartment from a steady flow of gangsters.

Across the street from the Water's Ebb, there was a cozy little Italian restaurant called Jerry's. One night, Pat and I joined Joey Adonis, Jr.—son of the infamous deported mobster Joey Adonis, Sr., known for his part in the 1931 murder of Mob leader Joe "The Boss" Masseria in Coney Island—and a couple of other wiseguys for a late dinner. Adonis was tall and athletic with salt-and-pepper hair and chiseled facial features. He was cut in the mold of his father, who'd changed his name to Adonis from Doto after arriving in the U.S. from Italy. The name change increased his reputation for vanity and womanizing.

The first thing I noticed was how everyone was kissing each other on the cheek—even Pat. I had not achieved inner-circle status yet, so the ritual didn't involve me, and that was just fine. Then Joey, Jr. reached into his pocket and pulled out what looked like two dozen quarters. He handed them to a busboy. "Put 'em all on A-4," Adonis instructed, motioning toward the jukebox.

As we all took our seats, A-4 started playing, and I heard the familiar, melancholy theme of *The Godfather*.

"You see the movie?" Adonis asked.

"Part One I seen ten times at least, Part Two maybe six or seven," one of Adonis's friends proudly answered.

It was an amazing sight to behold. Everywhere I went during this period, guys were always talking about "the movie" and how many times they'd seen it. *The Godfather* had come out in 1972, followed by *The Godfather Part II* in 1974. And Hollywood's treatment of Mafia life, based on the Mario Puzo book and the movies by Francis Ford Coppola, had an unbelievably powerful impact on the wiseguys I was getting to know. It was life imitating art. They were all like, "Ya gotta kiss." Everybody was kissing on the cheek.

The *Godfather* theme played on the jukebox nonstop through the whole dinner. "I love that song—I can never hear it too much," Adonis remarked, evoking a chorus of agreement at the table. But it wasn't just that Adonis had a soft spot for the movie theme: Playing it also served as a not-so-subtle message to the restaurant owner—and to the other patrons inside—that he had special guests on hand. Meantime, my role was to pick up the tab at the end of the evening.

The next day, Pat and I were back in our office. Our door was shut, but we knew that a handful of wiseguys were drinking, playing cards, and laughing it up in the social room two doors down the hall. A call came in for Pat, and he talked for five minutes, then hung up and stood up at his desk, starting his I'm-getting-ready-to-leave ritual: shuffling papers, looking for his car keys. "Where you headed?" I called out.

"Bobby, I got some business I gotta take care of," Pat replied, sounding mildly put out for having to explain.

"No, *we* have business to take care of!" I shouted, no longer concerned with dancing around a confrontation with Pat, no matter how vital he was to us. "And you'll take care of it . . . if I say you'll take care of it!"

The tension that had subsided for several weeks was now rushing out. But Pat was unfazed. Not wanting to draw the attention of the wiseguys, he whispered angrily back at me.

"I'm going because I know what I'm doing—I know Tino—you don't, and you'll just be in the way."

It wasn't something I'd planned to do, but in a blur of pent-up rage, I grabbed a chair, lifted it up, and heaved away full-force. It flew just over Pat's shoulder and crashed into the wall behind him. So much for not drawing attention. Pat froze in his tracks, staring at me with his mouth open. I had lost all control—a dangerous thing in an undercover setting, or any time in life for that matter.

Instantly, I knew I was wrong to let my anger take hold of me. But you know, the fight with your wife is never really over the dirty dishes; it's about all the stuff that's been mounting up before that. That's what was going on with me. It was the pressure of living undercover, the pressure of living two lives, the pressure of wearing a wire, and the pressure of managing every minute of the day to keep from being found out and possibly whacked. I'd been trying to act like Superman, like I could handle everything with no problem, but the reality was that I was showing the strain.

What if I'd hit Pat with the chair, and seriously hurt the guy? It could have been a disaster for the operation. Still, I had to let him know he wasn't running this show.

"We understand each other?" I said quietly, trying to act calm in spite of the pounding I felt inside my chest.

"Hey, you wanna be in charge? Be my guest," Pat responded, sitting back down. "Just tell me what you want to do."

"I wanna know everything you're doin', *everything*."

At that moment, there was a knock on our door and a voice called out loudly, "Hey, everything okay in there?" The door pushed open a crack and both Pat and I instantly turned to see Al Denny, whose office was right next to ours.

Al had yelled just loudly enough to create a smoke screen, making sure the Mafiaso in the room down the hall knew he was checking on the commotion. He stepped inside our office and shut the door behind him—his voice suddenly shifting to a low, angry whisper as he reverted from an Alamo employee to FBI man: "What the *fuck* are you guys doin'?" he chastised us. "You're gonna cause us all a problem, and I'm not here to babysit you two."

There was nothing I could say in my defense. I was wrong and I knew it. But sometimes you get lucky. From that point on, something changed for the better in how Pat and I worked together. Also, all that yelling and shouting, punctuated by the thud on the wall, made the wiseguys in the other room think I was a hard-ass, take-charge boss. It raised my stock in their eyes.

But it didn't solve all my problems. I was still getting constant pressure from the various Mafia factions that wanted Alamo under their own wing. Fiumara was the one I was most concerned about. I had met him a few times with Pat and had a gut feeling that something was brewing in his head.

On the job, I always projected an air of confidence and control. But inner turmoil—the feelings that erupted with Pat that day—continued to build. One night after dinner, I started to experience shortness of breath. The more I thought about it, the worse it became. I was convinced I was having a heart attack. I called Liddy and he arranged for me to see a doctor friend of his. In typical Liddy fashion, every detail was taken care of: The doctor never pressed me for any details about myself. He just ran all kinds of tests and stayed quiet until the end of the examination.

"Well, there's really nothing wrong with you that I can see—are you under a lot of stress these days?" he asked.

His words floated through my head in slow motion. All I could think was, "Stress? Are you fuckin' kidding me?" But I kept my answer brief: "Yeah, well, a little."

I drove back to Alamo, relieved that my heart was fine. Outside, it was dark and deserted, with the only sound coming from the steady rush of traffic overhead on the Hudson Bay Extension of the New Jersey Turnpike. I stood in front of the building, gazing across the black water of New York Harbor at the symbol of freedom in the distance, the Statue of Liberty. With all these Mafia guys wanting a piece of my time and my business, with the constant need to be painfully cautious about everything I said and did, I realized that my own sense of freedom was slowly slipping away.

CHAPTER SIX

NO GOOD FELLAS HERE

In a grimy sun-baked alley by a Newark warehouse, two young street thugs wait in the afternoon shadows, fidgeting silently against a brick wall and keeping a careful watch. They have a tractor-trailer load of stolen Peugeot bicycles to unload and are anxious to negotiate a final deal for the hot goods and get out. A white-and-maroon Chevy Malibu pulls slowly into the alley. Out steps a burly man in his early twenties with wavy dark brown hair. His gray T-shirt, sporting the message "Welcome to Beautiful Downtown Bayonne," hides the wire he is wearing, while he conceals the pounding in his chest with a cool, emotionless visage.

But instantly, Bobby Covert detects that something is not right.

He is expecting one man—the guy he had been dealing with all along—not two. "Who you bringin' along here?" he asks the ringleader casually, his pulse racing faster. "He's okay—he's in on it," the thug replies. He assures Covert that the deal is solid. But in the next moment, three other men—slickly dressed, gold-chained, wiseguy wanna-bes— turn the corner into the alley. "What the fuck is goin' on?" one of them yells, gun hanging at his side. Instantly, the two hoodlums hoping to deal the bikes reach toward their belts. "Hey fellas, whoa!" yells Covert, wondering if he has somehow walked into a trap and is seconds from taking a .38 caliber bullet.

As he tries to make sense of the unfolding confusion, he realizes the three slick punks with attitudes have already staked a claim to the load of Peugeots. They begin to berate the two others, threatening them with bodily harm. And now Covert is aware of a new sound—police sirens piercing through the neighborhood only blocks away. He doesn't know that the area is crawling with police cruisers, investigating the shooting death of Newark police officer Jack Snow, who had been killed that same afternoon, August 13, 1976, at a check-cashing store nearby off Route 1 & 9.

Yet he is certain of one thing: His life is in even greater jeopardy now. He could easily be caught in the crossfire of bullets should the police, at any minute, descend on the chaotic, gun-brandishing scene in the alley and assume he is one of the bad guys before he can explain otherwise. At the very least, he will be identified as a cop in front of criminals and his sixteen months undercover will instantly be over.

His thoughts spin with plausible reasons that he has to leave without appearing frightened or inadvertently drawing the wrath of the three late-comers to himself. Just then, one of them smashes the butt of his pistol into the face of the leader of the two thieves. As the man screams in pain and blood gushes from his nose, Covert realizes that the history between these two groups goes far beyond the deal at hand.

He seizes on the escalating tension to improvise an escape strategy. "Yo!!" he yells, the police sirens growing louder. "The people I'm with are not gonna like this. We're gonna let this lay. And when you figure it out, you know where to get me." The suggestion that he has ties to a powerful Mob family—one that won't be pleased with the bungled deal and might take some punitive action—has given him street credibility and an instant out. He screeches off in his Malibu and doesn't stop for fifteen minutes, until he finds a secluded stretch of highway off the Turnpike beyond Exit 14. He kneels down on the shoulder of the road beside his car and retches on the asphalt, repressed fear and the remnants of his lunch pouring out, leaving him dizzy and numb. That evening, he is still rattled, returning to his sparsely furnished apartment in Bayonne for a restless night's sleep.

Six months later, in the chill of a February evening, I stood outside on the second-floor balcony at the Water's Ebb Apartments, thinking back to that stolen-bike fiasco. I had moved up to fancy digs now—a modern, two-bedroom unit overlooking the shoreline of the Hudson River. In the distance, the George Washington Bridge glowed with a steady stream of headlights from rush-hour traffic crawling in and out of the city. My breath hit the cold night air like small puffs of smoke, which seemed fitting, considering how everything had heated up so fast. I found myself reflecting on the sudden success that had been made possible by my Mob-informant roomie, Pat Kelly—and where it was all going.

The bike deal seemed like child's play compared to how infinitely more complicated and dangerous life had become. Back then, with Project Alpha still in its early stages, I had been dealing with street criminals and low-level wiseguys. I didn't have any "people" in established crime families to back me up.

Now I had more people than I knew what to do with, entangling every move I made. John DiGilio was crude and heartless, a bearded man in his mid-forties who often wore a poor boy's cap over his brown hair and was built like a small bull, packing 180 pounds into his 5-foot-7 frame. He was definitely not someone you wanted to spend a lot of time around. But none of the mobsters I dealt with inspired more fear than Tino Fiumara.

Unlike the somewhat older DiGilio, Tino, in his late thirties, was a young Mob leader on the rise—a crew boss who reported directly to Peter LaPlaca, his capo in the Genovese Crime Family. Tino had thick black hair, leading-man looks, and a reputation for being particularly vicious. Waterfront shipping executives were terrified of him, and many of the wiseguys lower down the Genovese ladder were scared to refer to him by his real name, instead simply calling him "T" or "The Good-Looking Guy."

They had reason to be ultra-cautious. In addition to the piano-wire murder, Tino was reputed to have killed a number of other men, including the father of his own godson. Reliable informants had told the government that Tino had also murdered two brothers of one of his associates, Vinny Colucci, an ILA union boss. Yet Colucci remained unwavering in his loyalty to Fiumara. As frightening a figure as he was,

Tino officially claimed that his occupations were harmless: part-time salesman in an auto repair shop and occasional haberdasher.

Thanks to the respect Pat commanded from members of both the Bruno and Genovese Families, I was able to gain access to Fiumara's inner circle. We were beginning to do a lot of business together. So I wasn't surprised one night when the phone rang just after 8:00 p.m. and Tino's lieutenant, Michael Coppola, was on the other end. Still, I had an uneasy feeling about it when he said that he and Tino were on their way over. It was an unplanned visit.

Whenever I saw Tino, his cold, dark eyes made me think of a shark. He was a polished and formal man who was very much into the old-style Mob traditions, beginning with the kissing on the cheek. To Tino, the custom wasn't about mimicking a hit movie; it was a significant gesture of acceptance. Interestingly, Tino and Pat always exchanged kisses, but with me it was a handshake. Although I was at the kiss-on-the-cheek level with members of his crew, I never attained that status with Tino. It was his way of keeping me at bay. Tino wasn't real big—maybe 5-foot-11, 165 pounds—but he had a quiet, sinister presence that exuded his well-earned reputation for intimidation. He was not a man you crossed. And it was impossible to feel at ease in his presence, because I never knew what he was really thinking.

But somehow Pat often did. Tino liked Pat's charming, easy-going style and trusted him. In fact, all the Mob guys believed Pat's loyalty to be with them first and foremost. So I had a pretty strong sense of Tino's impending plan to muscle in on Alamo and make me his cash cow—freezing out the DiNorscios, and by extension the Brunos, and leaving DiGilio and Frigid Express out in the cold as well.

All along, as Bobby Covert, I had made it clear that I had no intention of aligning Alamo with one single family. We continued to follow the game plan laid down by my Project Alpha supervisor, Sergeant Liddy, requiring us to keep the scope of our investigation as wide as possible. As a result, each guy—Fiumara, DiNorscio, and DiGilio—worked harder to try to make exclusive deals with us. But they also held back business they could have been sending our way because they didn't want to share Alamo's growing profits with the other mobsters.

At a certain point, sharing the 25 percent of Alamo profits we were kicking back probably didn't look so good to them any more. I'm sure Tino would have liked all 25 percent for himself, and, in truth, probably more like 50 percent. He saw me as a reliable source of continuous income—an "earner" like Pat—so in that sense I didn't feel as if I was in any imminent danger. But by the same token, I never assumed that my status as head of the trucking company ensured my long-term safety. If things were to go south, who knew whether Tino would just as soon want me dead? Mobsters were reluctant to kill cops. But if you wore a wire virtually nonstop as I did, the danger was that they'd discover it and think I was an informant. And in that world, informants die.

Tino and Michael arrived at the Water's Ebb shortly after 11:00 p.m. They had been to our place once or twice before, along with a dozen or so other wiseguys we were dealing with at Alamo. Everyone seemed to love the view of the GW Bridge from the front balcony—and looked forward to the summertime view from the rear balcony of the swimming pool with all the sunbathing beauties.

Of course, they wouldn't have liked it had they known the place was entirely wired. There were recording devices in planters and in light fixtures, and when anyone came in, I'd hit a button and start recording. There was even a bug at the bottom of an ice bucket in the bar area—though, unfortunately, when anyone reached in for an ice cube, it sounded like an avalanche on the tape.

"So Bobby, how ya doin?" Coppola asked as Pat fixed Tino a vodka tonic at the bar.

"I'm good," I answered. "What do we have goin'?"

"Bobby, I got an idea for a new company, a tire company, and it'll make us all a lot of money," Tino said. "We can bring you more business than you ever dreamed of. And you'll be under my flag. Nobody will bother ya."

The thought shot through my head—yeah, nobody will bother me but *you.*

"I dunno, T, how's that going to play out?" I said.

I was thinking that DiGilio's watchdog, Anthony Pacilio, would instantly go running to his boss if he got wind that Tino was making a move like this.

"That kid Anthony, he's nothing but a weed, a *FUCKIN' WEED—* I'll cut him down," said Tino, pounding a fist on the top of the bar, his calm demeanor giving way to a flash of anger. "I'll take care of it. You just do what I say and watch the money roll in."

Tino laid out the basic idea for me—a new company called Liberty Tire & Trailer Service. It was to be located on the Alamo grounds, and the gist was this: We might, for instance, replace one tire on a truck and bill that company for five new tires. If the company objected, they might end up getting twenty-five tires slashed, and that cost a heck of a lot more than the five. Setting up a new company right on Alamo property was a brazen move, and it certainly wouldn't be met with approval by John DiGilio or Jackie DiNorscio and his Bruno Family connections, unless they could get a piece of Tino's action too.

I knew two things right away: It wouldn't be that easy to set up a separate operation, and it would put me smack in the middle of a power grab between three rival factions with a history of violence, doing what it took to obtain whatever they wanted. I would have to string Tino along, keep getting as much on tape as I could for Project Alpha and doing my best to stay safe. But I had a bad feeling in the pit of my stomach. I knew how much pressure he would exert to pull me away from the herd, and what might happen if he didn't get his way.

In addition to Tino's overtures, I was busy fending off constant demands from Jackie D. He might have been in a prison cell at Rahway less than thirty minutes away, but he never stopped trying to bully me into paying for this thing or that. Usually it involved his wife or his girlfriend. I knew he felt he was losing control of Alamo to the groups run by

Fiumara and DiGilio, and that made him even more of a headache.

One day I received a message that Jackie wanted to arrange a trip to Disney World in Orlando for his wife Marlene, their two kids, and his mother. The kicker was that he wanted Alamo Trucking to foot the entire bill. I sent word back to him at Rahway that the answer was "no."

The next day, a heavyset, muscular wiseguy showed up at my office. His name was William "Woody" Brown, and I knew his job description: He was Jackie's enforcer. Woody had come with a message for Pat and me.

"We need the money for the travel agency," he began.

"The tickets come to $1,325.29," Pat interjected.

"Right," said Woody, unfazed by the outrageousness of the request.

I jumped in, wondering aloud if Jackie would ask for even more if we came up with the money. At that point, Woody got to the bottom line.

"Well, Jackie said this is his wife and if we can't do this for him, he'll call Tino and Johnny and he'll shut everything down. There won't be nothing moving outta here."

I noticed something about Jackie's threat. Here was a member of the Bruno Crime Family claiming to have the ability to have members of the Genovese Crime Family shut us down. It was significant: Our investigation was continuing to show that—contrary to what law enforcement had always believed—distinctly separate Mob organizations worked together if there was money to be made. This cross-blending of family forces was a major revelation that would be underscored again and again in the years that followed.

Of course, in the meantime, we had the Magic Kingdom Mob dilemma to resolve. And we did what we had to do—pay more than $2,500 for the DiNorscio Family vacation to Disney World. Remember, this was $2,500 in the mid-seventies—quite a bit of cash.

Naturally, I was playing a role—saying "no" initially, and then appearing to wait for the hammer to fall before giving in. Yet it was a window into the plight of real business owners who faced similar threatening tactics, not knowing if they would lose their livelihoods, or even their lives, for noncompliance. My "business" had a steady source of funding from the federal government. It wasn't *my* money I was losing. Still, being threatened and manipulated by strongarm tactics infuriated me. I didn't sense the growing split in my identity then, but I'm sure some of that anger stemmed from continual immersion in my persona of Bobby Covert, a trucking businessman watching his profits being bled away by the Mafia.

Jackie DiNorscio, in his mid-thirties with a rap sheet as long as the Lincoln Tunnel, was shameless when it came to this kind of stunt. That's why it should have come as no surprise that his epic criminal trial in 1987—when he defended himself in court—became the longest trial in U.S. history and wound up as a major motion picture, *Find Me Guilty*, starring Vin Diesel. Even though he had plenty of cash funneling in from his various criminal pursuits, he made his wife apply for welfare while he was in prison so he could collect on that too.

Then there was his girlfriend, who also happened to be named Jackie. He ordered me to have her collect unemployment insurance because she was no longer working for Alamo. There was just one problem: She *never* had worked for Alamo, not even as one of those no-show employees we also had on the rolls—guys who collected a paycheck for doing nothing. Jackie insisted that I "fix it" for his girlfriend, and in the end I had no choice but to surrender to the pressure. The whole time, we were recording conversations and making meticulous reports of illegal acts—the kind that were crippling actual companies along the Jersey waterfront.

But we weren't done with Jackie—the girlfriend. I received a message from an intermediary to rent a car for $500 a month and bill it to Alamo so she had a way to get to the prison. It turned out that Jackie (the boyfriend) had figured out how to have sex with her during their visits. He'd sit in a chair while three of his men surrounded him to keep anyone from seeing. No wonder he wanted her to have a car so badly—conjugal visits were not part of the daily routine at Rahway State Prison.

I sent back my standard response to these ridiculous demands: "No."

Pat and I were sitting in our second-floor Alamo office when a call came the following day. Pat answered and motioned for me to start recording as he handed me the phone without telling me who it was, then started laughing when he saw the stunned look on my face. The familiar, raspy Jackie D. accent blasted in my ear.

"Bobby, you know who this is, right?"

"Oh, yeah, how ya doing?"

"Ah, did you tell me we could get that yesterday?"

"I told you I'm having a problem getting the money."

"You having a problem? Did I tell ya to lay it out personally?"

"I'm having a problem personally."

"Hey, Bobby, what are youse trying to do, make a fuckin' jerkoff out of somebody?"

"Hey, no, there's nothing like that being done."

"Nothin' like that. I mean what the fuck. You think that I'm a fuckin' beggar or something?"

"Nobody's saying that."

"Well, I asked ya for one motherfucking favor and youse are gonna tell me that youse are gonna have a problem with $500. I mean you want to see me blow my fuckin' top down there?"

"No, I don't want to see that. I don't want to have a problem with anybody."

There was a momentary pause.

"Bobby—how much can you give her today?"

"Deuce."

"I need $350 at least; it's got to be this morning."

"Ah, shit. You understand the problem I'm having, right?"

"Now I'm going to tell you what. I'm puttin' a fuckin' man down there, and I'll show youse all somethin' down there. I wanna see the fuckin' way the thing's being run. You understand what I'm sayin'?"

I heard a rustling on the line, and then Jackie's voice sounding distracted—"One minute, Ralph, I'll be off in one minute." He turned his attention back to me: "You understand what I'm saying?!"

Jackie's allotted minutes on the prison pay phone were up, and he left with the tirade still in full swing—I guess there was a time limit in prison for extortions over the telephone. But I understood what he was saying: If I didn't come up with the cash, he would shut us down. So again, I paid.

Soon after, Jackie somehow had it fixed so that he had his very own telephone in his jail cell. He'd gotten his hands on one of those little-girl Princess phones and had figured out where the prison phone lines were located. He found one near his cell and plugged an unauthorized extension into it. When the operator came on, he would simply have all his calls billed to Alamo—running up a bill in the thousands of dollars before the scam was discovered and shut down by the prison officials. It was good news for Bobby Covert, but bad news for the law-enforcement investigation, which had been privy to the phone numbers of all the Mob figures Jackie was calling around the country.

While the line was still active, he'd call to demand that I visit him at Rahway. That was one request I had to get around. There were too many guys I'd arrested as a young trooper who'd been sent to Rahway, any number of whom could have recognized me and blown my cover. When I refused to come, Jackie responded by sending Woody Brown and another beefy enforcer, Larry Maturo, to insist on the visit. Jackie knew that I had become somewhat friendly with Woody, so he sent along a guy who had no ties to me.

"It would be healthier for you to go to see Jackie," Maturo said ominously. "Just do what you're told and we'll leave it at that."

An undercover cop's greatest weapon isn't a gun; it's the ability to think on his feet. So I told Maturo that as a legitimate businessman, I couldn't risk hurting my reputation by visiting Jackie in prison. "Look, Larry, if I get called before Customs or the Waterfront Commission and my name shows up on a list as visiting prisons, that causes problems for all of us," I said, schmoozing to the best of my ability. No retribution followed—no attempts made to shut us down. The stall technique apparently worked.

It wasn't just Jackie DiNorscio soaking us every chance he could to pad his wallet. One day I got a bill for a soil test that had been performed, not on our property, but on Tino Fiumara's lawn. Another time, he billed us for appliances that had been bought for a bar and restaurant from which he got a percentage. He insisted that Alamo send truckers to his house on weekends to do odd jobs, anything from yard work to building him a back-yard barbecue. Unfortunately, the stonework on the barbecue wasn't to his liking, so he took a sledgehammer and smashed the whole thing apart, leaving the workers scared to death.

That image of Tino was very much on my mind in the days that followed the visit by Tino and Michael to the Water's Ebb. I didn't like the sound of entering into a private deal with him to start Liberty Tire right on Alamo property. But Tino was not a man who took no for an answer, nor someone with whom you wanted to have a conflict.

A week went by without a word. One night after work, Pat and I stood on the apartment balcony, talking over our options. "Look, Bobby, we'll work through it," he said. I gazed out at the flickering lights on the bridge, crossed by countless working people—citizens, as wiseguys called them—heading home to the comfort and love of their families from everyday jobs and normal lives. I wasn't sure how Tino's move was going to play out. But I did know I didn't like the direction things were heading.

CHAPTER SEVEN

THE BELLA VITA

On a balmy late-April night in early 1977, motorists barreling along Route 46 in Parsippany whip right past an elegant white-brick restaurant, unaware of the magnitude of an event unfolding inside. A tall, gregarious man in his fifties with thick gray hair, olive skin, and an engaging smile moves from table to table, greeting the patrons who fill his spacious dining room. They have come for the grand opening of the Bella Vita Ristorante, home of fine Italian cuisine and one man's lifelong dream.

Owner Louie Crescenzi, decked out in a black tuxedo, once wore a uniform with grease stains as the owner of a half dozen gas stations in northern Jersey. Yet he always imagined that this night would come, that he would save his earnings and finally parlay them into his true passion: his own dining establishment. Crescenzi, whose parents immigrated to the United States at the turn of the century, has chosen a name from his Italian heritage that captures what he wants his new place to represent—the good life.

Every detail is just right—the romantic, dimly lit dining room with candles burning at every table, the waiters with cummerbunds and white gloves delivering drinks from a large, crescent-shaped bar, the male singer crooning slow, jazzy love songs in a far corner, the Mediterranean vines painted beneath the crown molding along the ceiling, and the menu of traditional pasta dishes to die for.

But despite Crescenzi's exuberant mood and hearty laugh on this special evening, the good life is slowly taking a bad turn. Only a week earlier, he was stunned to learn that a man he had considered a friend— a person who had merely offered some advice and sales tips in launching the Bella Vita—insisted that he be given a 10-percent stake in the business. Crescenzi viewed the demand as preposterous and flatly rejected it. This so-called friend maintained that he was a legitimate business partner and, and in lieu of a percentage, said he would settle for a flat payment of $4,600.

Crescenzi has an entirely different view of the arrangement—he never made any promises of a partnership to this man, never signed a contract. Still, he can't get the problem off his mind even in the midst of his first big night in business. He knows a shakedown when he sees it, and worries what the con artist will pull next. In fact, the would-be associate has already made his next move, complaining to a friend with a Mob connection in New York City.

Several weeks later, after the restaurant's opening, a pair of Mafia crew members from Manhattan pay Crescenzi a visit and demand the money. They threaten him with bodily harm if he does not make good. The mere threat of violence is all that is required: The terrified restaurateur hands over $600, with the promise of four grand to follow soon after. Instead of paying the balance, however, Crescenzi reaches out to his own Mob connection, an old friend from Newark, Jerry Coppola. And Coppola immediately notifies his nephew, Michael Coppola— second in command to feared Genovese mobster Tino Fiumara.

Because the Bella Vita is based in New Jersey, virtually in his back yard, Fiumara decides that he has authority over the restaurant. He arranges a sitdown with the mobsters from New York and insists— albeit falsely—that he had already staked a claim to the restaurant.

Fiumara takes a strong stand with his counterpart and lets him know he's "trespassing," prompting the New York wiseguys to back off. He then dispatches Jerry Coppola to tell Crescenzi that his problems have been resolved. Crescenzi feels an immense weight lifting from his shoulders. He is so elated, he feels like crying. But he will soon shed tears over the newer, bigger problem he has unwittingly created for himself—a problem that, in a most unexpected turn of events, soon comes to the attention of Project Alpha.

As it turns out, Patrick John Kelly even has his finger on the pulse of this crime-in-the-making. His son-in-law happens to work as the head chef at—of all places—the Bella Vita restaurant. He casually mentions to Kelly the predicament ensnaring his boss, who promptly brings it to the attention of Alamo president Bobby Covert.

Covert is increasingly stressed by the constant demands on his time at Alamo, where he works 12-to-15-hour days, and by his own internal pressures, courtesy of Fiumara and his Mafia brethren. However, knowing Fiumara's track record, the potential extortion of a desperate restaurant owner cannot be ignored. So one afternoon, Covert sets off to find the Good Life—and perhaps a diversion from his own mounting difficulties.

The truth is, we would never have heard about Louie Crescenzi and how the Mob played "Guess Who's Coming to Dinner" at the Bella Vita—and decided never to leave—if Pat Kelly hadn't taken his family on a cruise.

A few years before Pat got pulled into his life as an informant, he was raking in money from who knows what kind of illegal enterprises and treated his wife, five daughters, and one son to a luxury trip around the Caribbean. As fate would have it, one of Pat's daughters, who was about twenty, met the head chef on board the ship, Angello Barone. He was a smooth-talking, good-looking guy, about ten years older than she, who clearly enjoyed the perks of his job—including flirting with the pretty girls aboard the cruise liner. Angello and Pat's daughter hit it off, got engaged a few months later, and, within the year, Pat had gained not only a son-in-law but one helluva good cook for Kelly family dinners. And, as it turned out, he also gained a future informant.

Angello eventually went looking for a new job to help support his bride. He had heard about a classy Italian restaurant opening in Parsippany and applied for the position of head chef. Louie Crescenzi couldn't believe his good fortune in landing a man with the kitchen skills Angello possessed. It was a perfect hire—at least, it wound up being perfect for us.

Angello had no idea, of course, that his father-in-law was in a new line of work with the New Jersey State Police and the FBI. But he did know that Pat was connected to the Mob. So when he heard that his boss had a problem with wiseguys across the river, Angello figured it was a situation worth mentioning; if nothing else, it was a chance to ingratiate himself to his wife's dad—and possibly get his own payoff down the road. Thanks to Angello, we got lucky. The young chef's decision to tell Pat gave us a key ingredient in our investigation: an important case that would provide direct evidence of how the Mafia took over a legitimate business, and that would ultimately help make cases we would never otherwise have been able to make.

"Hey, Bobby, it just keeps getting better," Pat said one morning. "You're gonna love this. I just found you a new best friend, and he owns the Bella Vita Restaurant."

Pat laid out the basics. Hearing that Tino was involved made it a no-brainer, despite all the headaches I was already dealing with at Alamo. I wasn't sure where this was going to take us, but I knew I'd had enough confrontations with Pat. At some point, I had to start agreeing with him or he might lose his motivation to bring in leads. Even though I wasn't crazy about a 45-minute drive to Parsippany for a bite to eat, it was a good time to stroke his ego.

"You make more cases in a week than most cops do in a month," I said. "I'm feeling kind of hungry anyway, so let's take a ride."

Off we went to the Bella Vita—the first of many lunches and dinners at the restaurant over the next few months. I just wanted to establish my presence at the place, meet Louie, and develop some rapport. I started eating lunch there two or three times a week, and dinner on the other nights. Pat often came along, and I gained instant credibility by being his partner. Louie thought Pat and I were best friends. I even told him that Pat was my mentor, which didn't hurt my standing at all, nor did the family connection between Pat and Angello.

Louie gradually began to open up. One Tuesday, after the lunch crowd had cleared out, Louie sat down with us at our table, and Pat said, bluntly, "Lou, Bobby knows what you're going through."

I jumped in the door Pat had opened for me. "Pat told me what you've been dealin' with, Louie. I've been down that road. It's very stressful. It's not easy."

The fact is, I knew that Louie was feeling some pressure from wiseguys from the City and that Michael Coppola and his uncle Jerry Coppola were looking for ways to make that problem disappear. I also had a pretty good idea that his problems were just beginning. From the moment I met Louie, it was clear that he wanted someone to talk to. He had seen his dream threatened, and the experience had shaken him. We were like two strangers sharing the bond of a common experience, and I was the sympathetic ear—like passengers seated next to each other on a plane engaged in a candid conversation. Maybe to calm your nerves from the fear of flying, you pour your life's story out to the person seated beside you just to make yourself feel better.

Louie poured out his story to me: all the details of what had transpired with the $4,600, and how Jerry Coppola had enlisted the support of his nephew Michael and this other man they referred to simply as "George" to make everything right.

Poor Louie. He didn't know that "George" was the secret code name Tino Fiumara frequently used so his real name wouldn't show up on wiretaps or be overheard by the wrong people in conversations. Ironically, to wiseguys, George meant a good person or good thing. So you might hear somebody describe a car as "George" or "Double George." Tino even went by the name "Mr. DeGeorge."

"I'm so thankful to George," Louie continued. "I'm going to show my appreciation and have him and all his people here for dinner, and they won't pay a dime—I'm buying. It's the least I can do to repay him for what he did for me."

I looked at Louie across the table and thought, "You think that's where this is going to end—you're going to buy them dinner one night and this will all be forgotten?"

Of course the tab would be higher than that. It's always been interesting to me that people don't turn to law enforcement in such situations. Here's a guy being shaken down, with two mobsters putting the muscle on him for $4,600, and there's no thought of going to the cops for help. I suppose we tend to look at informants as rats and stool pigeons, and people don't want to look at *themselves* like that.

People also gravitate toward the easy fix, instead of turning to the police, where cases have to be developed, arrests made, and trials held. All of that takes time. We all want our problems to go away, like that Etch-A-Sketch game we played as kids—just shake it, turn it over, and it comes back with a clean slate. But life doesn't work that way. With Louie, the easy fix was making a call to a connected friend in his old neighborhood, hoping he could make this problem disappear.

The next day, Pat took me aside and let me know what he'd heard from Michael Coppola. His uncle Jerry was going to pay Louie a visit and explain how everything was going to be resolved—that Louie would no longer have to worry about unwanted visits from New York mobsters and didn't have to ante up the additional $4,000. In exchange, however, Tino would be taking 25 percent of the weekly profits from the Bella Vita, and Louie would have to pay an additional $300 a week to support Jerry as a no-show employee on the payroll.

Jerry was going to meet Louie at his restaurant around 10:30 Friday morning, before the lunch-hour rush. I decided I'd go for a late lunch Friday, around 3:00 p.m. when the place would be empty, hoping Louie would need a shoulder to cry on.

As soon as I took my seat, I noticed that he looked distracted, shaken, the color drained from his normally tanned complexion. He was fiddling absent-mindedly at the bar with a small, empty cardboard box that had contained Bella Vita matchbooks, the souvenir kind that patrons picked up at the maitre-d' stand on the way out. He saw me and came right over to sit down, still holding the empty cardboard box—

unconsciously crushing and recrushing it. It seemed strangely appropriate that he was handling a box for matches; his entire vision of the good life had suddenly gone up in smoke.

"You all right, Louie?" I asked, even though I knew the answer.

He responded slowly, the words almost inaudible, as if he couldn't bear to hear what was coming out of his own mouth. It was as if he had been visited by the Ghost of Christmas Future in the Charles Dickens classic—and the road ahead was a terrifying one.

"Bobby, they're taking 25 percent of my business, and I have to pay $300 a week to Jerry. And he's not even going to be here, or do anything. I can't afford this. But they say I have no choice. I really have to pay them this money? This is my dream, Bobby—they're taking my dream."

For the next thirty minutes, Louie rambled on, repeating himself often. Even though I was sitting right across from him, he seemed to be talking to himself most of the time, drifting in and out of his own thoughts, trying to make sense of what he had been told by Jerry Coppola. As a trooper, I'd seen victims in shock. And Louie was in shock.

"They want 25 percent of the business—is that gross or net?" he asked. "I don't even know what they're talking about."

I hadn't seen this kind of despair in a long time, maybe ever. It was such an intense conversation, I barely touched my eggplant Parmesan and I had to get back to Alamo. I told him I was always available to talk, but he was barely listening. I patted him on the back and walked past the fancy porcelain statues by the hand-carved front door, leaving Louie alone with his tattered dream.

I continued coming to lunch for many months after that, gathering evidence and often wearing a wire. But honestly, this was personal—I was concerned for Louie, and I was checking in on him to see how he was holding up. Eventually, though, I had to realize I wasn't a social worker; I was an undercover state trooper working an intense case, and there wasn't a whole lot of time to be worrying about people other than myself.

One late May evening, Michael Coppola invited Pat and me to dinner at the Bella Vita. I arrived around 9:30 p.m. We sat at one table with Tino, Michael, and another one of Jerry's nephews, Paulie Coppola. Jerry and his wife sat at the table beside us, with their niece and her husband. Everybody seemed to be in good spirits, even Tino. And why shouldn't he be? He had just taken control of a high-end Italian restaurant to conduct business or just enjoy socializing. Every so often, he summoned people to his side to engage in private conversations. One long chat was with a wiseguy introduced to us as Bubble Eyes, and one look at his slightly bulging eyes explained that nickname more than adequately.

Then Tino leaned toward me. I'd been waiting for the other shoe to drop regarding his idea for turning Alamo into his own venture, Liberty Tire & Trailer Service. I was sure I was about to be given marching orders; but what I heard was, "Bobby, we're not going to move on that tire company."

It was the one thing I wasn't expecting to hear. I felt a huge sense of relief at not having to deal with his takeover attempt and all the ramifications triggered by such a move. I did all I could to maintain a poker face.

"Why's that, T?" I said seriously.

"Too complicated, Bobby. We start a new company on Alamo property and everybody wants a piece of it. Let it lay. I'll get somethin' goin'—and you'll be a rich man."

My relief shifted back to anxiety at the thought of being under Tino's flag—especially seeing what being under his flag was doing to Louie Crescenzi. At least I didn't have to deal with the tire company or any other imminent plans to take us over. Fortunately for me, Tino's greed had kicked into overdrive—he simply didn't want to share any profits with John DiGilio or Jackie DiNorscio. "Whatever you say," I replied. It was meant as a harmless affirmation, but Tino fired a stern look back at me that seemed to say, "You're fuckin'-A right it's whatever I say." Just like that, the conversation was over.

We were still there at 1:00 a.m., drinking and laughing, when Tino instructed Pat to "tell the Madam" to join us at the table—nodding his head in the direction of a solemn, sleepy-eyed Louie Crescenzi by the bar. The choice of word—madam—was revealing, an indication of who was getting screwed in this deal.

Louie shook himself to attention, walked over briskly, and sat down beside Tino. "The $600 has been taken care of," Tino informed him, referring to the money Louie had paid to the New York wiseguys. "Now I just want you to come to me if you have any problems. And always do the right thing." With that, Louie bowed his head, reached for Tino's hand and kissed it, then returned to the bar. It was a sad, pitiful sight and I felt terrible for Louie, knowing the humiliation, anger, and fear he must have been feeling at that moment.

I left soon after that. But Pat stayed behind. When I saw him the next day at Alamo, he told me Tino had gotten drunk, fallen asleep at the table, and stayed there until 7:00 a.m. Pat eventually got him into a car and drove him home.

Amid all the painful scenes I witnessed during this time, there were some light moments as well. One came when Joey Adonis, Jr., who loved sports almost as much as he savored the *Godfather* movies, challenged Alamo to a softball game with a bet on the line: Losers would treat the winning team to dinner at the Bella Vita.

We met outside the Water's Ebb Apartments—me, Pat, undercover agents Al Denny, Ralph Rascati, and Richard Blake, and an array of tough Alamo truckers, including Tony Ray, Frank Massaro, and Lenny Buzz. The plan was to meet Joey and his team at the Italianissimo Restaurant in Cliffside Park, but when we got there they were nowhere in sight. Hey, we thought we had a victory—and free dinner—by forfeit.

Finally, an hour later, Joey called the restaurant and we arranged to play the game at the Fort Lee Intermediate School. Al Denny—a great basketball player from Wake Forest—and I each held up our ends of the bargain, with a home run apiece, a couple of other hits, and a few nice plays in the field. We were winning something like 10–9 in the last inning, but damned if Joey didn't get the clutch hit that beat us by one run. It was just as well. As competitive as Joey was, it was better for me—even though I'd be picking up the tab—that he and his Bad News Wiseguy Bears won.

A week later, it was time to settle up. I arrived at the Bella Vita around 11:30 p.m. and was promptly ushered to a corner table with a dozen wiseguys. Joey couldn't wait to rub it in.

"Hey, Babe Ruth, nice game—hope ya got your wallet with ya," he yelled, as guffaws broke out at the table.

Everyone was there—Tino, the Coppolas, a Fiumara guy named Larry Ricci, and a wiseguy I recognized as Joe "The Indian" Polverino, among others. As softball faded from the conversation, Michael and Larry made a point of telling me that it would be in my best interest to convert Alamo trucks so they could handle both port work and a new kind of use involving landfills. I knew they wouldn't be broaching the topic if it hadn't come from Tino, so there was no doubt that the subject would resurface—perhaps in place of the tire idea that had gone flat—and I'd have to have a plan for dealing with it.

Then Jerry Coppola bent my ear about playing golf with him, and how once again it would be in my "best interest" to join the Upper Montclair Country Club because of all the political, high-ranking officials and big-time business people who played there and might be of help to me at Alamo. Truthfully, I just wanted to go home—or anywhere but here. I was tired, both from lack of sleep and from being in the constant presence of Mob guys. There's a big difference between enjoying a nice meal at a nice restaurant with your friends—and a nice restaurant and a nice meal with people who you have to make believe are your friends. And the more I had to make believe—talking like them, acting like them, thinking like them to fit in and survive—the more I started to lose sight of the line where Bob Delaney ended and Bobby Covert began.

It was getting close to 2:00 a.m., and I could see how distraught Louie was at seeing his vision for the Bella Vita being hijacked. He simply handed the restaurant keys to Larry Ricci and said, "*You* close up the place. I'll be back tomorrow." When I saw him do that, I knew he had given up. It was as if he was saying, "Here, take it all." Louie had always been the last one to leave, and now I was watching him walk out the door and never look back. He was probably wishing he had just paid the $4,600 to the other Mob guys from New York and been done with it. But the reality is that they'd have pegged him as weak and put their hooks into him the same way Tino had just done.

Back at my office the next day, I had little time to think about the demise of Louie Crescenzi or all the valuable hidden recordings we had been making of Tino's extortion game. There were new demands on my time and attention practically every time I turned around—most tied to my role as trucking-company president.

I had to meet with John DiGilio and Fat Anthony over money that Frigid Express had not yet paid Alamo. I reminded Anthony that I paid his cousin Neil Pacilio a percentage to keep this problem from occurring, and I was assured that the problem wouldn't happen again.

One of my Alamo drivers was hard up for cash. One day, he brought me a box, opened it, and pulled out a .25-caliber handgun he had picked up in Florida. He wanted to sell it to me for $100. It wasn't your normal employee–boss exchange, but I directed him to Ralph Rascati and Ralph made the buy, taking a weapon off the street and writing up a report on the illegal transaction.

I arrived at work one morning to be greeted by a man with a tractor-trailer load of stolen General Electric products. He pulled out some samples of the loot—a ten-band portable radio, an eight-track player called the Blaster, another called the Show Off, and a two-way radio. As I decided whether to meet the guy's asking price—45 percent of the wholesale value for the entire tractor-trailer load—word came in that we could purchase stolen truck tires at eighty bucks a pop in Elizabeth. I wrote out a check for $650 for a portion of the stolen GE products, and then jumped in my car to look into the stolen tires.

This is what my life had become, a blur of rip-off schemes that required constant evaluation and pulled me in multiple directions around the clock. And the whole time, there was Tino, lurking in the shadows like a circling shark, one that had just devoured a good man's dignity. There was no telling when he would strike again and what form the attack would take.

With my dad in front of his black-and-white New Jersey State Police troop car in 1953. Twenty years later, I would be wearing the uniform, too.

I wore No. 34 at Blessed John Neumann Prep and averaged 32 points a game in my junior year and 34 points in my senior year—the result of that hoop in my parents' backyard.

In 1969, my principal, Father Anthony Kowalski, and my basketball coach, Bob Plocinik, presenting me the ball with which I scored my one-thousandth point.

Receiving my badge, No. 2853, from my dad, Captain Delaney, No. 978 (center). To his right, Colonel David Kelly; to his left, Lieutenant Colonel Eugene Olaff.

That's me in front of the black-and-white troop car in 1973 with two of my cousins—before I started the undercover phase of my career.

Resigned 4-9-75 #2853
Delaney, R.J.

The official resignation photo taken on April 9, 1975 for State Police records indicating that I was no longer a Jersey Trooper—attention to detail was essential.

As soon as I started my undercover assignment, I thought I had to become an armpit with eyes, and a couple of times a week I'd put my hair in curlers to help create my new image.

Christmas 1976: Covert's look has changed to appear more like the wiseguys I hung around with—and man, was I putting on the pounds.

There was a lot of faking to make it all look real. Bobby Covert had credit cards, a driver's license, a social security number, a YMCA card, and even a criminal rap sheet in his name.

Bobby Covert, in 1976, on a loading dock. The beard is gone, and a Fu Manchu has become my signature.

Surveillance cameras were positioned throughout the trucking company offices, allowing us to preserve images of all visitors. Here is one of William "Woody" Brown, one of Jackie D's enforcers, who strong-armed me to pay for the DiNorscio Disney World vacation.

Ralph DiNorscio, brother of Jackie DiNorscio and son of Dominick DiNorscio (a.k.a. Tommy Adams), was a good example of how wiseguys have everyday problems. He was an alcoholic and ended up killing himself with booze and drugs.

Bobby Covert leading the way into the office of Mid-Atlantic Air & Sea Transportation, followed by wiseguys George "The Greek" Mavrodes in the checked pants and Nicky Paterno. The camera is hidden inside a stereo speaker mounted on the wall across the loading dock. It was our way of having a time stamp, back in 1975 before the digital technology. We had the sign documenting our location and the clock on the office back wall documenting the time; both would later be useful in court.

Bobby Covert's Lincoln Mark V in front of Alamo Transportation, 231 Communipaw Avenue, Jersey City, New Jersey.

The entrance to the truck yard, and just to the left—out of view—is where we stabled the horses that Pat Kelly persuaded me to keep.

Anthony Pacilio, a wiseguy out of the DiGilio crew.

Sitting at my Alamo desk in the second-floor office I shared with Pat Kelly.

Pat Kelly, a chain-smoker, seated at his desk on the other side of the office from me.

Surveillance photo taken in Hoboken, New Jersey, of two key Project Alpha targets: A. Joey Adonis (a.k.a. Joey A) and B. Tino Fiumara (a.k.a. "T," George, or Mr. DeGeorge).

The Sting Lounge in Bayonne, New Jersey, was one of my first hangouts as I started Bobby Covert's new life. I always loved the name of that bar.

Press conference on September 28, 1977, at the West Orange Armory, site of the raid command post. Back row (left to right): FBI Supervisor George DeHardy; Trooper Bob Weisert; Trooper Ralph Buono; myself; and Jack Liddy. Front row (left to right): Jim Golden, Law Enforcement Assistance Administration; Louis Giovanetti, special agent in charge of the New Jersey FBI office; New Jersey Attorney General William F. Hyland; and Colonel Clinton Pagano, New Jersey State Police.

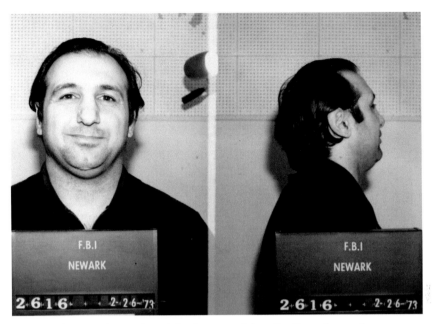

John DiGilio, a made member of the Genovese Crime Family, and one of my "partners" in Alamo Transportation.

In 1978, I attained the rank of Detective.

In 1979, after emerging from my life as Bobby Covert, I was now a detective but still enjoyed the opportunity to put on my State Police uniform. The blue ribbon above my left breast pocket is called the Blue Max, a distinguished honor recognizing troopers for outstanding performance in the line of duty. Mine was for my years infiltrating the Mob.

WILLIAM V. ROTH, JR., DEL., CHAIRMAN

CHARLES H. PERCY, ILL.   THOMAS F. EAGLETON, MO.
TED STEVENS, ALASKA   HENRY M. JACKSON, WASH.
CHARLES MC C. MATHIAS, JR., MD. LAWTON CHILES, FLA.
JOHN C. DANFORTH, MO.   SAM NUNN, GA.
WILLIAM S. COHEN, MAINE   JOHN GLENN, OHIO
DAVID DURENBERGER, MINN.   JIM SASSER, TENN.
MACK MATTINGLY, GA.   DAVID PRYOR, ARK.
WARREN B. RUDMAN, N.H.   CARL LEVIN, MICH.

JOAN M. MC ENTEE, STAFF DIRECTOR

SUBCOMMITTEE:

WILLIAM V. ROTH, JR., DEL., CHAIRMAN
WARREN B. RUDMAN, N.H., VICE CHAIRMAN

CHARLES H. PERCY, ILL.   SAM NUNN, GA.
CHARLES MC C. MATHIAS, JR., MD. HENRY M. JACKSON, WASH.
JOHN C. DANFORTH, MO.   LAWTON CHILES, FLA.
WILLIAM S. COHEN, MAINE   JOHN GLENN, OHIO
                               JIM SASSER, TENN.

S. CASE WEILAND
CHIEF COUNSEL
MICHAEL C. EBERHARDT
DEPUTY CHIEF COUNSEL
MARTY STEINBERG
CHIEF COUNSEL TO THE MINORITY

United States Senate

COMMITTEE ON
GOVERNMENTAL AFFAIRS
SENATE PERMANENT SUBCOMMITTEE
ON INVESTIGATIONS
WASHINGTON, D.C. 20510

March 11, 1981

Detective Robert Delaney
New Jersey State Police
Post Office Box 68
West Trenton, New Jersey   08625

Dear Bob:

I would like to thank you, on my own behalf and on behalf of the Permanent Subcommittee on Investigations, for your cooperation and testimony before the Subcommittee during our hearings on waterfront corruption.

Your testimony highlighted the important and crucial aspects of the need for undercover procedures in investigations of the organized criminal element. You are to be commended for the innovative and thorough work you achieved while serving in an undercover capacity during Project Alpha.

The function of this Subcommittee and others like it can be fully realized only with the full and complete cooperation of citizens like yourself. I personally commend you for the valuable service which you rendered to our effort.

Sincerely,

Sam Nunn
Ranking Minority Member

A letter I received from Senator Sam Nunn on March 11, 1981, commending me for the work done during Project Alpha and for testifying before his subcommittee.

My good friend and fellow trooper John Schroth, who first recognized my out-of-control behavior after my undercover days and confronted me about it.

Teaching at the New Jersey State Police Academy in 1983.

The Vince Lombardi quote hung over my desk at the New Jersey State Police Training Academy, where I developed the Institute on Organized Criminal Groups while I was assigned to the Criminal Science Unit.

Shaquille O'Neal's desire to enter law enforcement after his NBA career is well documented. When Shaq found out that I knew FBI director Louis Freeh, he asked me to help him get a job in the FBI. I told him he'd be great at surveillance—no one would ever recognize him.

Just another night at the office. Even Michael Jordan disagreed with some of my calls.

On April 2, 1995, Sunday afternoon, in a game at the New Jersey Meadowlands, I have to break up a fight between Patrick Ewing of the New York Knicks and Rick Mahorn—formerly one of the original Detroit Piston "Bad Boys"—then a New Jersey Net. I ejected both of them and found out later that they watched the game together in the locker room.

Ray Liotta, who played mobster Henry Hill in the movie *Goodfellas*, did the voice-over on the ESPN story about my undercover life—two Jersey boys who both played the role of a wiseguy.

With Martin Luther King III in 2006. His father's words have served me well, both on and off the court.

My induction into the New Jersey City University Athletic Hall of Fame on January 27, 2006. With me is my college basketball coach, Larry Schiner.

With my wife Billie and Charles Barkley at the Jimmy V Cancer Research Charity Golf Classic. I am the National Co-Chair of the Blow the Whistle on Cancer Campaign for the V Foundation, named in honor of the beloved coach, Jimmy Valvano.

Alive and well. Life is good. *(Photo credit: Aaron Lockwood Photography)*

CHAPTER EIGHT

REMEMBER THE ALAMO

On the fourth floor of the Union County Courthouse, a stately marble building towering over downtown Elizabeth, a man in a gray pinstriped suit stands before a grim-faced judge, awaiting his fate. The infraction is only a minor probation violation, but it carries immense conse-quences—not only for the defendant but for what has gradually evolved into a major investigation of organized crime on the New Jersey water-front. Pat Kelly has wriggled out of his share of tight spots before, but this one threatens to bring him down, and Project Alpha along with it.

Kelly has been brought in on a pending case tied to a real estate scam he'd run in Elizabeth, and the arresting officers, defense attorney, pros-ecutor, and judge have no idea of his invaluable status to an ongoing state and federal undercover operation. Kelly's court appearance has become an immediate concern to the head of the investigation, Jack Liddy, who coordinates a plan—based on word from Kelly—that his lawyer can fix the case and keep him out of prison. Inside Hanlon & Associates, Liddy hands an envelope with twenty-five $100 bills to Bob Delaney, who, in the guise of Bobby Covert, will do his best, an hour later, to buy his employee's freedom.

The proceedings are set for 2:30 p.m., and traffic is heavier than usual on Route 1 & 9 during the twenty-minute drive between Newark and Elizabeth. Covert, realizing that time is getting tight, beats most of the red lights and strides into the courtroom on the fourth floor at 2:25 p.m. He is just in time to see Kelly standing before the judge, with his lawyer, Dominick Mirabelli, to his right. Covert nonchalantly moves to the left side of the courtroom and takes a seat, where he will be easily visible to Mirabelli, who has relayed instructions through Kelly on what to do.

Five minutes later, Mirabelli, a portly middle-aged man with a pudgy face and thinning black hair, turns and nods affirmatively toward Covert, who nods back at the barrister. Mirabelli responds with a smile and a wink. Minutes later, Kelly pleads guilty to the charge related to his probation violation—part of the plan prearranged by Mirabelli to make the case go away. When the case is adjourned soon after, Covert follows Mirabelli and Kelly into a hallway. Mirabelli motions for Covert to follow him farther down the hall, through a doorway and into a fire-escape stairwell.

"Do you have the envelope?" he asks.

Covert reaches into his jacket pocket and pulls out a white Alamo Transportation envelope containing the cash. He hands it to Mirabelli, who counts the money slowly and smiles. "Very good, Bobby—it's all been taken care of," he says. Mirabelli has no idea that Covert is wearing a wire and has photocopied each bill so the serial numbers can be tracked. As a result, Project Alpha will eventually make a separate case against the corrupt attorney—who will plead guilty to an "accusation," as opposed to an indictment, and be disbarred for three years.

For now, Kelly hops into the passenger side of Covert's Lincoln Mark V parked on the busy street outside the courthouse. "You couldn't have been ten minutes earlier? I was starting to wonder if you were gonna even show up," Kelly says, giving his partner a good-natured jab.

"Hey, $2,500 doesn't grow on trees—unless the tree is in Jack Liddy's back yard," Covert responds with a smile. "But ya know, Pat, watching you squirm for a few seconds before you knew I was in that courtroom was worth the price of admission."

As they pull onto the highway for the drive back to Jersey City, a truck speeds past, doing at least seventy-five. It displays the familiar white sign on the side with a black border and burgundy lettering: "When Trucking, Remember the Alamo." "I'll remember not to pay that driver's ticket when he gets stopped for speeding by some trooper," Covert jokes to Kelly.

A half hour later, they arrive at Alamo, where the wiseguys' social room is filled with laughter and cigarette smoke and the usual stacks of phone messages and work orders are piled on their desks. Their lives have become chaotic in recent months, but are about to become more complicated than ever.

The phone rang at my desk just before I left to head back home to my apartment. I recognized Michael Coppola's voice instantly. There was an urgent tone to it. "Bobby, be at your place tonight—and tell Pat to be there too," he said. I knew better than to press him for details, especially over the phone.

Immediately I began to get a nervous stomach, a feeling that had been getting worse by the month, along with the sensation that my heart was beating too fast for its own good. The sense of relief I'd enjoyed at keeping Pat out of prison and by my side at Alamo suddenly gave way to anxiety over what Tino might have in mind now.

I drove home with the radio blaring—the FM station I tuned in was playing "Jungleland," by homegrown Jersey guy Bruce Springsteen, singing about gangs at midnight, cops, and the Jersey Turnpike. Add that all up, and you were talking about *my* jungle land. I rolled down the windows and opened the moon roof to let in the cool night air, trying to relax and not think about things I couldn't control.

Sometime after 9:00 p.m., the doorbell rang and I buzzed my guests through the security door to the apartment's lobby. A minute or so later, there was a knock on the door. Pat answered and Tino walked in, followed by Michael. They had been here several times since their initial visit to talk about the aborted tire enterprise, but this was the first time in a few months. As usual, Michael pointed to the stereo, a signal for me to crank up the volume on the radio to make sure any potential electronic surveillance would be blocked out. Pat prepared the vodka tonics for our guests, and Tino got right to the point.

"Bobby, we're starting a new company," he said.

"You mean trying the tire company again?" Pat jumped in.

"A new company, a trucking company," Tino continued.

"So you're talking about just putting Alamo to bed?" I asked him.

"Gradually, we'll just fade it right out," he replied.

Tino was finally making his move, and there was nothing subtle about it. He was tired of sharing profits with DiGilio and DiNorscio, and he believed Alamo's success was due to the business he had brought in anyway. This time, he would not have the problem of operating a new venture on Alamo property, because he intended to close us down altogether and move us out of Jersey City.

His idea was for us to become Liberty Trucking, opening a new terminal in the Down Neck area of Newark, where he exerted tremendous influence. We would work in and around the Newark port area with trucking companies he controlled. Specifically, we were to provide trucks for a company he operated called Airport Landfill Corp. In addition, he planned to make us the "house" trucker for shipping lines that had become part of his domain at the ports of Newark and Elizabeth.

What's more, Tino envisioned the new terminal employing non-union workers, which would circumvent rules that required union workers to load and unload—stuff and strip, as it was called—shipping containers. He had no intention of creating more business opportunities for us if they would benefit any other Mob factions. This would be his baby, and, though he didn't say it, the implication was clear: All the kickbacks would go directly into his pocket.

"House truckers, Bobby, you're gonna be house truckers," he said enthusiastically, as if trying to make us feel as excited as he did. "I got three other lines for you. Just move out of there, move the operation, for Pete's sake." Did I really hear him say "for Pete's sake"? Tino sounded positively giddy, more like a happy kid than a cutthroat gangster who punctuated his sentences with profanity more times than not. But in an unguarded moment, his expression of emotion and accomplishment was the same as any law-abiding citizen—it just happened to be attached to an illegal pursuit.

"Good, we'll start makin' changes," I said, while thinking to myself, "There's nothing good about this."

"I'll get back to you," he said, finishing off his drink and putting it down on the bar. "Beautiful night, isn't it?" he added, looking out through the open balcony across the Hudson. With that, Tino turned and headed to the door, Coppola following behind him.

Pat and I waited a few seconds to make sure they were well on their way, and then tried to figure out how we were going to deal with a blatant, bold takeover of our trucking company—one that was certain to be met with resistance and anger from two other Mob groups.

"How the hell are we gonna get through this?" I asked Pat.

"I dunno. Tino's a bulldog—it's not gonna go away," he said.

I walked over to the bar and poured myself a Scotch and water, a stiff one. This wasn't going to be easy. If we played it right, we would likely gather valuable evidence against Tino and his crew, and who knows how many other wiseguys along the way. At the same time, the constant pressure of living with a fictitious self, always one step from a potentially lethal mistake, continued to build.

Only four and a half years earlier, I had been a junior in college, set to follow my father's footsteps into the New Jersey State Police. Now I was starting to feel like I didn't know who I was. I felt agitated, trapped in a role that was planned to last six months but at this point had stretched well past two years with no clear end in sight.

"Pat, I gotta clear my head. I'm gonna take a ride—and not on one of your freakin' horses," I said, grabbing my car keys.

I pulled out of the Water's Ebb parking lot, and just started driving with no particular destination in mind. Maybe instinctively, I found myself on Interstate 80 heading west to Paterson and thinking about old times.

I remembered an incident as a young state trooper, right before I went undercover. I was stationed in Somerville and made a car stop, arrested two guys with about thirty pounds of marijuana, then heard over the State Police radio that another troop car was close by and would back me up. When you're making an arrest, you're aware that you have backup, but you don't look to see who it is; you keep your full attention on the criminals. It wasn't until I had the cuffs on the bad guys that I realized the other trooper was my father. From that day forward, we always joked that the family that arrests people together stays together. But in a larger sense, I always knew Dad had my back.

When I passed the sign announcing Paterson's city limits just after 11:00 p.m., I pulled off at a gas station and dialed the number of my parents' house. My dad picked up.

"You guys still awake?" I asked.

"Rob, how are you?" he responded, and I could hear the concern in his voice.

"Dad, everything's fine—I'm just in the area, five minutes away, and thought I'd stop by to say hello."

"Okay, good. I'll get my car out of the garage for you."

Leave it to a veteran State Police officer to anticipate what I was thinking: I didn't want to leave my Mark V on the street to attract attention, so this way I could just pull into the garage and keep as low a profile as possible. I steered slowly past the familiar streets of my old neighborhood—Union, Lexington, Arlington, Emerson, Elberon, and finally Maitland. It had been more than a year since I'd been there when my grandmother had passed away, but it still felt like another lifetime. Driving on the roads of my childhood—passing the houses where the DiLellas, the Luizis, and the Picarellis lived—was comforting compared to the names that entwined my world now, like DiGilio, Coppola, and Fiumara.

My mom rushed over to give me a warm hug as I walked into the house. Then my dad and I embraced. Parents have a way of knowing what's going on with their kids, no matter how old they are, and I think they could see something in me—maybe fatigue, maybe just a look of distraction that I wasn't able to conceal, despite how skilled I had become at hiding my true feelings in the company I now kept around the clock.

"I'm good, I'm good," I said, sitting down on the living room sofa where I had spent countless hours talking to my parents and watching TV as a kid.

When she heard I was coming, my mom had warmed up leftover chicken and rice from dinner, and put it, along with milk and a slice of chocolate cake, on a tray which she carried over to me. In that moment, it felt really good to be home, even though I wasn't sure why I had come or if it was even a good idea to begin with. I asked how they were doing, about my sister Kath, about my grandparents. But as soon as they asked how I was doing, I found myself closing up. I didn't really want to answer any questions, and there wasn't much I could say anyway. I just wanted to sit for a while and savor the feeling of home—a life raft I could cling to in stormy waters.

My mom went back into the kitchen to get me a second helping, and Dad moved closer. "How are you doing, Rob?" he asked quietly.

"I'm fine, Dad, just got so many fuckin' things to take care of all the time," I said.

"Rob," he said, holding up an index finger in front of his lips. "Watch the language; your mother—she might overhear."

I hadn't even realized I'd dropped in the f-word, something I'd never done in the strict Catholic household where I was raised. I apologized just as my mom returned with another tray full of food.

Unfortunately, after fifteen minutes or so, I started feeling antsy, as if I couldn't relax even in the no-pressure, stable confines of my old home. It was a sensation I'd felt when I'd come to the house two years before to tell my grandparents about my undercover assignment, and it wouldn't be the last time I'd feel it. Every time I sought out a place from my past to find a little peace or equilibrium, I wanted to figure out how to get away almost as soon as I arrived. "Mom, Dad—it's great to see you, but I gotta get back, lots of work to do tomorrow," I said, hugging them and heading to my car. I watched in my rearview mirror as my dad closed the garage door. Then I pulled onto Maitland, unsure of when I would return.

The next morning, I arrived at Alamo and instantly faced the first crisis of the day. Ray Suarez, one of Patty Mack's guys and terminal manager for Frigid Express, was on the phone. "Bobby, we got a problem," he said. A load of frozen shrimp and frog's legs had gone bad because of a glitch with the refrigeration system in one of our trucks. That represented a lot of money down the drain for Patty, and I'd have to deal with the repercussions.

I stalled Ray, telling him I had other meetings scheduled the next day at the Holiday Inn across from Newark International Airport; I'd call and let him know what room I was in, and he could meet me there. That gave me time to get together with the electronic surveillance unit guys, rent a room at the Holiday Inn, and make sure all the recording equipment could be set up in the next room. There was way too much going on at any given moment at Alamo, and I didn't want to take a chance at anything interrupting an important meeting that was tied to Patty Mack.

Like clockwork, Ray met me in Room 224 the next day. With the ESU team listening in from 226, Ray explained the solution to me—we'd get the money from the insurance company to fix the bad unit and cover the lost load, but instead of dumping the spoiled seafood as required, we'd truck it down through Brownsville, Texas, and into Mexico, refreeze it, truck it back up here, and then sell it in Canada as if it were perfectly fresh.

I listened to Ray, stunned at the plan he was laying out. There was no way I could let this happen as Trooper Robert J. Delaney, but trucking boss Bobby Covert had to appear unfazed by the outrageous idea.

"Let me ask you something: Do people get sick from this?" I asked.

"Oh, yeah," he replied matter-of-factly.

"I mean, can somebody die?" I pressed him.

"Yeah, I guess so," he answered, as if we were talking about whether it might rain tomorrow.

I realized that I had to change my line of questioning or I would appear overly concerned about the public's health and welfare, rather than reflecting how a wiseguy would view it—all about making money.

"Is that gonna tie back to us?" I asked.

"No, no. We break the loads up—we sell 'em here and there around Canada. Nobody has a clue where it came from."

We never made a case on the spoiled loads because, obviously, we could never allow it to actually take place. But we took the evidence we gathered and eventually presented it to the Toronto Metropolitan Police, who shared it with the Royal Canadian Mounted Police. And they worked it from their end. Four years later, a writer from the *Toronto Globe & Mail* named Peter Moon wrote an in-depth story exposing the situation. Ray Suarez and his company, to my knowledge, never got to do any more trucking business in Canada, so at least some justice was later served.

At the moment it was happening, all I could do was put Suarez on hold and move on to the endless flow of pressing matters. Pat and I had to drive to a Sheraton Inn outside Philadelphia, where we met with a pair of Bruno associates, including the president of local No. 30 of the city's Roofers Union, John McCullough. Pat asked them to help get Alamo new business in Port Camden, and they said they'd call their contacts to make it happen—more good evidence for the investigation.

Meanwhile, Anthony Pacilio was still pushing me to align with Johnny D, floating the enticement of full union cooperation and freedom from the normal restrictions imposed by the Teamsters and the ILA.

"We can handle the problems," Fat Anthony told Pat and me. "Johnny *is* the union; and don't tell anyone this, but he took a guy off a forklift and made him president of a big union." I had to give him credit: During our entire time in the operation, we hadn't had a single union representative visit Alamo to determine if we were a union shop.

"Yeah, but what unions will our drivers and other employees have to join if we get more work around Port Newark?" Pat asked him.

"We may start our own local union and put our own man in as shop steward," he answered, as if there was no issue at all.

Fiumara's group had sunk its teeth into the unions, too. We learned that one group of dockworkers had an unusual dental-plan payment— consisting of paying Larry Ricci $15 in cash when he came around every two weeks. Ricci bragged that he was an ILA officer with Local No. 17 in Manhattan and also earned $45,000 running a shipping operation, Primmi Lines, for Tino at Port Newark—explaining that he just watched TV, put his feet on his desk, or slept on the job. Anyway, one poor dockworker needed to get some dental work done for his little boy and wanted to know more about the plan he'd been paying his hard-earned money into. His supervisor advised him to ask Larry. The next time Ricci showed up to collect dental funds, the dockworker approached him with his question. Ricci hit the guy in the chest with the back of his hand and said in a menacing voice, "The dental plan—that's designed to keep your own fuckin' teeth. Any more questions?"

The question for us continued to be what DiGilio had in mind for Alamo Trucking. He didn't like that we were dragging our feet joining him. So he soon began moving ahead with his own plan to shift Alamo into his camp, opening up new trucking opportunities at the port.

Naturally, we'd have to return the favor to him in some form or another. The first time came in April 1977, when the ILA Locals 1587-1588 held a dinner-dance. DiGilio made it known that I was to buy a table for ten people at a cost of $400. I also paid another $150 for a full-page ad in the dinner-dance program—a grand total of $550. In 1977, that was many people's salary for at least two weeks. The event was not exactly a top-shelf night on the town—wooden meeting tables covered by white cloths, a two-bit jazz combo in the back, men chomping on stogies in clouds of cigar smoke, wives in beehive hairdos talking among themselves. During the dinner, the head of that union, Donald Carson, made a point of stopping by our table and introducing himself to Pat and me. "Give my regards to where they have to go," he told us. Once again, everybody we dealt with was talking in some kind of code—but there was no doubt that Carson was talking about John DiGilio.

The dinner was a microcosm of what had been going on with the Mob and unions for years. Organized crime's infiltration of labor unions—especially on the New Jersey waterfront, where it could control the ebb and flow of shipping commerce—had long been a target of law enforcement. Project Alpha underscored our working knowledge of how the Mafia corrupted union leaders and workers, through threats and coercion, to gain control of the docks.

Lingering in the background of our investigation was the mysterious disappearance of Teamsters president Jimmy Hoffa, who had vanished in July 1975. He was last seen alive at the Machus Red Fox Inn in Bloomfield Township, Michigan, since renamed the Andiamo Italia West Restaurant. All law-enforcement eyes were out for any clues relating to Hoffa's whereabouts or fate. Rumors were rampant about him while we were conducting Project Alpha—including a joke that he had been buried in the end zone of Giants Stadium at the Meadowlands, which was under construction at the time. I could just imagine the bosses at the FBI and the State Police thinking we'd be the ones to get the crucial information, because we were right in the middle of the Mob and the waterfront unions with our trucking operation.

But amazingly, there was deafening silence on Hoffa. I never heard word one about it, and most of what I learned was from reading articles in the *Newark Star-Ledger*. When you're in the eye of the storm, you're not exposed to everything. Either the Mob guys we were around didn't know, or it was so high up the line that everybody knew better than to talk about it. And I certainly couldn't bring it up. If the Mob guys weren't talking about Hoffa and I started asking questions, that would have been an instant red flag. They'd have thought, "Why the hell does he care about this murder?" As an undercover cop, you can't ask questions like that, because you'll sound too inquisitive. They wouldn't kill you over it, but they'd pull back and say "Cut him loose." That would have been disastrous for us.

Pat and I definitely didn't hear anything about Mr. Hoffa at Donald Carson's deadly dull union dinner-dance. Afterward, we drove back to the Water's Ebb around midnight, talking about the moves in progress by Johnny Dee and Tino. And we knew that the DiNorscios and Brunos were out there too, though we didn't know what they were planning. As we drove, Pat recalled the time Jackie DiNorscio, years before he went to prison, wanted to test Pat to make sure he was a stand-up guy and see how well he could handle pressure. One night, Jackie D. had Pat take a ride with him. Pat was driving and Jackie was in the passenger seat, with another wiseguy in the back seat. Right out of the blue, Jackie pulled out a gun, turned around, and shot the man repeatedly. Pat was shocked but managed to keep his cool at the wheel. Seconds later, Jackie—and the man in the back seat—started laughing their heads off. It was a fake hit, just to see how Pat would react. He passed the test, his first big step to being accepted by the DiNorscios.

I winced as Pat recounted the story—wondering how frightening and sickening it must have felt to be part of that. But that was only part one. Pat then opened up with me about two individuals from Brooklyn, one named Graziano and the other Juicy, who were driving around with Frankie Valli, the lead singer of the Four Seasons. With Frankie watching in horror, one of the wiseguys pulled a gun and faked a hit on the other guy. Frankie thought he'd witnessed a real murder, and he was later extorted in the scheme—made to pay up or be turned in to the police for not reporting the crime. Years later, this scenario would be played out in Broadway's version of a *hit*—the musical production *Jersey Boys*—about the life of Valli and his legendary group.

Hits were just one way the Mob did its business, and they were reserved for extreme situations. As we continued toward Edgewater, Pat told me how he had once heard from Fat Anthony why a guy named Vinny Capone was killed in Hoboken. He was shot with a .22—a hit allegedly ordered by John DiGilio, who was upset when he didn't receive a piece of the action in a narcotics deal that Capone had directed. Interestingly, Johnny Dee had Tino Fiumara's people carry out the hit. Our two business partners were capable of a lot more than opening doors for trucks.

They had started out sharing our kickbacks, but now each guy definitely wanted Alamo to himself. I met on and off with Liddy at Hanlon & Associates over the next few weeks about how to deal with these simultaneous aggressive advances. His solution took me by surprise at first, but it made sense. Liddy was bringing in another undercover trooper, Detective Robert Weisert, to help out with the investigation.

The move wasn't just to give us another man to work with the wiseguys. The episode with my heart problem was still on Liddy's mind, and he knew I was overloaded with work, with Tino and Johnny Dee pulling me in different directions. I think he could tell that the stress of the job was taking its toll, and he wanted to relieve me of some of the pressure I was under. Bringing in Weisert, a tall, blond-haired guy who had worked in the organized crime and narcotics units, was designed to do just that. The cover story was that he was an old friend of mine who had a lot of money and wanted to invest in Alamo.

I have to say that Weisert was a real trooper—in every sense of the word. You can imagine how difficult it was for him to simply be thrown into a complex, perilous operation that had been going on almost two years. He had to get up to speed practically overnight. And he needed to know everything about me, because we had to act like old friends in front of the wiseguys—and be convincing at it. Liddy and I spent a lot of time prepping him at Hanlon & Associates, but he still only had a few weeks to get ready.

Our specific plan called for me to tell Anthony Pacilio, Anthony Ray, and the mobsters in the loop that we weren't making as much money as we'd thought we would, so I needed a financial boost from my old buddy. Weisert became Bobby Hesse and showed up one day driving a brand-new tan 1977 Corvette. Just as we'd hoped, Fat Anthony noticed the fancy ride and introduced himself right away. He knew a money guy when he saw one, and he started romancing Weisert the same way they had romanced me.

Meanwhile, my orders were to stick with Tino—go along with his plan to eventually phase out Alamo. We hadn't made a decision yet on whether to open the new company he had in mind, Liberty Trucking. But the plan was to stay in his camp and see where things might lead. The idea of spending even more time with Tino was hardly cause for celebration, but it was the only move that would work. I knew how the guy operated and could tell he was starting to trust me.

The wheels were in motion, with Bobby Hesse and Bobby Covert traveling down a road with a fork up ahead. Hesse would steer his way to the DiGilios—and Covert would continue following the uncertain, treacherous route paved by Tino Fiumara.

CHAPTER NINE
GOING, GOING, GONE

The threatening, profane calls to Alamo from Jackie DiNorscio never cease while he does his time at Rahway. He continues to think he owns Pat Kelly and can dictate the direction of the trucking company. But even behind bars, he has heard rumblings of the DiGilio and Fiumara takeover plans. It only makes his calls to the man he knows as Bobby Covert more abusive and blustery, though the threats seem increasingly hollow as he loses ground to the two competing Genovese factions.

His latest demand is that $500 be diverted from Alamo profits to the woman Covert has been told is the matriarch of the DiNorscios, living at home in nearby Irvington, New Jersey, in advance of Mother's Day.

"She needs the money and I don't want to hear any muthafuckin' excuses, Bobby," DiNorscio says.

"We're not doin' as good down here as you think," Bobby answers with the usual stall tactic.

"Find a fuckin' way," DiNorscio snaps. He pauses for a moment and his tone unexpectedly softens. "C'mon, Bobby, this is my mom."

DiNorscio, like countless mobsters through the decades, has no problem inflicting pain on anyone who gets in his way. But when the topic turns to their mothers, sentimentality takes over and turns them into momma's boys. Among the most famous was Jimmy "The Gent" Burke. The architect of the $5.8-million Lufthansa robbery, later portrayed by Robert DeNiro in the 1990 movie GoodFellas, *was said to have spent hundreds of dollars on red roses to hand out to the mothers of his imprisoned Lucchese Family colleagues every Mother's Day. In fact, the day has always been a sacred one among mobsters, when violence is temporarily shelved to honor the women who gave them life,* nurtured them, made their favorite pasta and gravy, and always offered unconditional love.

Jackie DiNorscio is no different, and Covert decides not to spar any longer than necessary with him over the payment to his mother.

The DiNorscios have occasionally gone by the surname Adams over the years, primarily because Dominick often hung out as a young thug on Adams Street in Newark. Law enforcement also knows him as Tommy Adams, and his two sons as Jackie and Ralph Adams—a dysfunctional, scary trio if ever there was one. And as Covert drives off, the theme song of the 1960s TV sitcom runs through his head—he is off to see the First Lady of the Adams Family.

Getting away from the office feels good as he cruises out of Jersey City over the Pulaski Skyway—nearly three decades before Tony Soprano would make the same spot famous at the start of each episode in the HBO series about the life of a New Jersey Mob family. He winds his way through Newark and exits twenty minutes later in a wooded suburb, where jets can be heard overhead beginning their thunderous descent to the nearby airport.

He drives down Chancellor Avenue and parks on Nesbit Terrace across from her house. She is sitting on the front porch in a floral print dress. Her eyes are glazed from crying, and her straggly brown hair is in need of a trip to the beauty parlor. She appears to be about sixty, but the heavy makeup on her once-pretty face can't hide the hard years she has lived as a Mob wife and mother. Life has gotten even tougher lately.

"What's wrong, Mrs. D?" her visitor asks.

"Everything," she answers. "My husband is in the federal pen, Jackie's at Rahway, and Ralphie is in the county jail. And today the dogcatcher came and took my dog away. My whole family's in the fuckin' can."

Dumbfounded, Covert wants to say something comforting, but no words come to mind. He thinks to himself, "There's no Hallmark card for this situation." The unfolding scene may appear comical, but he feels genuinely bad for her, studying her pained, distant expression. All he can do is place a hand on her shoulder and hold the envelope out to her. "Here, I hope this helps," he says sympathetically. But Mrs. DiNorscio is so distraught that she doesn't even notice. He lays the envelope with the cash gently in her lap—not sure whether to hug her or to console her. Instead, he opts for the easy way out and walks back to his car.

But there is nothing easy about this job, he thinks, and nothing normal about a world that has become part of his everyday abnormal reality.

Instead of driving straight to Jersey City and whatever may be awaiting him at Alamo, Covert takes a detour through downtown Newark. He passes his usual destination there, Hanlon & Associates, and heads to the Down Neck area, a clean, close-knit Italian-American enclave where many honest, hardworking citizens reside. Despite the tidy environs, it has also been a breeding ground for organized crime—a place where the man in his sights, Tino Fiumara, grew up and now rules with an iron grip. This is the section of town where Fiumara has told Covert he will soon have to live and work.

The streets are jammed with clusters of old brick row houses. Cozy Italian restaurants with colorful awnings and social clubs dot the neighborhood blocks. Many of those clubs, he knows, are Mob hangouts— usually identifiable by the man sitting on a chair outside, keeping watch. These are haunts in which Fiumara likely learned his trade during his formative years as a young wiseguy.

Minutes later, Covert decides to end his morning travels, hopping on U.S. 1 & 9 for the ride back to Jersey City. But another trip he never imagined is in the works.

For months, the Brunos had been hovering in the background. Now they were making their own move and bringing in some big guns. A call came in to Pat one afternoon at Alamo from Bruno Family captain Johnny Simone, also known as Johnny Keyes, inviting us to South Florida for a luncheon meeting the next day. Many high-ranking Bruno members would be in attendance to talk about new opportunities for Alamo's trucking business.

I had no time to think it through. I reacted totally in the mode of Bobby Covert, head of Alamo Trucking. I was in his skin, as if there was no higher-up to consult, no permission to seek. I didn't bother calling my bosses to clear the trip; the idea didn't even occur to me. In my mind, I was the boss, the final decision-maker. My primary thought was: This is a great opportunity to expand my business and make money with the trucks.

For the moment, I had stopped thinking like Bob Delaney, undercover state trooper; ignored any potential danger involved in meeting a new wiseguy group; and failed to plan for surveillance teams and anything else related to my role as a law-enforcement officer. As far as I was concerned, I was on top of the situation and knew exactly what I was doing. All the angst I had been feeling as my alter ego in recent months—that sense of being trapped in an endless, dangerous investigation—seemed to evaporate with the adrenaline rush of making an instinctive command decision. I felt invigorated, strangely comfortable all of a sudden as Bobby Covert—as if the role were a kind of armor that gave me control and security.

As for Pat, he loved the intrigue of it all, loved having another chance to keep the game alive for himself. So the informant and the trooper bought first-class tickets, got up the next morning, and boarded an Eastern Airlines flight to Fort Lauderdale—attaching our wires in the lavatory before the plane landed. We were met by Simone; Carl "Pappy" Ippolito, a member of the Bruno organization; and Edward "Brownie" Bralynski, a Bruno associate.

Right away, I began to have second thoughts. Pat was put in one car and I was put in another, and we began to drive. It hit me like a ton of bricks that none of my superiors had any idea where we were. I felt a knot in my stomach, but kept up the banter with Brownie. What if we had walked blindly into a setup, maybe as payback for having gotten too close to Tino? We could be whacked, and nobody in the chain of command would have any idea what happened.

In about twenty minutes, we were in Hollywood, Florida, and pulling into Joe Sonken's Gold Coast Restaurant, an upscale, tropical-themed place with big windows and a view of boats tied up at the dock. There were no regular customers inside, just a half dozen tables covered by white cloths, at which more than a dozen major players in organized crime—Mob bosses and underbosses—were already seated when we came in.

Many were connected to the Bruno organization. I recognized Russ Bufalino, head of the Bufalino Crime Family of upstate New York, Pennsylvania, and parts of Jersey, who was considered a prime suspect in the Jimmy Hoffa disappearance. Kelly and Simone sat at one table having a private conversation, while various offers related to Alamo's trucking services were relayed from one table to the next and finally to me. Somebody might say, "We'll pay this much, we'll do this but not that," and negotiations would then go back and forth, with modifications and changes. The Mob bosses employed this pass-it-down-the-line mode of communication—kind of like the old game of telephone— thinking that they could beat a conspiracy rap by claiming that they never talked to anybody directly. But I'm pretty sure that having an undercover cop witness the whole thing was not part of their plan.

When the lunch meeting ended, Simone, a grandfatherly-looking guy with white hair and a great tan, told me he would do everything he could to help strengthen Alamo. He was a very formal man, deeply steeped in Mob tradition. As we shook hands, he clasped his free hand over mine so I basically couldn't pull away until he was ready. Then, tapping his top hand in rhythm with the words, he said quietly, "Do the right thing, Bobby." I knew that meant to show a sign of good faith and the proper respect. So I reached into my pocket and slipped a pair of $100 bills into his hand. And that's how easy it was. When you're dealing with the Mob, if you put the right amount of money in the right hands at the right time, the right doors open. We walked out of the restaurant with lanes open to Florida, and with the opportunity to become one of the more successful trucking lines in the eastern United States.

When we returned, I immediately called Liddy to tell him about what we had accomplished. But I could tell right away from the quiet, deliberate tone in his voice that we'd crossed the line with our impromptu spring break with the Brunos.

"I don't have to tell you that you compromised the integrity of this investigation," Liddy said, sounding like a disappointed dad. He didn't raise his voice or scream during the call, and that really got to me. Here was a man who always stood up for me, always went the extra mile to make sure I had everything I needed in the toughest of circumstances, always stayed flexible with me instead of enforcing a rigid, by-the-book approach, the man I had the greatest respect for. I'd let down the best boss I'd ever had.

"You could have gotten yourself killed," he continued. "You could have gotten Kelly killed."

There wasn't much I could say in my defense. I had broken the chain of command. Funny, that's exactly what I'd often gotten angry at Pat for doing; now I'd gone and done the same thing to Jack. In short, I'd screwed up. Maybe I was getting too relaxed with some of the wiseguys I was hanging around, and had been getting a little too friendly with them over the past year. You can't spend so much time around people and not develop some attachments.

Like when Charlie "Cup of Coffee" and his wife had me over to their house and I met their little handicapped boy. Charlie was really proud that his son was able to feed himself with his own knife and fork. Or when a guy named Ronnie Sardella invited me to his family's house for get-togethers and various holidays, and they all made me feel very welcome. Even a guy like Joey Adonis, Jr. was always friendly to me. He had a fun-loving personality and was easy to be around, whether or not he was beating us in softball. And the one guy I found I could truly trust by now was the ace Mob infiltrator I'd butted heads with so often, my friend Pat Kelly.

In several meetings with my supervisors that followed the Florida trip, I wound up defending many of the mid-level wiseguys I associated with, saying things like, "He's not such a bad guy. He's not hurting people. He's just doing stolen loads." My morality had begun to shift, and I hadn't even noticed.

My manner had also begun to change, taking on more of a confrontational edge and swagger. One day, the entire undercover team was summoned by Liddy to a meeting with two attorneys, Mark Malone, a deputy attorney general with the New Jersey Criminal Justice Department, and Carl LoPresti from the attorney general's office in Newark. They had been assigned to head the prosecution side of the investigation. Up to this point, we'd had no attorneys involved in the investigation at all, and the fact that they had now arrived on the scene should have been a clue to me that Project Alpha was entering its final stage. But I was too immersed in the everyday routine of my undercover life to see that.

They had a million questions about every facet of what we'd been doing and were fascinated by what we had accomplished. And now that we were making major strides, they were suddenly an integral part of Project Alpha, trying to play catch-up since they were the people who would be shepherding these cases into court. Malone and LoPresti were thrilled with the mountain of recordings and related evidence we'd gathered over the past two years, saying things like "this is absolutely tremendous."

Then LoPresti jumped in and said, "This will allow us to make strong racketeering cases because we have verbal threats, coupled with extortion, and all we need is physical violence."

I'd been slouching in my chair, listening to the guy talk without reacting, but as soon as he made that comment, I blurted out, "Who the fuck's your victim?" All of a sudden the room got deathly quiet. "I'm not getting smacked around for anybody," I continued, glancing over to Liddy with an expression of anger. All I could think was, thank God they hadn't been involved in the front end of the operation—or we'd never have gotten anything accomplished. Typical attorneys—you never had enough evidence for them. They always wanted more and more. From my standpoint, I was thinking, "If you can't make the case with the evidence I have, what the hell's wrong with you?" When I look back, this was not one of my proudest moments. The arrogance and brashness—those traits weren't part of my true personality. I can tell you that LoPresti and Malone were two of the most dedicated prosecutors I ever worked with, but I was so freakin' aggravated, so fed up with everything going on around me, nobody could do right in my eyes no matter what they did.

LoPresti tried to explain himself further, but Liddy, sensing that tensions might boil over at any second, pulled the plug on the discussion. "That won't be happenin'," he said to the attorneys. The topic changed and I calmed down. But the point was, in 1975 I probably would have said "Yes, sir." After nearly three years of living this life, I didn't care if the attorney general himself was sitting in front me, I was speaking up. I had gone from being a subservient trooper at age twenty-three to a guy who, in only two years, basically said, "Fuck you. This ain't happenin'. You ain't tellin' me what to do in this thing. This is my show." My behavior, I would later learn, wasn't going unnoticed by my State Police supervisors.

One of them, Capt. Harold Spedding, pulled me aside before I left and looked me straight in the eye. "I hope you get assigned to me when this is over," he said in a low, seething voice. "I'm coming down on you with both feet." At the time, all I thought was, "Who the hell do you think you're talkin' to?" But I now know he was right, and what he was trying to say to me was, "Hey, kid, you're too big for your own britches." There was an interesting role reversal going on: You had captains and bosses who had to defer to Jack Liddy as a sergeant first class and me as a trooper, because we had the pulse of Project Alpha. Under the circumstances, it was probably natural that I would get an inflated view of my status—but it was equally natural for Capt. Spedding to have a bad reaction to my cocky attitude. We were like two trains speeding on a collision course.

This was all part of the turmoil I was experiencing: One minute I was sticking up for the wiseguys, the next I was getting in the face of government officials and insisting cases would be made *my* way. And more and more, I just wanted to get away from the Mob altogether, get back to enjoying a normal life, whatever that was.

I could see it was something my old friend Jimmy DiLella was enjoying now; he had gotten married to his childhood sweetheart Laura Decker. About a year into my undercover life, I shared with Jimmy and Laura what I was doing, and they did what they could to provide emotional support. There were nights I would call them and say I was coming over for a little while. Jimmy was doing well in the business world and had moved to an upscale neighborhood in Bergen County, so all he had to do was open one bay of his three-car garage to let me in. I'd stay for dinner, make small talk, and then be on my way. Those visits, brief though they were, were therapeutic. Jimmy owned some horses—trotters—and I'd occasionally drive up to the Meadowlands Racetrack knowing that he and Laura would be there. It wasn't as if I was going there to socialize with them—just seeing them from a distance was comforting to me. But I told them that if they ever saw me, they shouldn't approach or even acknowledge me.

Meanwhile, both business proposals from the Bruno and Genovese Families were in the works and the walls were pushing in on me from all directions. One night soon after returning from Florida, I went to dinner at the Bella Vita, mostly to see how Louie was doing. I joined Tino and the usual crowd of wiseguys at the corner table, where some mobster I didn't recognize was telling a story of a man who hadn't made good on a loan. This guy and his associate dragged the poor kid into a restaurant freezer and left him inside for four or five hours. They then went back to the freezer with a Louisville Slugger and took batting practice on his legs.

Everybody at the table laughed like it was the most hilarious thing they'd heard all year. And I did my best to laugh along too—even though the thought made me lose my appetite. Tino gave me a look, and I wondered if he noticed my half-hearted reaction. "You all right, Bobby? You don't look so hot," he said.

"I'm good—just a little tired, T, long day," I replied.

On the way home to my apartment, I pulled off Route 46 and parked on the shoulder. There in the darkness, as I had done in Bayonne and on several other occasions when the tension grew too high, I knelt in the grass and puked my guts out.

The next night, Pat and I were at our apartment when we got a call from Michael Coppola. He told us Tino wanted to meet us in an hour at a diner about two miles from Alamo. It sounded strange. I mean, why wouldn't he have just come here? "Whaddya think it is?" I asked Pat. "No idea," he replied, and the fact that he was baffled didn't make me feel any better. Just to be safe, we both decided it would be better if we didn't wear the Nagra recorders. The only thing I decided to carry was the beige leather briefcase I always brought along to meetings.

Maybe Tino had learned about our trip to Florida and was going to quiz us on it. We drove to the diner, reviewing what we might say if that was the case. We stayed in our car. About five minutes after we got there, a plain black sedan pulled alongside of us. The front passenger window rolled down and there was Tino—as always traveling in a nondescript vehicle to draw less attention to himself. He looked serious and motioned for us to get in.

It was showtime. My heart was beating fast, but I was totally focused, ready for whatever might come. Pat and I got out of our car and slid into his back seat.

Larry Ricci was in the driver's seat, and he nodded to us. "How ya doin'," he said. I took a seat directly behind Tino with my briefcase on my lap. And the first thought I had was "Oh, shit, where the hell are they going to take us?" Whenever you're being driven someplace with Mob guys, you don't have control of the situation. There's always an underlying fear of what will happen next.

But to our surprise, we didn't go anywhere.

Tino just wanted to talk. The Brunos never came up at all. Instead, he began explaining in detail his plan to accelerate Alamo's transformation into Liberty Trucking. The longer the conversation stretched on, the more I relaxed. Before I knew it, I was back to thinking like Bobby Covert, wondering how much money we might make with the new arrangement.

To answer his questions, I had to check some trucking papers, so I popped the latch on my briefcase. It made the usual harmless clicking sound. And bam!

All hell broke loose. In a heartbeat, Tino violently swung his arm over his seat, lunged toward me, and hit my briefcase.

"Whoa!! Whoa!" I yelled, unable to get out any other words.

"T! T! T! It's okay! It's okay!" Pat shouted.

Larry put his hand on Tino's shoulder to calm him down. My popping the briefcase latch had apparently sounded to Tino exactly like the sound of the hammer of a gun being cocked. An awkward silence hung over us for what seemed like an eternity.

My stomach was churning like crazy, and I gave Pat a look out the corner of my eye, like "Say something. Make this right." All of us had to re-gather our wits. Finally, Tino said, "It's okay, Bobby, you're okay." And we went on with the conversation. But something had changed.

Tino had unwittingly showed a weakness. In a moment of panic, he let me have control of the situation, if only for a second. In the days that followed, I couldn't get the thought out of my head.

What if next time I actually had a gun in my briefcase?

I could end this whole freaking mess. I could click open the briefcase and this time Tino wouldn't notice. I would pull out a pistol and fire into the back of his head. Before Larry could react, I would shoot him too. And to make sure there were no witnesses, I would have to turn the gun on Pat—hard as it might be—and squeeze the trigger.

In moments of despair, a person can rationalize anything. I would say it was all in self-defense and nobody could prove otherwise. I'd be saving society from the cost of a long trial of a very bad guy. I might even be hailed as a hero. But now all I really wanted was to get out. I wanted my life back.

So I started making plans, pondering the unthinkable.

CHAPTER TEN

THE RAID

In a thick, late-night fog rising from Port Newark, union workers hurry to load a massive tanker bound for Europe, one of the Maersk Line ships controlled by Tino Fiumara. A forklift operator maneuvering into position to lift a stack of boxes looks down and makes eye contact with Bobby Covert, lingering in the darkness of the docks, and smiles. Covert, wanting not to be recognized, quickly looks away. Then he hurries to an empty street near the Port, waiting for a car that's to meet him at midnight. A black sedan, headlights off, emerges from the gray mist. Fiumara steps out of the passenger side, Larry Ricci the driver's side. Covert moves silently through the shadows from behind, as if floating on air. He grips a snub-nosed detective special, aims first at the back of Ricci's head, calmly squeezes the trigger. But, inexplicably, the gun jams. Ricci hears a sound, wheels around, and whips out a firearm from his belt, while Fiumara's look of shock turns to laughter as he spits out, "We knew, Bobby. We always knew."

Covert bolts upright in his bed.

The alarm clock on the nightstand reads 3:17 a.m. The sheets are soaked from perspiration, as they have been the past two nights. Sleep only comes in small waves. Ever since the moment Covert opened his briefcase, and a window of opportunity along with it, he has been consumed with thoughts of taking matters into his own hands, his gun hand, and ending this investigation with a few well-placed bullets. Imagining the scene—the blood and brain matter splattered against windows—makes him nauseous and on edge. But the feeling is not enough to push the thoughts away.

Even at work, sitting alongside Pat Kelly, they creep into his mind—he pictures Kelly's stunned expression in the millisecond before he would have to blow him away, his body slumping lifelessly against the inside car door moments later.

He is suddenly aware of Kelly's voice. "Bobby, do you want to grab some lunch or not?" he says. "I'm starving."

"Nah, not hungry, you go ahead," Covert replies, continuing to review invoices. He wonders how Alamo will close down without causing an uproar among DiGilio and DiNorscio, and sees himself being uprooted to Down Neck, starting an entirely new operation with Fiumara breathing down his neck at all times. Six months has become nearly three years and counting—and who's to say there won't be a fourth or fifth year now if Liberty Tire becomes a gold mine of evidence?

That evening, Covert, wearing his body wire, finds himself back at the Bella Vita, sitting at a table with Fiumara, Ricci, and the Coppolas. Michael Coppola excuses himself from the table and tells Fiumara that he needs to go to his car to get something out of the trunk. Fiumara jokes, "Michael, you're getting something out? Aren't you usually putting something in?" The comment, meant to imply dead bodies, is greeted by raucous laughter. Fiumara looks across the table and smiles directly at Covert, locking eyes momentarily—as if to convey a hint of intimidation and what he is capable of doing.

When Covert drives home, he looks at the leather briefcase on the passenger seat and thinks about sliding his .38 inside it the next day.

Back at his apartment, he stands on the balcony and watches the nighttime traffic flow across the George Washington Bridge, pondering what he is capable of doing. Shortly after collapsing into his bed, he drifts off, sweat soon pouring from his body like toxic fluid as he tosses and turns in the grip of another nightmare. In his exhaustion, he falls into a deeper sleep than usual, and awakens only to the abrupt sound of Kelly knocking on his door. "Hey, we gotta get movin'," Kelly yells. "Lots to do today."

We all know the feeling of waking up from a horrible dream that seems all too real, leaving you shaken and uneasy. For several days, I frightened myself into thinking that I might actually commit this violent act. Looking back, I guess I had to fully imagine the details in order to finally realize, deep in my gut, that I wasn't capable of ever doing such a thing.

As a trooper, I knew I would be able to pull the trigger to defend myself or anyone else whose life was in danger; but I couldn't pull the trigger just to eliminate someone.

In the days that followed the briefcase incident, I had to wrestle myself away from the gruesome fantasies that gripped my thoughts. In times of relentless stress, like the draining emotional ride I was taking with some very bad people, your thoughts can be pulled into dark places where they would never otherwise go. But something inside you—your upbringing, your character, and your values—prevents you from taking that next step. We all have within us the capacity to dream of doing something terrible—and this was the ultimate destructive dream for me. But that's what it was: a nightmare. Not an act. That's the crucial difference—crossing the line between dreaming and doing—that separates people who stay within the laws of society and those who perform the worst kind of criminal acts.

There was one scenario that never entered my mind during this whole episode in August 1977, but was about to surface and jolt my world in a completely new direction. One afternoon, I received a message from Liddy to meet him at Hanlon & Associates the next morning.

"We're getting ready to shut down," he said, concise as always.

I couldn't believe what I was hearing, especially after everything I'd been contemplating. But I could mask my emotions as well as anybody—better than most, by now—so hiding my relief wasn't all that hard.

"When?" I asked him, stone-faced.

"Soon as we can," he replied. "The attorneys are going through everything, planning out all the cases."

Liddy didn't have to say so, but the trip Pat and I had taken to Florida was probably the clincher. He and the other Project Alpha leaders must have sensed that I was getting in too deep—getting a little too confident in my ability to handle things on my own—and perhaps the next time I wouldn't be so lucky if we prolonged the operation any further.

The good news was that the top brass felt that there was more than enough evidence—for starters, 400-plus hours of recorded conversations involving Pat, myself, and the rest of the undercover team—for this thing to go to trial.

I sat there, still trying to process this new development. After more than two and a half years, my job of living two lives simultaneously was actually going to end. I felt like a soldier on the front lines being told, suddenly, that his tour of duty was over and he could return home. The words should have made me feel like celebrating, thrusting a triumphant fist in the air. But living with the Mob had made it hard for me to express any emotion other than anger.

At first, listening to Liddy talk, I felt numb. But as the news sank in, a surge of pride over what we'd been doing all this time swept through me—a welcome change from the storm of stress and conflict I'd been dwelling on so much in recent months.

But there wasn't time to think about these changes. We still had work to do. While the attorneys prepared their cases, it was essential that we continue on our current course, consorting with the wiseguys until just the right moment, or we could risk jeopardizing everything.

One of the first things on the agenda was Pat. The longer the operation had played out, the happier I think he was, no matter how complicated it made our lives.

The reason was simple. Our investigation kept Pat on the street, living the exciting life he was accustomed to, with no shortage of perks—including having all his bills paid by the government. The end of Project Alpha meant his life would be disrupted, redefined in a huge way. He would have to testify against mobsters who had considered him a trusted friend—and, from then on, live an uncertain, perhaps not entirely safe, new life in the Witness Protection Program.

I decided to break the news to Pat gently. Weisert was living at our apartment by then, too, and he'd been part of the Project Alpha shutdown meeting that day. When I got back to the apartment around 7:00 p.m., they were both there and I told Bobby I wanted to speak to Pat alone. "Hey, you wanna go for a swim?" I asked. We went downstairs to the pool. Pretty soon, we were just dangling in the deep end, hanging from the side and making small talk. When the moment was right, I just said, "Pat, I talked to Jack today. We're gonna be shuttin' this thing down, probably in three weeks to a month. It's gonna stop. And we gotta start doin' things about getting you ready for the Program."

He didn't want to hear it. In classic Pat Kelly style, he immediately began reeling off convincing reasons why we should keep the operation going. I'd seen him in this mode many times before, but this was different. I looked in his eyes and could sense he was scared; the slick con man seemed more like a vulnerable kid. "This thing can go so much further, and we can get so much more," he protested. "We're just startin'." Then he added things like I know I can get this guy, I know I can get that guy, and started throwing out names of heavy hitters up the ladder, wiseguys all over the United States—and getting in even closer to Tino. I just let him talk, almost the way you let the air out of a balloon. Finally I interjected: "Pat. The decision's been made for us. We did good. But it's done."

For so long, I had been walking in Pat's world, following his lead. Now he was suddenly thrown into mine. I was going to have to put together his application for the Witness Protection Program. "I'm working with the Feds," I told him. "And we gotta get movin' on it."

Pat looked up into the beautiful summer night sky over the Hudson and let the words sink in. It had been a good ride, but now it was over. And though I'd miss Pat's company, I felt as if I had a new lease on life. I wouldn't have to stuff a tape recorder inside my pants and run wires up my sides any more, worrying if this was the time I would be found out. I wouldn't have to oversee a chaotic trucking operation where even my own employees were trying to sell me guns and stolen property, let alone dealing with the wiseguys who had become part of our enterprise. Now there would be only one kickback: me kicking back and having a chance to breathe freely again. All I wanted to do was embrace a long-awaited moment of closure.

Much to Pat's dismay, in late August of 1977, I drove him to the Federal Building at St. Andrew's Place in New York City to have an initial Witness Protection meeting. He would move to the first location for three months, followed by a second six months later, and finally a third six months after that—then he'd be on his own starting a new life. There was absolutely no question that Pat qualified for and needed to be in that program: He'd be dead in five minutes if he wasn't relocated by the government and given a new identity. Even so, an application had to be properly submitted, and I did my part by writing a detailed, two-page, single-spaced letter of recommendation to Major Baum, the State Police commander who had interviewed me for the undercover assignment in 1975. A portion of it read:

"Patrick J. Kelly became actively involved in Project Alpha, working with the undercover operatives and through Patrick J. Kelly's efforts, Project Alpha changed from a small business front dealing in stolen property, to a full scale trucking operation which is totally under Mob influence. . . . It is my estimation that Patrick J. Kelly has been a great aid to law enforcement in learning about and fighting organized crime. I would hope that every possible consideration be given to Mr. Patrick J. Kelly and his family for Relocation at the culmination of Project Alpha."

On the other hand, moving his whole family was going to be no easy feat. Not only was Pat married and the father of six kids; at the time he joined Project Alpha, he was living with his wife's *sister* and having an affair with her. So the question became, were we going to relocate his wife or his wife's sister? It didn't take him long to decide. "I want my wife to go with me," he said. I pictured myself having to speak to the two sisters when the time came—trust me, working with the Mafia would be child's play compared to the hell-hath-no-fury-like-two-women-scorned reaction that lay ahead. No one could ever accuse Pat of living a boring life.

Meanwhile, our work at Alamo was just as intense as ever, as we completed our final weeks of operation. Perhaps to convince us that we shouldn't pull the plug so quickly, Pat reported back to us about a conversation between Larry Ricci, president of Tino's Airport Landfill Corporation, and a jailed trucker about the illegal dumping of chemicals in Newark. In addition, Pat was taping conversations with Tino and Michael at a place called Frisky's Tavern, getting more evidence against Tino and Jerry Coppola on the extortion of Lou Crescenzi at the Bella Vita.

While Pat worked so diligently, I continued meeting with U.S. Marshals and our attorneys to make sure everything was going smoothly with Relocation plans for Pat and his family. We also had a serious matter to contend with: Threats of physical harm had been made to Bob Weisert by members of the DiGilio camp. They'd been courting Weisert aggressively because of the money he flaunted. Some of his cash wound up as loan-sharking money out on the street, and now they were coming after him hard over loan-shark money they wanted to take *away* from him. Fat Anthony was relentless, and though the specific threat was to Weisert, there was a broader threat to all of us at Alamo. The upside was this: Every last bit of evidence was going to bolster our cases.

Tino clearly had no idea what was coming down. By the third week of August, he had instructed Pat to start wearing a beeper at all times so he could be reached at a moment's notice regarding the phasing of Alamo into Liberty. That's not all Tino had on his mind. When I stopped by the Bella Vita for lunch a week later, the place was being prepared for an upcoming wedding reception for Tino's sister. What a guy—takes over a restaurant and makes it a full-service operation for his whole family. While I was ordering lunch, he and Michael Coppola saw me and beckoned me to come over. Tino was pleased to tell me that he'd lined up a contract for me to haul packaged beef and a few other products now that the "other guy"—meaning DiGilio—was out of the picture. It was a nice parting gift from Tino, straight to my hidden tape recorder.

Two days later, on August 30, the State Police moving company showed up at the Water's Ebb apartments and moved my undercover belongings to a new residence —better known as New Jersey State Police Headquarters—all in preparation for what was to come next: the raid.

In late September, two days before it was to take place, Jack Liddy, his FBI counterpart George DeHardy, and I went to the apartment where the Crescenzis lived. Liddy had me stand off to the side and knocked on the door. He and DeHardy identified themselves, and Louie greeted them. And as soon as he did, Liddy and DeHardy stepped away, according to plan, and I stepped forward and said, "Louie, I'm Trooper Bob Delaney, New Jersey State Police."

His jaw dropped and his face lit up. "Oh my God, Bobby, I knew you weren't like them," he said with jubilation. We stayed an hour or so, talking to Louie in his living room, sharing with him selective details of Project Alpha. Early in the investigation, we had played things close to the vest and tried to develop relationships. Now, since the raid was on the horizon, we could afford to be more aggressive, swing for the fences, in trying to tie down loose ends to make cases. We made our pitch to Louie and asked him if he would wear a wire when he made the next $300 payoff to Jerry Coppola. "I'm gonna get this guy, I'm gonna *get* this guy," Louie said. He was so excited to finally have the opportunity to expose the man who had stolen his dream.

I was feeling pretty excited myself. All the work I had done on Project Alpha was about to pay off. On September 28, 1977, at 3:00 a.m., about two hundred troopers and FBI agents from all over New Jersey were told to report to the West Orange Armory. A makeshift stage had been erected inside the armory, and there I stood with my undercover partners—including FBI agent Lenny Perrone, our dear "departed" trucking colleague, miraculously back from the dead. We were flanked by Liddy and a half dozen or so high-ranking State Police officers.

I looked out at the crowd and noticed how all the uniformed troopers stayed among themselves, the State Police detectives by themselves, and the FBI agents with their own. It reminded me of the lines that had divided our undercover team in the early stages of Project Alpha—even though we had proven how well different agencies could eventually work together without rivalry and jealousies. It was apparent that the three separate groups I was looking at had a long way to go in terms of cross-agency cooperation.

The armory rumbled with the din of several hundred conversations, but everyone realized something significant was about to take place. Law enforcement knows all about the circadian clock, which governs sleep patterns. People are in their deepest sleep at four in the morning, and the element of surprise can be at its highest. That's the reason for the early-morning raids.

Each trooper was handed a packet that contained paperwork about which wiseguy they were to go out and arrest, along with search warrants and bags to collect evidence that would need to be processed.

Shortly before everyone was to be given the order to move out, I surveyed the room and saw troopers sipping coffee and renewing acquaintances with guys they hadn't seen in months or years. More than a few were looking up at me, probably wondering who the hell I was. I know I couldn't have looked all that familiar, wearing a blue three-piece suit and weighing a good thirty pounds more than I had in 1975 from all the nervous eating, late-night pasta meals at the Bella Vita, and a schedule that never left time for working out. I'd shaved my Fu Manchu, the signature of my undercover look, and waited with a sense of pride and growing anticipation. That's when I heard someone shout my name loud enough to cut through the clatter.

"Delaney!"

I looked in the direction of the sound and my eyes stopped at a familiar face just off to the side of the platform, no more than twenty feet away. All I could do was smile. It was my original State Police partner, Bobby Scott, standing there with his mouth open and a look of complete surprise. "Hey, Bobby!" I yelled back, climbing down from the stage.

"I don't know whether to hug ya or hit ya," he said as he reached me. We embraced, and I tried to explain: "Bobby, I wanted to tell ya right away." He cut me off, clearly having figured out what I was doing there in plain clothes, basking in the spotlight. "Looks to me like you've been busy," he said. "We have some work to do right now 'cause of you." Then he added with a smile, "But I can't wait to hear *this* story."

Minutes later, Bobby Scott and several hundred fellow troopers and FBI men were out the door in groups of four—two troopers, one State Police detective, one FBI agent—ready to pay an early-morning visit to the names on the arrest warrants.

By about 5:00 a.m., the troop cars were starting to return to the armory. Two troopers would get out with a handcuffed mobster, a photograph would be taken, and he would be brought to the basement for processing. That's where the fingerprinting and booking took place. In several adjacent rooms, detectives and FBI agents were looking to find the next Pat Kelly, questioning anybody who might have value as an informant and want to join our side. I was still upstairs while this all was taking place. Detective Barry Lardiere asked me if I wanted to see what was happening. I said sure, and we headed down the steps making small talk.

But as soon as I walked into the processing room, a reality that I had completely overlooked began to settle in. In my zeal to move on from my undercover life and bask in the glory of the outcome, I hadn't focused on a cold fact: I would now be face to face with people who I had been associated with for close to three years, in some cases guys who I had actually gotten to like.

The first few groups were on their way in, with handcuffed, stunned men squinting in the bright fluorescent lights. I recognized brawny Woody Brown, one of the enforcers Jackie D. had sent to Alamo. His brown hair was disheveled and he looked disoriented. Across the room, I could make out "Uncle Charlie" Cannizzo, glum and silent in a rumpled sports jacket he wore over a black western shirt. One usually dapper wiseguy, Vito Pizzolato, looked particularly ticked off, perhaps because he had been dragged in without his ever-present toupee. No one noticed me, but I looked up a minute later and saw two troopers leading a man past me. Ronnie Sardella—a nice guy who'd had me over for dinners with his family—stared at me, barely three feet away.

I was standing in the military position known as "parade rest"—with my hands behind my back—subconsciously trying to act as if I was part of the paramilitary world of law enforcement. To Ronnie, it must have appeared that I was handcuffed just like he was.

"Bobby, what'd they pinch ya for?" he asked.

Before I could answer, Detective Lardiere, standing beside me, leaned forward and proclaimed to Ronnie, "He's with *us*. He's a Jersey Trooper."

I'll never forget the look on Ronnie's face. His eyes widened, but not in anger. He just looked at me with genuine hurt in his eyes, and then said something that etched itself in my memory banks: "Bobby, you're a friend of mine. How could you do this to me?"

Freeze the frame. Go back in time to my fourth-grade class at St. Mary's Grammar School in Paterson. Sister Joseph Rosaire caught me doing something—I can't even remember what—and my immediate reaction was to say, "Jimmy DiLella's doin' it, too." I gave up my best friend in a heartbeat. And in the next heartbeat, she hit me. You know that ring that says they're married to God? Bullshit. The ring is there to put welts on your head. She gave me a crack and said, "Delaney, you don't tell on your friends."

Now roll the tape forward a dozen years. I was twenty-one and it was the first time I'd ever driven a troop car by myself. Internal Affairs was interviewing various troopers as part of an investigation into misuse of an unmarked troop car for personal reasons. I had to go from the barracks in Flemington, where I was stationed, to division headquarters in Trenton. When I left Flemington, it was as if I was leaving a family house, because all the senior troopers were standing outside and saying to me, "You don't tell 'em nothin', kid." They were waving to me as I was leaving; and when I came back a few hours later, they asked me what had happened. "They just asked me to fill out this report," I said, showing them a document. My trooper colleague's instructions were simple: "Just write 'I have no knowledge of the aforementioned.' That's all you tell Internal Affairs."

I've been conditioned—most of us have—not to tell on my friends. So when Ronnie Sardella gave me that look, I knew exactly what he was thinking. I felt as if I had betrayed a socially accepted, and constantly reinforced, credo—and, by extension, that I had betrayed a friend who trusted me. Of course, I would later realize it was Bobby *Covert* who had done that, not Bob Delaney—but I was suffering so much in that moment because the line between Covert and Delaney, trucker and trooper, had become hopelessly blurred.

That's why, in a million years, nothing I could think to say would change Ronnie's mind. I felt like I was the biggest bum in the entire world. For the rest of that morning and well into the day, I could tell you what everybody was wearing on their feet, because I had a hard time lifting my head up.

Obviously, I glanced around the room from time to time, but I avoided making eye contact with anybody. Tino and Michael Coppola weren't picked up during the raid—there was a different strategy in mind for them. I did catch a glimpse of John DiGilio, Anthony Pacilio, George Mavrodes, Nicky Paterno, Danny Roche, and many other mobsters with whom I'd associated while undercover. Some were left on the street for strategic purposes, making them think they'd gotten away with something and might unwittingly lead us to more breakthroughs.

Amid all the organized chaos, Liddy sought me out. Unaware of the tremendous pangs of guilt I was experiencing, he said, "Nice work, Trooper."

"Thank you, sir," I responded, then looked down, to the side, anywhere but into the eyes of the nearly three dozen wiseguys brought in by Project Alpha in one fell swoop.

At some point, I can't remember when, I got out of my three-piece suit and changed into my State Police uniform for the first time since 1975. We then moved upstairs and stood on the platform for a press conference. Reporters, photographers, and film crews from media outlets in New Jersey, New York, and Pennsylvania pressed in to hear Project Alpha officials sing the praises of the biggest organized crime investigation in the history of the state—with more than a hundred cases that the prosecutors intended to make.

And all I wanted was to get away from there. Something had changed inside me. I couldn't just go back to being Trooper Robert J. Delaney. Bobby Covert and the wiseguy world were now part of who I was. I had thought this would be the crowning moment of my career—but I'd never felt more miserable and alone in my life.

CHAPTER ELEVEN

SPIRALING DOWNWARD

In the wake of the raid, Project Alpha dominates the media across the Northeast. Headlines proclaim that thirty-five organized-crime members have been arrested as a result of the joint State Police–FBI investigation. TV footage airs on local newscasts showing mobsters being led away in handcuffs. And eight days after the massive bust, the man in the eye of the storm receives his own news bulletin.

Bob Delaney is told to report the next morning to New Jersey State Police Division Headquarters in Trenton for a meeting with Major Bill Baum.

He and fellow undercover trooper Ralph Buono/Rascati have already been assigned to the State Police's Organized Crime Central Unit. That has caused some initial resentment among the unit's leaders, because Delaney and Buono will not actually be available to do any work—they'll be too busy with grand jury presentations and preparing for Project Alpha cases.

Now, Delaney arrives at headquarters and is told to go directly to the Major's office, where a handful of captains and lieutenants are engaged in conversation.

Delaney has only been in this office once before, that day in 1975 when he interviewed for the undercover job—under the influence of three or four beers, courtesy of Jack Liddy. He settles into the same chair from that session so long ago and looks at the major on the other side of the desk. Baum gets right to the point.

"We have some information that we've received through an informant and additional information from a wiretap that indicates that there may be a threat on your life," he says.

Delaney stares at the major impassively, but the words startle him, as if he has just been given a grim prognosis by his doctor. Baum reads Delaney's tense body language, which belies his stoic facade, and decides it would be best to excuse the other officers from the room. He comes around his desk to take a chair next to Delaney, shifting the tone of the meeting from business to personal. He wants his words—firm and carefully measured—to have impact.

"We are not taking this lightly, and we know it's serious, but I don't want you to think you're alone," he says. He pauses, and then tries a new strategy.

"Think about this. When these guys are sitting around, do you think they're going to be saying, 'How about that Bobby? What an actor! How about him pulling this act off on us? Maybe we should get together and have dinner.' Of course not."

Baum tells him that cops react in similar fashion when one of their own is killed in the line of duty. "We hear troopers say, those cop killers are coming in on a slab—and then, they come in wearing handcuffs. It's an emotional reaction, and wiseguys are no different. They're going to call you every name in the book and badmouth you to everyone who will listen."

"This is a helluva way to start the day, Major," Delaney replies with a smile, trying to defuse the tension with a quip, a technique that has always helped him lighten the load in serious situations.

Baum sees the comment for what it is and looks him straight in the eye, choosing words he hopes will resonate.

"We are on this. We'll act on it. You're a trooper, and you'll have troopers with you at all times until I have this to where I want it." Delaney reads something comforting into the Major's message: Both of them are part of the law-enforcement gang, and that's one hell of a Mob, too.

Major Baum's comments have given even more weight to remarks made by New Jersey State Police Colonel Clinton Pagano during the post-raid press conference. Pagano took the opportunity to send a *veiled warning to any Mafioso watching on TV or reading the next day's papers.*

"These troopers did what they were told to do. I'm clearly identifying them," he said, pointing to Delaney, Ralph Buono, and Bobby Weisert. "They are members of the New Jersey State Police." A reporter asked Pagano if his comment was meant to put the Mafia on notice: that if it sought retribution on Delaney or any others from the undercover team, it would face the full weight of the State Police and the FBI.

"Those aren't my words, they're yours," Pagano responded. "But I like your words a lot better."

In the weeks that follow, Delaney is given round-the-clock State Police protection, with troopers posted outside and inside his home. FBI and State Police intelligence continues to monitor the word on the street, and Baum eventually becomes convinced that the danger has diminished. But that is little consolation to Delaney as he sets out trying to live again—to find his place in a world where nothing feels quite the same.

I knew that one thing Major Baum had told me was absolutely true: I was a trooper. I understood that. If only it could have been as simple as his statement.

But nothing was simple. A man named Bobby Covert had lived inside the body of Bob Delaney for nearly three years. And Bobby Covert was an informant. I had actually come to see myself as two distinctly different people: One had just come out from under cover for the New Jersey State Police and received accolades for a good job well done; the other was a snitch who had sold out people who trusted him.

When I looked in the mirror, I saw Bob Delaney.

When I looked into my soul, I felt the guilt and fear that haunted Bobby Covert. From one moment to the next, I didn't know who was winning the tug-of-war inside of me. I do know that the Mob guys weren't troubled by a case of double vision—they just saw an undercover trooper who had played the role of a trucking company president and ruined their lives. But there was nothing I could do to shake free from the subconscious grip Bobby Covert had on my self-image, the part that created the intense turmoil—seeing danger in the most mundane events, feeling waves of paranoia at every turn, knowing that informants face an unforgiving judgment in the Mob world.

It didn't matter what kind of reassurances I received, nothing could truly put me at ease now. The granite foundation of my self-image preceding my undercover assignment had given way to shifting sands of doubt and worry. Suddenly, everything became a potential threat to my security, because I knew—no matter how the major tried to explain it to me—my perception was that the Mafia wanted me as dead as they did Pat Kelly, who was under the protection of the State Police and the FBI.

This was a time in my life when I should have been celebrating, enjoying the end of my undercover life and the reemergence of my personal life. But that was hard to do with troopers living inside my bi-level house, monitoring a police radio at all times. It was hard to do with the persistent anxiety that prompted me to keep a shotgun within reach of the bed. I had trouble sleeping, sometimes lying there for hours, letting my mind imagine all kinds of threatening scenarios and how I would respond to them in the split second I'd have. That made falling asleep even more difficult, and every time I glanced at the clock by my bed, time seemed to taunt me with how slowly it moved.

The round-the-clock protection lasted about two weeks. It wasn't long after it ended that I thought I heard a noise as I lay in bed, trying to make myself fall asleep. The sound—muffled voices, as best as I could tell—was coming from outside the bedroom window. Instantly, every muscle in my body tensed and I reached for the shotgun and peered out the window. I couldn't see anything. Rather than go outside, completely vulnerable to whatever unknown danger was lurking there, I calmed myself and called the local police. They had been alerted to my situation and, within minutes, a pair of squad cars rushed to my street—lights and sirens off to avoid alerting any wrongdoers. The only problem was that the wiseguy suspects I had in mind turned out to be a couple of regular guys trying to change a flat tire nearby, after a night of partying. The officers got them on their way and I apologized, feeling foolish that I'd overreacted. Falling asleep after that was next to impossible, so I sat in a chair by the TV, watching some grade-B movie until I nodded off.

These kinds of incidents didn't happen on a daily basis, but they happened more often than I would have liked. There was the time I opened the door to get the paper in the driveway. I'd barely stepped onto the front step when a rapid-fire, mechanical roar overhead made me freeze. I saw a helicopter, flying abnormally low, just over the trees, heading toward my house. My senses were attuned to filtering everything I encountered as a possible threat to me and my family, and I had to do it without having the luxury of time to analyze what I was seeing. I was so paranoid by now, so self-absorbed with my fears and insecurity, that I imagined people hiding behind every tree. My reality had become skewed to the point that virtually anything could appear as an imminent danger; I'd lost the ability to evaluate situations normally. So when I saw the helicopter, my mind flashed—*protect* myself. I quickly stepped back inside, slammed the door, and ducked—as if I could shut the door on all my problems.

A minute or so passed, and I noticed that the sound of the helicopter circling around the neighborhood persisted. I edged to the living room window and looked up to see that the helicopter was from Ocean County Mosquito Control, out on a detail to hunt down flying insects. I stood against the living room wall, and let out a sigh. My heart still pounded hard, as if I'd actually been under attack. And I guess, in a way, I was—from within.

Life at home was continuing to become increasingly stressful. It was barely a month after the end of Project Alpha, and I attended a Halloween party at the house of a fellow trooper, Jimmy Mulholland, a few towns away on the Jersey Shore. It was a chance to get reacquainted with the State Police social circle. Jimmy and I knew each other from Paterson. We were members of the 88th New Jersey State Police class and went through training together. I went to the party as

Zorro, complete with the mask, black hat, cape, and sword. I made small talk with the guys—ripping the Jets, who were off to a terrible start in the NFL; reliving Reggie Jackson's home run heroics in the Yankees' World Series championship a few weeks earlier. But the longer I stayed there, the more restless and uncomfortable I became.

At some point, I remember that I didn't feel like talking any more and walked into the empty kitchen. I noticed an open spot between the refrigerator and the corner of the countertop, and that's where I retreated to, standing alone, clearing my head. Everybody at the party knew I'd been through a tough period, but nobody wanted to broach the subject for fear of saying the wrong thing. Nobody wanted to acknowledge that maybe I was different now. The result was that they wanted to talk to me as if nothing at all had happened, as if I was the exact same guy they'd known back in 1975. Everything they said, while well-intentioned, sounded fake. All I wanted to do was get away.

Jimmy hadn't seen me in those three years, but he was a good friend and knew something wasn't right. He came into the kitchen. "You okay?" he said, offering me a bottle of beer.

I paused, trying to think of how to express what I was feeling. "For the last three years, all I've been doin' is acting," I said after a few seconds. "I've been in costume playing Halloween each and every day, and I'm tired of it." I spoke the words slowly, and as I was talking I was taking the costume off—as if trying to shed the layers of Bobby Covert. Needless to say, I didn't stick around the party much longer.

That incident was only a sample of the turbulence that disrupted my life in the months that followed. I was constantly irritable and impatient, and arguments in my personal life over little things were commonplace. My language was crude and coarse, as if I was still hanging with wiseguys. The compass in my life wasn't functioning properly any more. I tried to move forward but constantly found myself pulled back into the past—still feeling guilt over betraying friendships I had made, oddly longing for the rush of excitement that marked my life undercover. I wanted that lifestyle to end, but when it was over, I began craving it again—almost as if I was being drawn back into the web.

It felt as if nobody understood me at all. And when people asked how I was doing, I knew they really wouldn't understand, because I didn't understand myself. My standard response became "I'm good." It was easier than trying to explain, and that's what people wanted to hear anyway.

It wasn't any better at work, either. I had grown accustomed to being on center stage, constantly conferring with top brass of the State Police and the FBI—and having my opinions and insights matter. Now I was in a routine job, transcribing tape recordings for hours on end, conferring with prosecutors about potential cases, and, on occasion, driving one of the State Police cars to the motor pool for a monthly inspection.

More than a few fellow troopers, and even supervisors, resented all the attention I had received from Project Alpha, and I could constantly feel it. That was especially true after I no longer had the Lincoln Mark V and all the other undercover toys that had been provided by the federal grant. I was now assigned a State Police vehicle—a nice, fully equipped Chevy Impala surveillance car—that had been driven by senior detective Pete Hallock. It was the best car in the unit, appearing to be a regular vehicle with all the police devices hidden inside. Here I was, a kid coming out of nowhere, being assigned the best car as a reward for the undercover job I'd just completed—taking it from the most senior man in the unit. No one was happy about this, because they all had more of a right to that car than I did. Everything in society has a pecking order, and when you upset that order, it creates jealousies and resentments.

That situation wasn't my fault. But my behavior was to blame for other problems that developed. I was frequently argumentative and foulmouthed with colleagues, another throwback to my life with the Mob, where qualities such as bullying and boasting came with the territory. Though it might seem odd that I failed to realize how arrogant and boorish I'd become, I honestly didn't even think about it. For the better part of my first year back as a trooper, working in the Organized

Crime Unit, I acted like a wiseguy and continued to dress the part, too. I wore a diamond pinky ring, a leather jacket, and open-collar shirts that revealed the gold chain around my neck. I'd wanted more than anything to escape that world, but seemed to be doing everything I could to relive that part of my life.

It was common in our unit to finish surveillance at 2:00 a.m. and then go out to dinner or hit a bar. Often, when I went out with fellow detectives, I'd fall back into my Bobby Covert routine, throwing money around as if it was still coming from a government grant to investigate the Mafia. I'd leave big tips and buy rounds of drinks for all my friends, still unable to separate myself from the lifestyle in which I'd been thoroughly immersed. I even went so far as to carry on the kiss-on-the-cheek wiseguy tradition, unconcerned that it bothered the heck out of my trooper colleagues on the receiving end. It was all part of who I'd become, and I didn't care what anyone thought.

That's what was happening on the outside. Inside, I was confused and angry, and there was nobody I could turn to for help. This was still the 1970s, and many agencies such as the State Police had not yet instituted high-level employee support programs, and nobody was going to use what they did have available anyway for fear of the stigma attached to anyone with "mental problems." I was on my own, dreading the prospect of eventually testifying against people I had come to know and like, despite their line of work. I was frustrated, because I couldn't figure out what was going on inside me, going back and forth in my mind about who I was.

What I didn't know then was that unresolved frustration often leads to aggression. On several occasions, the rage growing inside me flared and I punched the walls inside my house—behaving exactly like a little boy who becomes frustrated with a toy and then throws it at something or someone. The difference here was that my fist left gaping holes that had to be covered by picture frames, so nobody visiting would know I had a problem. But I knew it. I would stand there in silence, eyes glazed, wondering how many more walls I'd have to hit before I found an answer. I felt depressed, detached from emotions of genuine happiness, more isolated from the world than ever.

Luckily for me, somebody was watching—John Schroth, a fellow detective from the Organized Crime Central Unit in Keyport, New Jersey, who had also been assigned to the criminal prosecution phase of Project Alpha. He couldn't help but notice my pattern of reckless, obnoxious behavior. Schroth had been a psychology major at Rutgers, and he recognized that I was following a highly destructive path.

He didn't walk up to me and try to set me straight the first time he observed me acting out. It took a few months before he even said anything. Think about it—when we know a co-worker who's an alcoholic or has a drug problem, we don't approach them right away and start making suggestions. It's hard to intervene. We may see behavior in the workplace that concerns us, but we often don't say anything. It takes a special person to take a co-worker aside and tell them that they have a problem. You have to do it in just the right way, because you're taking one hell of a risk. It could end up with a quick "Fuck you" and that's the end of the conversation.

After one late-night surveillance, Schroth and I stopped off at the Headliner Bar in Belmar, New Jersey to have a few drinks. I must have been carrying on again, because when we walked back to the car an hour later, Schroth took me aside in the parking lot and said, "Bobby, you're not with those guys any more; stop acting like you are. And all that money you're throwing around—that's not government money, that's your *mortgage* money."

I didn't want to hear it—probably because I was in denial. Even though I knew deep down that Schroth had it right, I just wasn't ready to be honest with myself. Maybe maintaining the charade of wealth and success made it easier to avoid facing the reality that my life had profoundly changed. I was trapped between two lives—Covert's and Delaney's—and I had become a different, even an unpleasant, person in the process.

But now I had Schroth—a man with good street sense, a solid

law-enforcement background, and a psychology degree—stepping forward to give me a reality check.

We continued our conversations over the course of the next year, with these talks eventually becoming informal sit-down sessions. They helped me immensely. Even though Schroth wasn't a trained psychologist, he knew enough to help me put some of my feelings in perspective. I wouldn't say that I changed overnight, but I did begin to tone down some of my over-the-top behavior thanks to him. And that helped me get through the grueling three-year court trial phase of Project Alpha better than I otherwise would have.

There was another person during that time, in the wake of Project Alpha, who helped me separate the personas of Delaney and Covert. When I'd been a student at Jersey City State College, I'd had a psychology professor named Dr. Hank Campbell. I happened to run into him at a police seminar where I was sharing my undercover experience and he was presenting his research into law-enforcement psychology, helping agencies around the United States. Afterward, we started talking about what I'd been through, and it felt good to open up to a trained professional. We continued to speak periodically, and I laid out what I'd been through and what I was feeling—the guilt over arresting people who I'd become friendly with, the vomiting, the sweats in the middle of the night. The more I talked to him, the more I wanted to share, and I did.

Hank explained to me that I was having normal reactions to abnormal situations, that I had become very good at repressing basic responses to fear. Typically, our brains react with a fight-or-flight syndrome when facing danger. Or in a fear-inducing situation, we experience sweaty palms or sweating on the back. Some type of physical manifestation is normal under such circumstances. I repressed those responses, but they still had to come out somehow, some way. So when I would be in the most relaxed state—sleeping—I would perspire heavily. I was good at acting calm when I had the recorder on me in the company of Mob guys; but when I would get two miles down the road, in a relaxed state, no longer with my guard up, I would vomit or get diarrhea. I never told anybody I was going through any of that, because I didn't want to come across as weak. In fact, Dr. Campbell was the first person I confided in about everything I'd been through.

The more I talked to him, the more the negative emotions that had been weighing me down gradually began to lift. Hank stopped me in my tracks when he told me, "You're in Post-Traumatic Stress."

I knew the term from reading newspaper accounts of soldiers coming back from Vietnam in the 1960s and '70s. But that was the last thing I thought would have applied to me. Hank explained to me how it was a clinical disorder that affected people who'd endured a terrifying ordeal—faced the real possibility of death—and then suffered repercussions from the experience, feeling anxious, angry, or emotionally numb. I'd felt all of those things. "Bob, you went through a very traumatic experience," he said. "You were not put on this earth to be two people. Yet you became another person. In the medical profession, if we knew of a person with two personalities, we'd call them schizophrenic. But as an undercover agent, we're asking a person to do this. It's a tremendous investigative skill, though the toll it takes on an undercover agent can be immense."

I thought about what Hank said, and the words made sense to me. Just hearing that there was a reason for my troubled state was a huge relief. It's not that I changed instantly; but I somehow felt different, as if his diagnosis had defused the pressure mounting inside me.

We talked a lot about how I'd felt comfortable hanging around some of the mobsters—more comfortable than I felt with some of the good guys. I explained how I'd become protective of them when talking to my superiors. Hank likened my reactions to the Stockholm Syndrome, which drew its name from the famous 1973 bank robbery in Sweden committed by Jan-Erik Olsson. During the 144-hour ordeal, the hostages began to identify with, sympathize with, and become attached to their captors. Hank felt that I had experienced elements of that as a survival strategy and coping mechanism—as if I had been held hostage by my undercover lifestyle.

Talking to Hank created an increased self-awareness, which I embraced. I realized that the street changes you, you don't change the street. I did things I'd never have done if I had not become Bobby Covert. It's like a mascot at NBA games. They get to run around the stands, pull people's shoes off, throw popcorn, clown with the players. But that person would never be able to do all that if he wasn't in a mascot outfit. For me, Bobby Covert was a costume I was able to wear to enter a different side of life.

The court cases stemming from Project Alpha took up most of my time. I testified in front of grand juries and in criminal cases all around New York, New Jersey, and Pennsylvania, coming face to face with mobsters who now regarded me as the scum of the earth, especially Tino Fiumara. I just viewed him now as one more defendant I was testifying against. I would occasionally get glares or dirty looks. But it was hard for him or any of the mobsters to use intimidation techniques, because troopers were all over the place and there was strength in numbers. Still, that didn't make the whole process of being in court virtually day after day—for one case after another—any easier. It was as grueling being on the stand the last year as it had been the first. I found testifying to be the most draining experience imaginable.

I have a similar experience in my line of work today—working a playoff game, where everything is magnified and there's so much at stake. You're not *physically* exhausted when you hit the locker room at the end of a game, you're mentally exhausted. That's what I tell my fellow officials: "Now you know what it's like to be on the stand for three hours in a criminal case."

I always prided myself in not coloring testimony against the wiseguys. I never tried to paint them worse than they were. There was stuff I knew about them—maybe about women, booze, drugs—that had nothing to do with the case. I was simply not comfortable alluding to any of it during my testimony. Funny as it may sound, if I were sitting there on trial, I wouldn't want someone doing that to me. In the end, if you're being straight with what you're talking about and only dealing with the pertinent facts, then you've been fair to the person you're testifying against. They can't claim you portrayed them in a bad light. You just did your job.

I was the same on the stand talking about a "made" guy like John DiGilio as I was about someone from a crew like Ronnie Sardella. Again, I relate it to the fairness that's needed in my current profession. I don't see a difference between a Michael Jordan and the twelfth guy on the other team when making a call—contrary to what fans and announcers may say and think. There are no Jordan rules for me, and there were no Mob rules back then. And I didn't feel differently testifying against one mobster compared to another—contrary to what the wiseguys may have thought.

On the other hand, restaurateur Louie Crescenzi struggled when the time came for him to take the stand. Though he had told us how he couldn't wait to make Tino and the Coppolas pay for destroying his dream, he was not nearly as cooperative a witness as we had hoped. As Louie left the witness stand, prosecutor Carl LoPresti improvised one of the all-time great courtroom lines. He pointed to the floor and said to the jury in a dramatic tone: "What you see there are the footsteps of fear."

Pat did his job well, too, and it was probably harder for him than me. At the end of testifying each day, I at least went home, while he went to a hotel or a safe house, surrounded by U.S. Marshals with whom he had nothing in common. It was part of the role reversal that had taken place. The loneliness I had felt undercover, he now experienced as part of the government team. We often had to sneak him in and out of the courtroom for his own safety, making him lie down on the floorboards of cars for security reasons.

When the final case was over, Pat and I embraced and said our goodbyes. He was gone from the face of the earth, off into the anonymity of Witness Protection. And I was gradually finding my way back into the real world, about to step onto a larger stage than I could ever have imagined.

CHAPTER TWELVE
WHISTLE-BLOWER

October 14, 1982. Bob Delaney weaves his way through late-afternoon traffic in lower Manhattan, passing the bustling Wall Street district en route to the Battery Maritime ferry terminal for a quick boat ride to Governor's Island. He is heading to a dinner party honoring FBI agent Joe Pistone—a.k.a. Donnie Brasco—who worked undercover from 1976 to 1981 infiltrating New York's infamous Bonanno Crime Family.

Delaney is attending the Pistone tribute at the urging of FBI Special Agent Louis Freeh, a man he has come to know well and deeply respect.

Between 1979 and 1981, the trooper-turned-detective had worked on multiple cases with Freeh, more than a decade before the Bureau's New York field supervisor would become the fifteenth director of the FBI. The two Jersey natives developed a good working relationship and a strong rapport, allowing Delaney to share with Freeh some of the emotional burdens and feelings of guilt that lingered from his undercover work.

Freeh hadn't been at liberty to share any information about the Bonanno operation with Delaney while Pistone was still on the street. But now Pistone is the toast of law enforcement—his lengthy Mafia investigation hailed as a landmark—and Freeh knows Delaney will benefit from meeting the heralded FBI undercover agent at the dinner.

"It'd be good for you to be there," Freeh tells him.

Reflecting about Project Alpha on the trip from New Jersey to Governor's Island, Delaney's mind wanders back to another long trip south he took as Bobby Covert on July 15, 1977—eleven weeks before the end of the operation.

It was a welcome breather, a chance to escape the tension at Alamo Trucking for a day. Wearing an Alamo golf shirt, slacks, and a wire, he drove from Jersey City to Longport, a beachfront town just south of Atlantic City, to meet with the underboss of Angelo Bruno, head of the Bruno Crime Family. Another kickback payment had to be made.

The mobster's name was Pete Casella, a gray-haired, older man who greeted Delaney at his quaint summer cottage clad in shorts and a white sleeveless undershirt that barely concealed his ample paunch. They reclined on the front porch in high-backed green and white lawn chairs, sipping lemonade, enjoying the cool ocean breeze, and making light conversation.

Casella sang the praises of Pat Kelly and promised more trucking business for Alamo. But soon the subject turned to the hottest of topics in New Jersey: legalized gambling in Atlantic City.

The state had approved the gambling referendum in 1976, and the first casinos along the Atlantic City boardwalk were scheduled to open in 1978. This was a matter of intense interest to the Mob. Wiseguys saw the town as fertile territory, but there was the question of who would control the potential gold mine.

Covert listened as Casella lamented a new complication: Governor Brendan Byrne had announced that a Gaming Commission would work with the State Police to prevent Atlantic City from falling under Mob influence as it had in Las Vegas.

"They're gonna have problems in Atlantic City," Casella warned. "The lawmen are gonna fuck this whole thing up."

"Whaddya mean?" asked Covert.

"Everything they're doin' is gonna be set up to keep organized crime out—but if they keep organized crime out, they got a bigger problem 'cause they'll have disorganized crime, and disorganized crime is worse than us," Casella replied.

Covert could not believe what he was hearing, so he simply tried to keep the senior wiseguy speaking. "That makes sense, Pete," he said.

"Bobby," Casella continued, "any guy with a tank of gas can take a ride to AC and knock people over the head as they come outta the casino. That's what disorganized crime does. We had it right in Vegas.

You had to have money to get there, and we controlled everything so there were no problems. But here any mutt can jump in a car and be there in an hour."

Delaney chuckles at the memory of the story as he is directed by NYPD officers to a fenced-in parking lot at the Battery Terminal docks. Boarding the ferry, he is fully aware of the security offered by the island—only one way on, only one way off. Stepping inside, he sees that the banquet hall itself has a heavy police presence, beyond the law-enforcement dinner guests. This is no surprise, considering that the Mob has placed a $500,000 bounty on Pistone's head.

Delaney looks around the room and realizes that he is the only New Jersey state trooper in the crowd of several hundred federal agents and prosecutors, making him feel like a distant relation at a family party.

Suddenly, even before seeing them, he hears the distinctive, melancholy sound of the NYPD bagpipers. They lead Pistone into the room, where he takes his seat at the head table, surrounded by FBI agents and attorneys wearing three-piece suits and wingtip shoes. Everyone is in awe of Pistone, whose story will be told years later in the 1997 movie Donnie Brasco *with Johnny Depp in the title role and Al Pacino as Bonanno member Benjamin "Lefty" Ruggiero.*

The reaction reminds Delaney of the excitement the prosecutors had exuded when they first heard him describe the details of Project Alpha.

At the end of the night, with guests filtering out of the room, Freeh introduces Delaney to Pistone. The two undercover agents sit alone at the head table and talk for more than an hour. Of all the hundreds of people who attended the banquet, they are the only two who completely understand what the other has gone through. They talk about their Paterson roots, their formative years, and develop an instant connection. Delaney shares with Pistone his conflicted feelings over putting away mobsters he had come to know and like.

Pistone, some ten years older than the thirty-year-old Delaney, offers Godfather-like words: "Bobby, this was our job. It was business—nothing more, nothing less." He will become a close friend and confidant, *someone to help Delaney deal with the emotional scars of undercover work. On this night, they spend most of their time sharing war stories from their lives with the Mob. They are like two long-lost brothers, looking back on their separate childhoods in search of common ground. They are convinced that sometime during their undercover lives, their paths must have crossed—without either of them being aware of the other's true identity.*

Delaney knows this evening is Pistone's moment of recognition, one he has earned after a dangerous six-year roller-coaster ride that ultimately will deal a severe blow to the Mafia's power base.

Of course, only eight months earlier, Delaney had his own moment on top of the hill—the hill in the heart of the nation's capital, where he told his story and came away a changed person.

Louie Freeh was right. That night talking to Joe Pistone at Governor's Island did help. What Joe said struck a chord with me. It underlined what Dr. Hank Campbell was telling me about normal: Don't look for what you knew as normal; accept a *new* normal.

Little by little, the words seemed to be sinking in. And one event would serve as a crucial stepping stone in that process of understanding and acceptance, helping me see the job I did in a new light.

It was the day I testified before the United States Senate.

My road to Congress began with the announcement that Senate hearings on waterfront corruption, chaired by Senator Sam Nunn of Georgia, were scheduled for mid-February 1981. The committee's official name was a mouthful: Hearings Before the Permanent Subcommittee on Investigations of the Committee on Governmental Affairs, United States Senate. The work we had done on Project Alpha was going to play a central role—and I was being called upon to appear before the distinguished panel to give a detailed account of the entire undercover operation.

Committee representatives came to New Jersey in December 1980 to interview me. Soon after that, I began traveling to Washington once a week to prepare my testimony, and by late January 1981 I was in D.C.

three or four days every week, working with members of Senator Nunn's committee as the hearings neared.

Six years earlier, I had sat in frustration at my metal desk at Mid-Atlantic Air-Sea Transportation, screaming at George Mavrodes and his wiseguys about the value of stolen unemployment compensation checks.

Now I'd be sitting at an antique mahogany table inside the massive Everett Dirksen Building on Constitution Avenue—before an eye-opening roll call of senators that included, in addition to Senator Nunn, Warren Rudman of New Hampshire, John Glenn of Ohio, Charles Percy of Illinois, Charles Mathias of Maryland, Henry "Scoop" Jackson of Washington, John Danforth of Missouri, William Cohen of Maine, and Lawton Chiles of Florida. I was only twenty-nine—a year shy of the minimum age requirement to be a U.S. Senator—but those lawmakers and others crowding the chamber would be listening to my every word in an historic place where critical issues and policies had been debated and decided through the decades.

In addition to Louie Freeh, one of the committee members who helped me prepare my testimony was FBI agent Ray Maria. Ray had handled waterfront corruption cases in south Florida and had worked related cases since 1975. We worked together closely, spending hours fine-tuning my formal statement and sharing stories of cases we had both worked. Our stories were strikingly similar; only the names of the characters were different. The hearings were ambitious in their scope, set for February 17, 18, 19, 25, 26, and 27, 1981, with more than three dozen people scheduled to appear. Some would be nonwilling participants; several imprisoned Mafia figures of note, including Tino Fiumara and Russ Bufalino, were on the list.

There was a standing-room-only crowd every day. The hearings began on a Tuesday morning, and the tone was set immediately by Joseph Teitelbaum, a steamship agency official operating out of the Port of Miami, who told the committee tales of extortion and threats—and a business devastated by Mob tactics.

"When I first met Ray Maria," Teitelbaum told Senator Nunn, "he asked me, 'How far do you want to go with this, Joe?' I said all the way to the Senate committee so maybe we can get some new labor laws—so my kids do not have to live under the threat of payoffs like I had to."

My appearance was scheduled for Thursday, February 26. I arrived with Jack Liddy, now *Lieutenant* Jack Liddy, along with John J. Degnan, attorney general for the state of New Jersey. Due to concerns about further exposing my identity, the only stipulation regarding my appearance was that I would remain behind a screen while testifying.

Degnan introduced Colonel Pagano and then set the stage for Jack and me. "The story in New Jersey begins in 1967, when *Life* magazine dubbed our state 'the most corrupt in the nation,'" Degnan told the committee. "Frankly, I wouldn't mention that embarrassing motto were it not for the stunning turnaround we have effected in New Jersey since that time, a process worth recounting for a few moments since it culminated with Project Alpha, which you will hear a great deal about this morning."

Degnan proceeded to put our efforts into perspective for the panel.

"Project Alpha provides us with a case history of organized crime's influence in this area and the success New Jersey, the FBI, and the Justice Department have had in uncovering the key details," he said.

After Degnan wrapped up his comments, Liddy spoke. He explained the learning curve we went through, moving from the small operation of Mid-Atlantic to the larger and more magnetic Alamo trucking company. "Detective Delaney was designated owner of the firm," Liddy told the committee. "The undercover operatives knew how to assume the lifestyles and mannerisms that would enable them to blend in with organized crime figures in the Genovese and Bruno families."

I listened out of view, as committee members paid close attention to my old boss talking about me and Pat Kelly—and I couldn't help but wonder where Pat was at this moment.

"The undercover personnel succeeded in ingratiating themselves with the Newark underworld because of a very cooperative informant. The agents, particularly Detective Delaney, had many contacts with precisely the higher-level organized crime figures we have previously identified."

Liddy concluded with a point that hit at the heart of our investigation into the extortion of small businesses, such as Louie Crescenzi's Bella Vita Ristorante. He told of the ever-present threat of physical violence, stating: "It is the view of law-enforcement officials that what happened to Alamo Transportation was an accurate reflection of what happens to many businesses in the Newark Port area. . . . Alamo Transportation proved to be a laboratory for law enforcement to study organized crime's infiltration of legitimate businesses."

I was up next. Senator Nunn asked that the room be cleared so a screen could be set up, allowing me to give my testimony without compromising my identity. When I was in position, I was about ten feet from the panel with the screen to my back, shielding me from the rest of the chamber: The senators could see me, but the people in the gallery could not. The senator made it clear that no photographs would be taken of me—and then provided a warning, in case anybody wanted to leave the room before I began speaking: The taped conversations of mobsters I would play throughout my testimony came straight from the street. The "motherfuckers," "cocksuckers," and related F-word terms of endearment would be echoing loud and clear in the hallowed halls of the Senate.

My gift of gab has always had its advantages, and it worked for me now. I wasn't the slightest bit nervous about the momentous nature of my appearance. Of course, I had my prepared remarks to read first.

"In my undercover assignment, I presented myself as a rich, young, unmarried man who was interested in becoming involved in the trucking industry. I also let it be known that I was willing to become associated with members of the criminal underworld."

The room was completely silent as I went on to talk about the person who made the operation possible, Patrick John Kelly.

"Patrick Kelly is an extraordinary man, a very successful businessman whose interests in real estate, construction, and other ventures had made him quite comfortable financially. Kelly had cut some corners, made some questionable transactions, and had come to the attention of law enforcement."

I laid out all the high points of our work together in Project Alpha, explaining the gist of the secret recordings Pat and I had made along the way with Tino Fiumara, Jackie DiNorscio, John DiGilio, Michael Coppola, and others. The senators were fascinated with the workings of the Mafia. They had all kinds of questions about the tapes, and I walked them through the contents of each one.

I related the story of Joey Adonis, Jr., and how he'd handed the busboy at Jerry's restaurant a fistful of quarters to keep the *Godfather* theme playing nonstop, and how all the wiseguys mimicked what they'd seen on the screen. That whetted Senator Nunn's appetite for more details: "In other words, you are saying sometimes they go to the movie to see how they themselves are supposed to behave, is that right?"

"That is true," I answered. "They had a lot of things taught to them through *The Godfather*. They try to live up to it. The movie was telling them how to act. Life imitates art over and over."

That provided a lighter moment in the testimony—one that would generate subsequent news coverage—but I quickly shifted the tone to a more somber one, re-emphasizing Liddy's points about the impact of extortion on legitimate waterfront businesses.

"I would like to comment on the high price, financially and emotionally, organized criminals extract from businessmen they victimize," I said. "I have a great sympathy for legitimate businessmen who are caught up in the kind of situation that confronted Alamo Transportation."

I described the fear of threats I had experienced as head of Alamo, and explained that mobsters benefited from their image in the media— with a reputation of enforcing their will through assault and murder. "Once that threatened enforcement mechanism is perceived as real in the mind of their victims, the victims bend very easily in any direction the mobsters want them to bend. Actual violence may not be necessary, once the threat is perceived as genuine."

I then talked about the hopelessness that comes with the realization that one is subservient to the whims of organized criminals. But, I pointed out, I was a law-enforcement officer, and I could have ended my undercover role had I found myself in personal danger.

"Although I assumed the role of the owner of the company, it was not my money at stake. It wasn't my savings and my years of hard work and sacrifice that were being torn away ruthlessly by mobsters. But having seen how the system works first-hand, I have an idea of the impact it must have on honest people whose only objective is to run their business successfully."

Senator Rudman was curious whether an extorted business owner could buy his way out of trouble with a large lump sum of cash.

"I don't feel that is a reality," I answered. "I think once you make yourself available or become involved with organized crime, and you have opened that door, they are just going to keep coming back at you. They are not going to let you off the hook."

The senator from New Hampshire still had the floor, and wanted to know about the pressures of living undercover for nearly three years. I could have given a doctoral dissertation on that topic, but I opted to offer the *Cliff Notes* version.

"It is a difficult position to be in because you take on a lifestyle that is not one that you have been brought up in. It is not a lifestyle that is your own. In fact, it's the opposite. A person who is in law enforcement has a set of ideals, or morality, and in many ways you had to learn a whole new way of thinking.

"When they referred to someone as being a 'good cop,' that didn't mean he was a good police officer; that meant he was the kind of guy you could buy off. Now you had to start changing your whole way of thinking, and after you do it for close to three years, it is not easy to change back again to the way that you were before. So yes, to answer your question, Senator, it is a very stressful situation to live undercover."

Senator Rudman wanted to know more about Fiumara, asking me: "During the years that this operation was going on, did you see a definite ascension of his power in that structure of organized crime, that he was wielding more and more power?"

"Yes," I answered. "Mr. Fiumara was an expert in demeanor. He would be able to come into a room, and you could tell he was there by the way his people would handle themselves around him, the way he handled himself, the way he spoke. You knew he was in charge. And it was even spoken about by other organized crime figures that Tino was an up-and-coming guy; he would be someone to be reckoned with over the next few years."

I then provided a glossary of wiseguy terminology, and followed that by revealing what had happened to the mobsters we'd investigated. For instance, a year before, Angelo Bruno had been murdered by a rival with a shotgun blast to his head as he sat in his car.

As a footnote, Bruno's successor, Philip "Chicken Man" Testa, was later killed by a homemade bomb that contained construction nails. It was not a normal Mob-style hit, but it was suspected that the crime may have been connected to the man who'd served me lemonade on his beachfront porch and mused about "disorganized crime," Pete Casella.

As my two-hour testimony wound to a close, Senator Rudman finished his questioning with words of praise for me, though I knew they were meant for every member of our undercover team.

"Trooper Delaney, I think you have exemplified the highest standards of law enforcement. I have been familiar with the use of undercover agents in the state operation. I realize what considerable risk you put yourself and your family through, and we are indeed fortunate to have people who are willing to take those risks, because, in my view, the only way that evidence of this kind can be produced is either through undercover work or through the use of electronic surveillance. You are certainly to be commended."

When my testimony was over, any misgivings and difficulties I'd experienced during Project Alpha faded into the background, replaced, in all honesty, by a strong sense of having done my duty to my state and country. The words of thanks and praise by the panel, along with a sense of being surrounded by history, of being close to the heart of our government, reinforced my feelings of patriotism. Senator Nunn called for an hour-long recess. I heard him say, "We will clear the room and ask that cameras be turned in a downward position and Mr. Delaney will leave the room."

I had barely had a chance to move when I was approached by Senators Nunn and Rudman, who promptly convened their own session with me. They wanted to talk further, hear more stories of what it had been like undercover—much as folks do today, hoping this ref will share what it's like running the floor in the NBA. We spoke for forty-five minutes. And though the rest of the New Jersey contingent returned home, I was asked to stay behind for the remainder of the hearings in case my insight or perspective would be needed to answer questions that might arise.

Tino made his appearance on the final day of testimony—summoned from his Leavenworth, Kansas, prison cell. He was serving a 25-year federal sentence for convictions in Project Alpha and a landmark UNIRAC—Union Racketeering—case in New York involving Genovese heavyweight Michael Clemente.

Clemente, leader of the International Longshoreman Local 856 in Manhattan, was a major figure in organized crime dating back to the 1950s. He was a contemporary of the notorious Vito Genovese and Albert Anastasia. Both Clemente and Anastasia—who was gunned down in a bloody barbershop hit in 1957—served as inspiration for the crime boss played by actor Lee J. Cobb in *On the Waterfront*. Clemente was the man who put Tino in charge of the Jersey waterfront—and now they were doing time together. Clemente was sentenced to twenty years, while Tino's ever-faithful underling Vinny Colucci got five and a half years, and his loyal lieutenant, Michael Coppola, thirteen years.

But when Tino spoke at the hearings, it was mostly to invoke the Fifth Amendment—his first ten responses, twelve times in all—as well as invoking attorney–client privilege a total of four times.

That night, we all gathered in the offices of the subcommittee in the old Russell Building next door. A lot of people who'd contributed—from the Justice Department, the FBI, and other staffers—came by to celebrate. There were about fifty people in the room, and the TV was tuned to the *NBC Evening News* with John Chancellor. We got great coverage and Senator Nunn was elated.

Every cop knows that great feeling you have on the day you get your badge—you believe you've just become part of something that can make a difference. That sentiment was duplicated for me when my assignment in Washington ended. And, in fact, the Waterfront Corruption hearings would produce labor-racketeering amendments to the Comprehensive Crime Control Act of 1984. Among other things, the amendments substantially increased penalties for violations of the Labor-Management Relations Act of 1947, also known as the Taft–Hartley Act.

I left for New Jersey the next day feeling the best I'd ever felt about my role in Project Alpha. Shortly afterward, I received an envelope with a return address I recognized. The letter inside, from Senator Nunn, gave me an additional boost of pride. It read, in part:

"Your testimony highlighted the importance and crucial aspects of the need for undercover procedures in investigations of the organized criminal element. You are to be commended for the innovative and thorough work you achieved while serving in an undercover capacity during Project Alpha."

But there was little time to bask in the glow of my trip to Washington. When I returned to the New Jersey State Police in early March, my job with the Intelligence Bureau was waiting for me—which meant more organized-crime investigations, along with the prospect of more work on the street, or in the toilet as I now called it—and the longer you're in the toilet, the more you start to stink.

I hadn't been part of that world for the past two months; testifying in D.C. had dominated my life. Being away from the street brought my mind into focus. It was time for a change. I knew there was an instructor position opening at the State Police Academy in Sea Girt, New Jersey. The Training Bureau was under the Administrative Section, which meant no "street work" would be involved. So I approached Colonel Pagano about my desire to leave organized-crime investigations for the classroom. He was sensitive to my situation and empathetic in his response. "I understand," he said. "You've done a lot of good work for us and we appreciate it."

A new challenge was about to unfold, even though, as an instructor, I quickly found myself immersed in a familiar topic. When I arrived at the Academy, I was assigned to the Criminal Science Unit and told I would be taking over what was then known as the Organized Crime School. In short order, I changed the concept and name to the Institute on Organized Criminal Groups and created a two-week program that dealt with all kinds of criminal enterprises. No longer was the focus simply on traditional organized crime, a.k.a. the Mafia.

I started delving into domestic and international terrorist groups, outlaw motorcycle gangs, Colombian drug cartels, and many others. Experts from different agencies—contacts I'd made over the years—helped make the Institute a well-known, sought-after law-enforcement education program.

My undercover years were officially over. I had closed the book on a defining chapter of my life that day in the nation's capital, adding my words into the permanent transcripts of the U.S. Senate.

In a way, I felt that I was leaving a part of Bobby Covert behind in the small print of a landmark Congressional report. But maybe part of him would always remain inside me. As I moved on as Bob Delaney of the New Jersey State Police, I found myself still searching for balance and meaning in a world that had been turned upside down for a very long time. I discovered what I was looking for not on the marble floors of the Capitol, but on the hardwood floors of my youth.

CHAPTER THIRTEEN

A NEW LIFE THROUGH HOOPS

Inside a high school gym, two junior varsity teams race up and down the basketball court, and the man with the whistle jogs alongside the mob in motion, keeping order with a keen eye.

Bob Delaney blows the whistle and rotates his hands as a player drives toward the rim. "That's a travel!" he says, taking the ball and handing it to the opposing team.

He has yet to shed the extra thirty pounds he gained from his years undercover and the stressful ride that followed. He is out of shape and slightly winded—a far cry from the All-State player he had been at Blessed John Neumann Prep and the team captain at Jersey City State. But something about being back on the court, amid the wholesome high school atmosphere, feels invigorating to him. It gives him a sense of peace.

He has found happiness through hoops therapy.

Families are in the stands shouting their support. Cheerleaders are chanting and waving pompons. Delaney savors the pure, positive energy of the scene, having spent so much of his life surrounded by the dark side of human nature. Something about this feels right—even more than it did when he played on the State Police basketball team as a young trooper, and more than it did when he dabbled in officiating before going undercover.

Back then, Delaney knew that his basketball playing skills were never going to take him to the next competitive level, so he focused on staying involved in the game of his youth in a different way: as a referee. He became a member of the Tri-County Officials Association headed by collegiate basketball referee guru Edgar Cartotto of Paterson. Soon, Delaney was officiating CYO and recreation league games, working his way up to high school contests. Then came Project Alpha, and his officiating hobby was shelved for nearly six years.

But now, after so many years spent in court, being on the court is a renewed source of pleasure for Delaney. It is a way to get back to his roots, his old playing weight, the camaraderie and fun he was missing—and, most of all, a sense of normality.

Officiating serves as the perfect release from his work with the State Police and his new position teaching at the Academy in Sea Girt, a short drive from his Jersey Shore home. He applies to the International Association of Approved Basketball Officials, takes the test for Local Board No. 194, and passes with ease. That opens the door to officiating freshman, JV, and varsity games at area high schools.

One Friday night after a round of games, the coaches and referees gather as usual at Peterson's Riviera Inn along the Manasquan River to share stories about the key plays from the contests—coaches at one end of the bar, officials at the other. In this pre-VCR era, talking about the highlights takes the place of fast-forwarding and rewinding tape—and the discussions become a constant source of new knowledge for Delaney. He is busy bantering about basketball when Larry Hennessy, athletic director and basketball coach at Neptune High School, approaches the zebras' end of the bar. Hennessy is impressed by Delaney's ability and style. The coach tells the young ref he is the commissioner of the Jersey Shore Summer Pro League and adds, "We're always looking for good officials—you oughta give it a try."

It becomes Delaney's official introduction to professional basketball. Working around his State Police schedule, he stands out in the Jersey Shore Summer Pro League, and his confident, authoritative ways catch the attention of Darrell Garretson, the supervisor of officials for the NBA.

Garretson sees Delaney as a capable guy—meaning he has the potential to become an NBA referee, not what it meant when he was in the Mob world. He takes Delaney to California in 1983 to work in the Los Angeles Summer Pro League. Using vacation time from the Outfit, Delaney officiates games featuring dozens of current and *up-and-coming NBA players—Rick Carlisle, Greg Kite, Eddie Jordan, Terry Cummings, and many others. Delaney returns to the L.A. league in the summers of 1984 and 1985, and Garretson decides to bring him to Canada in 1986 for a mini-camp featuring four NBA teams and a then-tattooless, low-key Dennis Rodman.*

Doors continue to open, as Garretson hires Delaney as an official in the Continental Basketball Association in 1984. He works games, continuing to hone his reputation as a tough but fair official. For three years, he manages to juggle forty to fifty CBA games per season, dozens of high school games, and his full-time gig standing in front of a classroom at the State Police Academy sharing his law-enforcement experiences.

From 1983 to 1986, Delaney fortifies his skills as a potential NBA ref by working the preseason training camps for the New York Knicks, New Jersey Nets, and Philadelphia 76ers, traveling between St. Joe's University for the 76ers, Princeton University for the Nets, and Monmouth College for the Knicks.

He is on the verge of a dream job.

The Knicks were often a topic of conversation among the wiseguys at Alamo Trucking. Now, here I was in October 1985, rushing off to referee one of New York's training-camp scrimmages. It was amazing. I'd gone from jumping through hoops in the Mob shadows—to officiating hoops in the sports spotlight.

One afternoon, I finished work at the Academy and drove from Sea Girt to Monmouth College to officiate a 3:00 p.m. Knicks intrasquad scrimmage—about thirty minutes away. Well, twenty minutes in a troop car. The autumn day had started off on the cool side, so my attire included a shirt and tie, penny loafers, and a nice wool sweater. But by noon, the weather had become unseasonably warm, so I took off the tie and wrapped the blue sweater around my neck. And when I walked into the arena holding my referee bag, I looked unintentionally like an Ivy League grad student.

Hubie Brown was the Knicks' coach then, and he was on the basketball court conducting practice. The team then included players like Darrell Walker, Bill Cartwright, Pat Cummings—and a rookie named Patrick Ewing. I was heading to the locker room, and as I walked through the gymnasium, I heard a voice yell, "Hey, *Delaney,* if you're gonna dress like that, go over and work at Princeton with the Nets—your preppy look will fit in just fine."

It was Coach Brown's inimitable voice. His players looked at me and started to laugh.

I turned, looked, and smiled—knowing I couldn't win with any kind of comeback in that situation. This was Hubie's show. So I smiled, accepted that I was the butt of the joke, nodded, and continued on my way. I worked the scrimmage, which lasted about an hour. A break for the players followed, and then I officiated an evening scrimmage before driving home dog-tired.

The next day, I made a stop at my State Police locker before heading to Monmouth College for another Knick scrimmage. Aside from being quick with a quip, Hubie Brown is always teaching, with a daily lesson plan for his players. When I entered the gymnasium, Hubie was at midcourt, a spot that doubled as his classroom. All eyes were on him. Because of his concentrated focus on teaching, he didn't notice as I walked up behind him and said, "Hey, Coach, you got a problem with the way I'm dressed today?"

He turned around and did a double-take and said, "Not at all, Trooper. Have a good day." I was standing there in my full State Police uniform—the military-style blue and gold, complete with black leather belts and holster.

Hubie's expression wasn't all that different from the look Major Baum had given me when I'd stood up to him in my undercover job interview a decade earlier. Think about how fortunate I was here in my post-undercover life. I had the opportunity to work scrimmages with Hubie Brown as coach. People pay big bucks for that kind of clinic. Learning from a Hall of Fame coach helped to build the foundation of my officiating career, just as I'd learned from other masters in the two preceding years when the Knicks trained at Upsala College. Hubie had Rick Pitino and Richie Adubato as assistants, and I was exposed to both of those great basketball minds—long before Pitino became an institution at the University of Louisville and Adubato an NBA head coach for Detroit, Dallas, and Orlando, and later New York and Washington in the WNBA.

Being around guys like Hubie, Matty Guokas of the Sixers, Bob McKinnon of the Nets, and many others was an amazing learning experience. Now I got to see plays that teams were running and how top coaches approached every nuance of the game. It gave me a hell of an education—a doctorate in the game of basketball.

The learning process continued every night in the CBA. For instance, in 1986, I was working a game between the Baltimore Lightning and the Bay State Bombardiers of Worcester, Massachusetts, coached by Hall of Famer and former Celtics great Dave Cowens. The Bombardiers had a mascot, Colonel P.J., who dressed in a day-glo orange jumpsuit, aviator helmet, and goggles. During time-outs, he'd always come running onto the court and "fly" around in circles with the lights off, then finish his act with a head-first dive, sliding across the floor.

As the second period started, we had a problem with the net, and my partner, Danny Crawford, and I had to wait for a custodian to replace it. So we had an extended officials' time-out. I was standing a few feet away from the free-throw line, supervising the hanging of the new twine. Meanwhile, P.J. started going into his act. I could tell from the crowd noise and background music that he was going into his dive-bomb routine. Suddenly, the whole atmosphere changed. I caught a glimpse of him as I glanced over my shoulder and realized that I was his target. Colonel P.J. was on a kamikaze mission, entering my airspace.

I jumped at the last instant, avoiding a full-scale collision as P.J., who had apparently misjudged his landing, slid underneath me. I had to tilt at an angle, almost falling, to catch my balance. I couldn't give him a technical foul, but I did the next best thing: I ejected him. P.J. walked sheepishly off the court as the organist played "Hit the Road, Jack."

CBA Commissioner Jimmy Drucker put P.J. on "mascot probation," and the story ended up in newspapers across the country—from the *Sporting News* on down. Granted, this is a comical story. But there has to be a respect for the game, night in and night out, and that includes respect for the officials. Colonel P.J. was demoted to Captain P.J. by Drucker, but he couldn't have been happier, because I'd made him a star. Talk about an ironic twist in my life. I busted a guy—and he liked it.

Early on, I learned that my role in basketball was to be a referee, that I wasn't an evaluator of talent. Some people are very good at that, but not me. If you want proof, I refereed Charles Barkley's first intrasquad scrimmage at St. Joe's University after he was drafted by the 76ers in 1984, when Matt Guokas was the coach and Julius Erving was still playing. The scrimmage started, and by the end of the first half, I'd called six offensive fouls on Barkley. That would have knocked him out of a regular NBA game, of course, but in the scrimmage it didn't matter: Nobody fouls out of a scrimmage. On the way to the locker room at halftime, though, I remember saying to my officiating partner, Tommy Lowenstein, "That guy will *never* make it in the NBA." Now, let's take a look at Sir Charles's career: one of the top fifty NBA Players of all time, Hall of Famer, and Top 25 all-time leaders in scoring and rebounds. You get my point. Clearly, I wasn't on the road to becoming an NBA talent scout.

But I was gaining skill as a referee. And working in the CBA—getting a taste of NBA games during the preseason—was invaluable.

The CBA was a very competitive league—and it was made up of a lot of people who didn't want to be there. The players didn't want to be there; the coaches didn't want to be there—everybody wanted to move up to the NBA. You had coaches who were trying to hone their skills, like Phil Jackson, George Karl, Flip Saunders, and Bill Musselman. And some players had already been in the NBA but had slipped out of the league and were maintaining their comeback hopes by playing in the CBA.

Game management was as important as, if not more important than, calling the block charge foul correctly. Players like Kenny Bannister weren't afraid to take a guy's head off with an elbow. And you had to deal with some tough street players who couldn't make it in the college game, so they ended up in the CBA. These situations forced me to learn how to control games and work with all kinds of players and coaches. The skills I had developed during my years in law enforcement—interacting with people, sensing when tensions were starting to rise, and understanding nonverbal communication—helped me handle those challenges.

The road to becoming an NBA referee requires an enormous commitment of time, and having a demanding day job makes the process even more complicated. But then if it was easy, everybody would be doing it. The average person will drop by the wayside because of the level of commitment and dedication needed. I compare it to my becoming a New Jersey state trooper. There were three thousand people who took the written test—one of five steps in the selection process—and that number was whittled down to 102 candidates who entered the Academy on March 17, 1973. And only 54 graduated three months later on June 22. I've been very fortunate to have been part of two elite organizations, considering how intense and difficult the selection process is for each group.

In 1987, Darrell Garretson and Rod Thorn had made up their minds. I was sitting in my office at the State Police Academy when Rod called. He started out with small talk, asked how I was doing and how I thought the preseason had gone with the four NBA games I'd worked. My response was, "More important, Rod, how do *you* think I did?"

Over the phone line, I heard Rod's characteristic staccato chuckle, followed by "Hey, big fella, we're gonna hire you."

The feeling that gave me was second to none. When the call had come in, I knew Rod was either going to tell me I was hired or would be sent to the CBA for another year. For anyone who's ever received a promotion in any profession, it's an unforgettable moment, filled with pride and excitement. After Rod told me I was hired, I don't remember what I said to him, and I don't remember what he said to me; but when the call ended, I just sat there for a few minutes to let the news sink in. They say your life passes before your eyes when you die. But when you accomplish something you've been working so hard to achieve, all the steps you took along the way seem to pass before your eyes as well.

I found myself thinking back to the people who'd gotten me there—my mom and dad, putting that hoop up in the back yard; my high school basketball coach, Bob Plocinik; my college coach, Larry Schiner; and all my teammates over the years. I thought about getting cut from the team in seventh grade and then working as hard as I could to make the team the next season. I also thought about all the time I'd spent traveling around the country: When other people were home at night, I'd be driving to Albany to work a CBA game, or catching a flight home from LaCrosse, Wisconsin. I remember driving past Madison Square Garden in Manhattan to referee summer pro league games—on the way to some cramped high school gym in the city—and thinking, "Some day I'm going to work in there."

The news got around fast, and after work I met many of my colleagues at Harrigan's Bar in Sea Girt. I bought one round of drinks—not rounds all night long, as I had done in earlier, troubled times. Among all the people who were there patting me on the back—and asking me for free tickets to NBA games—was the detective who'd helped put me on the right path, John Schroth.

The State Police and NBA agreed to let me maintain both positions for a while. I'd travel around the country to work my assigned games. On my days off, the State Police honored the teaching commitments I had to other law-enforcement training centers. Finally, on January 22, 1988, I officially resigned from the State Police. This time it was for real, not a cover story like the one concocted when I'd gone undercover thirteen years earlier.

It was a whole new world, but my old one followed me. My rookie year, I was refereeing a game in Utah, and Karl Malone, one of the greatest power forwards in NBA history, looked at me said, "I know about you."

"Oh, yeah?" I said.

"Yeah, you're the man on the floor—and you're *the man* off the floor," he answered with a wink.

It was the Mailman's way of acknowledging my law-enforcement background. Back then, there were only twenty-three teams, and the NBA network was—and remains—a small family. There are no secrets.

Darrell Garretson minimized my law-enforcement past as I came into the league. And I realize now what he was doing. He wanted players, coaches, and general managers to know me as a referee, not as the ex-trooper or the undercover guy. He wanted my basketball reputation to be developed. There was only one story done about me and my underground background early on, and that was by my hometown newspaper, the *Asbury Park Press*. Other than that, my Project Alpha days were a non-issue.

There was a fine balance between my past, present, and future, and Darrell's management decisions got me to where I am today. When I look back, Darrell handled my situation perfectly, because his approach allowed me to create an identity and reputation separate from my law-enforcement life.

I had to make adjustments in a hurry when I came into the league, the first being the constant travel. Working as an NBA official means you're living a frequent-flier existence, and destinations become a blur of endless hotel lobbies, room-service meals, and basketball arenas.

Spending a good portion of your time on airplanes is a major part of the lifestyle. That took some getting used to; and, with the heightened security since September 11, 2001, air travel has become even more challenging. I take about twenty-plus flights a month during the 82-game season. And I travel to thirty NBA cities across the U.S. and Canada. I've seen just about every conceivable scenario in the friendly skies: from aborted landings and takeoffs, to blown tires and electrical fires. I've been in the company of screaming and vomiting passengers—even one guy who took matters into his own hands and urinated into his airsick bag because the small plane didn't have a lavatory.

I've cut my share of deals with God when we're at 30,000 feet and that plane is shaking and rolling—I start off praying and offering to put $1,000 in the collection envelope that Sunday. As the plane starts to smooth out, I'm down to about $500. And by the time we land, another zero has dropped and I'm at $50. Thankfully, the Good Lord has a sense of humor.

Getting proper rest on the road is another priority. Even though you're going to all these towns around the country, you're not on vacation. You have to get the sightseeing out of your system. You're there because it's your job. As Wally Rooney, one of the all-time great referees, told me early on, "The boys in the pub don't make the club." He was referring to that lobby bar in the hotel, and his message was clear: You're here to work. It's not party time.

There was one other key adjustment I had to make when I started in the league: getting accustomed to the speed, quickness, and size of the players. There's no way you can learn about "bigs"—the term for NBA centers and power forwards—until you're on the floor with them. Because if they're any good, they're going to be in the league and that's the only place you can referee "true bigs." You'll have quick guards, quick forwards, and great shooters at every level of basketball. But when you get to the NBA, you have size and strength. Size means play above the rim. And playing above the rim on a consistent basis, combined with the quickness and strength, makes for the best basketball on the planet.

The only way you know if somebody can referee at the NBA level is to have him or her referee an NBA game. You can surmise that they've got it, but you can't know for sure until they get onto that floor and start working with some of the greatest athletes in the world. One of the first memorable tests of my NBA career occurred in a preseason game I was working with Jack Madden in Corpus Christi, Texas. San Antonio was hosting Dallas, and each team had impressive centers—7-foot-2, 260-pound Artis Gilmore for the Spurs and 7-foot-2, 275-pound James

Donaldson for the Mavericks. I was in the lead position as Gilmore and Donaldson jostled in the post. I saw it as a collision. I mean, to me it seemed like a hard hit. I blew the whistle, but didn't even know what I was going to call. I had never seen two players bang up against each other like that. Everybody stopped and looked at me with a why-are-you-blowing-the-whistle expression.

"I got a foul on—" came out of my mouth. But before I could finish the sentence, Artis said, "This happens every night in the league. If you're gonna call a foul on that, we're gonna be here all night."

Jack Madden came over to me, took the ball out of my hands, and said quietly, "All they're doin' is bodying up." Then he called out for everyone to hear, "Inadvertent whistle. Side out. Let's go."

I'll tell you this: When you see a pair of 7-foot-2 behemoths "body up" against each other and hear that *thud,* it definitely gets your attention.

There were other light moments as well, early on. In my first season in the league, I was officiating a game at the Forum in Los Angeles—the new NBA ref with the slicked-back hair meets the veteran coach with the slicked-back hair, Pat Riley of the Lakers. At some point during the game, I made a call that Riley didn't like, and his reactions resulted in my giving him a technical foul. Without missing a beat, Magic Johnson, the Hall of Fame Laker, walked over to me and said with his million-dollar smile, "He doesn't like you being in the league because you got better hair than he does."

Being back on the court continued to give me the peace I was seeking, a refuge from the life I had lived a decade earlier. I understood that 94-by-50-foot world—the dimensions of a basketball court, a dimension of life that had become my comfort zone. I felt at home with the running, the adrenaline rush, the responsibility for officiating the game and enforcing the rules, allowing the athleticism of the players to unfold. That was a therapy for me, coming from the chaos I had lived through. This had structure and discipline, and with that came a sense of emotional security. Basketball was my way of feeling safe. I understand you may be thinking: How is it safe to be out there in front of twenty thousand people, working in such a high-profile job after living the life I did? But living in plain sight made sense to me.

Officiating has done more for me than just allow me to stay close to the game and make a living; it's offered me something much greater—a way of restoring my place in mainstream life. It felt like that when I came into the league, and it still feels that way more than twenty years later. When I go on that court for those three hours, nothing else matters.

That doesn't mean it's all good at all times. The feeling of failure and disappointment in the game of basketball comes with the territory. In a game between Minnesota and San Antonio in March 1993, the Timberwolves were down by three points with a few seconds left. They in-bounded the ball and Chuck "The Rifleman" Person went up for a shot, lofting a three-point attempt that could tie the game and send it to overtime. But I thought Person was fouled and blew the whistle—an instant before the ball swished through the net to tie the score.

Right there I had a problem: The key was that I "thought" I saw contact, as opposed to actually *seeing* it. And that's not the only thing I didn't see. As I faced the scorer's table—holding out both arms to indicate the basket was a good three-point goal, and about to signal which player the foul was on—Person completely caught me off-guard. He was so excited over having a chance to win the game at the foul line that he raced over, wrapped his arms around me, and lifted me several feet off the floor. I'd never had that happen in my entire career and have never had it happen since. I was yelling, "Put me down, Chuck!" Person obliged, then sank the winning free throw, and Minnesota left the court celebrating a buzzer-beating victory with a rare four-point play.

But I soon went from a spontaneous elevated moment—literally, thanks to Person's bench-pressing me—to a genuine low moment.

Back in the hotel room, the crew watched the VHS game tape. The thing about tape is that it doesn't lie. There was no foul. I didn't sleep that night because of the knot I had in my stomach. This is what referees call a "gamer"—a call that affects the outcome of the game. It's one thing to kick a call in the first, second, or third quarter, and of course you don't even want to do that. But when you kick it and there's only a second or two left on the clock in a tight game, it's a gamer. In my profession, there's no worse feeling in the world.

Darrell called me the next day and said, "Okay, it's going to eat at your gut until you get back on the horse. When's your next game?" I told him it was in two days, and he replied, "There's nothing I can do to make it any better for the next two days. But when you get back on the horse, you're gonna be fine. You've got a long career ahead of you. It's going to be okay."

I've been asked, "At what point did you master the officiating craft?" My answer is, "I never feel that way." There's a level of confidence that grows. But you know this is not something you entirely master. Every night you go out looking for that perfect game, but in reality you know it's never going to happen. You're never going to get every call right. Either you'll miss something you should have called or you'll call something incorrectly. It's a challenge every time you're on the court.

There's another factor in the mix as well. When physical activity is part of your job, it's a fact that your physical abilities will diminish with age. I can't run as fast as I did at thirty-five, but I can get to the right spots on the floor because of my experience, and I still run well. Everyone ages differently, so it's a matter of understanding your own body. It's no different from a pilot who constantly makes critical judgments in all kinds of conditions. If your physical abilities become diminished, it's time to think about retirement.

When I was coming up in the CBA, I would watch NBA officials such as Darrell Garretson, Hugh Evans, Jake O'Donnell, Ed T. Rush, and Jack Madden. I was about the same size as those guys. They were successful at what they did, and I wanted to adapt their styles to my personality. Hugh's retired now, but he helped me tremendously along the way, talking for hours about game situations and this business of ours.

And I always remember what he told me about retirement. But I've got to be honest, it didn't really make sense until recently, knowing I'm on the back nine of my career. "Your body will tell you when it's time to leave the game," he said. "We can all work the playoffs for many years, because the adrenaline is so high and the games are spaced apart. The real question is how your body feels in January or February when you have to work every night or every other night. When you start feeling worn down early in the season—physically or mentally—it's time to get out."

With all the time I spend in hotel rooms, ESPN's SportsCenter has been a constant companion, and over the years I've observed that some college officials work five or six nights in a row. They're working more games than I do in a week and their season is shorter. There's no way any official can work six nights in a row and be ready for every game. It's too physically demanding. And forget about the games; just consider the travel. If we're going to be serving the game, we have to be well-rested, well-prepared, and ready to work every contest. At this point in my career, I don't work back-to-back games any more, like some of our officials do, and that allows me to be better rested and better prepared. Now, that means more time away from home, but there's a give-and-take in everything.

Darrell Garretson practiced his own type of give-and-take. If you were doing well, he'd give you a hard time—nit-picking you, and not allowing you to relax or think you were so damn good. But if you had a problem, like making a bad call, he'd take the time to phone you two and three times a day, asking, "How you doing? Everything all right?" He was there to pick you up, brush you off, and help restore your confidence. He was one hell of a leader.

Darrell retired as our boss in 1998 after seventeen years as director of officials and twenty-seven as an official himself—including thirteen years in which he did both jobs simultaneously. He was the man who opened the doors to the NBA for me. He was a true genius on the subject of basketball officiating, and he implemented a system that is still used today, making an impact at all levels of basketball. It was Darrell, for instance, who coined the terminology "referee the defense"—meaning that a referee should direct his or her eyes toward the defensive player, as opposed to watching the ball. They would then see any illegal actions by the defender; and if the offensive player initiated the action, that would also be clearly seen. That's just one of his countless contributions. The man should be in the Hall of Fame, and I was lucky to be around him.

I was lucky in other ways, too. In my second year in the NBA, the league went from two referees in a crew to three. That change improved the quality of the officiating, because it allowed us to see the game from an angle we had never had before—sideline-to-sideline. When there were only two officials, you were always running from baseline to baseline, looking down toward the basket and out from the basket. When we went to the third person, it gave us the same side view the coaches and players sitting on the bench have, as well as the fans sitting behind and across from the scorer's table. And it allows us to identify more fouls and violations.

The door of opportunity opened for me because more officials were needed to work the playoffs by going to a three-person crew. Thanks to that change in the landscape, I've refereed in the playoffs since 1989. That's unheard of today. You have veteran officials who haven't offici-ated in the playoffs yet. There are only so many spots available in the post-season, and our staff doesn't have a great deal of turnover. People don't retire every year, so playoff assignments are limited. Working beyond the regular season enhances your credibility, but it also adds to your experience. I know what it's like on that floor—the intensity level that takes place in the first, second, and third rounds, and the Finals. I've also experienced that pressure from my undercover work and in law enforcement. I understand when your heart starts to race and you have to look as if you're in full control. It's exactly the same.

Naturally, I've heard my share of comments from players and fans about my undercover life over the years. A few seasons ago when Grant Hill of the Orlando Magic was out with an injury, sitting on the bench, he came up to me during a TV timeout and started to pat me down. "You still wired, Delaney?" he asked with a grin. I actually was wearing a wire, since the game was being broadcast by ABC. I gave Grant my best deadpan expression and answered, "Yeah, I'm wired—and the last time I wore a wire, fifty people went to jail."

In February 2007, I was officiating a game at the Continental Airlines Arena between the New Jersey Nets and Sacramento Kings. I saw actor Vincent Curatola, a.k.a. Johnny Sack of *The Sopranos,* sitting courtside. I went over to him and said, "You're the only made guy I didn't lock up in Jersey," and he stuck out his wrists as if to be led away in cuffs.

The fans get into the act, too, yelling things like "Hey, Covert, after that call, they should put *you* in the Witness Protection Program." Or the guy seated courtside who held up a cell phone and called out, "Hey, John Gotti wants to talk to you."

And there are plenty of fans whose comments have nothing to do with my past life—like director Spike Lee, for example. A few years ago, he was complaining about a call I had made against the Knicks in Miami. Several weeks after that, I saw him at a Knicks–Indianapolis Pacers playoff game, and he started up again about the Miami call. I smiled at him and said, "Spike, I've seen every one of your movies—and they weren't all hits, either."

The fact is, I've seen about everything during my years on this earth, but I also know that life is full of rude awakenings. I was home the morning of July 20, 2007, when I learned of the *New York Post's* front-page story that the FBI was investigating an NBA referee involved with gambling.

The NBA instructed all employees to pass on media inquiries about Tim Donaghy to the league office. I did just that when I was contacted by various news organizations, explaining, "I am not allowed to comment due to a directive by the NBA and the ongoing investigation—so I cannot share my anger, outrage, and disgust regarding the situation." My mom taught me a long time ago, if you've got nothing good to say, don't say anything at all. And that's exactly what I intend to do.

Many improvements to our officiating craft have been made under the various bosses I've had along the way.

For the record, I've worked for three different supervisors and a handful of operations directors. First, there was Darrell Garretson, whose title was Chief of Staff, with Scotty Stirling as Vice President of Operations, followed by Rod Thorn. Eddie T. Rush later took over from Darrell with a new title, Director of Officials, and Stu Jackson became the Vice President of Operations. Since 2003, Ronnie Nunn has been the Director of Officials with Stu still in the same position.

There's a new face in the mix now—Bernie Fryer. I was one of his partners when he worked his last game in the 2007 Finals and announced his retirement that night. The rocking-chair lifestyle was short-lived. He's the new Assistant Director of Officials, a great addition to the NBA management team.

When I came into the league, Darrell was the *only* one running the show. It was very similar to how teams were in the early days of the NBA—one head coach, no assistants. Red Auerbach didn't have an assistant, nor did Red Holzman. But gradually, the NBA developed to where each team now has three or more assistants, as well as a behind-the-scenes staff working with the team. The same thing happened with our team. The transition began under Eddie T. Rush and now has grown into a full-blown operation under Stu Jackson and Ronnie Nunn—they have four group supervisors, an observer in each of the thirty arenas, and an entire staff that's responsible for the officials.

During Darrell's tenure, the current boom we enjoy in technology had not yet occurred, so the scrutiny of officials simply wasn't as intense as it is today. In my years as an NBA referee, that scrutiny has increased 150 percent. We've gone from having a handful of camera angles during telecasts to games with fourteen to twenty-four camera angles. As a result, the responsibilities have increased for every subsequent generation of management.

Just to show you how far we've come, when I started out in 1987, officials had no game tape to review. By 1988, once in a while we'd get a tape, and it was this big VHS cassette that would arrive about a week after the game. Darrell was the only one provided with a VCR, and he'd mail you the tape for review after he received it—but it was only shot by some guy in the stands from *one* angle.

By 1989 or '90, we had tapes available to watch, and we'd take them back to the hotel. The problem was, how the hell were we going to play them? But NBA referees are very resourceful. Blockbuster Video had a deal they offered—if you rented a certain number of tapes, the store would provide the VCR for free. So we would go to the nearest Blockbuster outlet during the afternoon on game day, rent five videos we'd never watch just to get the VCR, bring it back to the hotel room, and hook it up to a TV. That way, when we came back to the hotel after the game, we could just throw the game tape in.

But here's the kicker: The next morning, we'd be on a 6:00 flight to the next city. Well, Blockbuster wasn't open. So you had to pay the bellman an extra ten bucks to take the VCR back for you.

Things have definitely progressed since the Blockbuster Stone Age of the early 1990s—VHS gave way to 8-mm and Hi-8 tapes on portable mini-cams that the league bought for us, followed by computers and state-of-the-art "flip discs" that allow us to tape the game right in our locker room. On top of that, we get Hi-Definition DVDs of the telecasts. We used to watch all this on a laptop computer screen. But we now have small projectors that attach to our laptops, so we can review the game in the hotel room on a big screen. And what I've just explained isn't even the whole system.

We also have a Web site that allows the operations department to communicate with us on a daily basis. There are nearly sixty officials on staff, spread across the country, but if something takes place in Chicago on a Monday night, by Tuesday morning every official will have viewed that play and know exactly how the league wants anything similar to be called. We also have a weekly written test that leads to discussions on rules. Over the course of the season, we can have 300-plus "Web Plays" sent to us. You can be told something, sure; but when you see it, you learn from it immediately. The reason that we watch so much video is that it reinforces what you're doing right—and immediately shows you what needs to be corrected. Finding ways to do our jobs more effectively has been an evolutionary process—starting with Darrell, moving on to Eddie, continuing with Ronnie, and also involving Rod and Stu. And it all stems from a higher authority, Commissioner David Stern.

In the end, it's like any business concerned with quality control: You're always looking for ways to make the product better.

In addition to the changes in technology, there are always changes in management style. We all have experienced changes in leadership, no matter our walk of life. If you're going to be successful, you better adjust your sails. You can disagree with superiors and offer your opinions, but the bottom line is, the reason they have the title is because they are in charge. There's a too-prevalent belief in our society that if we follow somebody, we're not being leaders ourselves. That's not true. Good leaders allow themselves to be led—and I've witnessed that in the New Jersey State Police and the National Basketball Association.

There are far too many NBA recollections to recount here. That'll have to wait for another book. One memory stands out for me, though. It was my first regular-season game ever—and Darrell arranged, through Vice President of Scheduling Matt Winick, for me to officiate close to home at Madison Square Garden. I had a limo pick up my family and bring them to my official debut in style.

I was working with Jess Kersey. Early in the first period, I made a horrendous call on my mother's all-time favorite player, Patrick Ewing. It was his second foul—*terrible*. The second foul on a player is big in the first quarter; the player ends up on the bench because the coach doesn't want to take a chance on him getting his third or fourth foul before halftime.

Patrick, all seven feet of him, was standing over me and looking down with a glare, as if to say, "What the hell kind of call is that?" I could feel what officials call "the house coming down on you." You can hear the crowd shouting and booing, and it literally seems as if they're on top of you. There's no place to hide, no place to turn—you just have to wait for the free throw to take place and move on. My parents were sitting behind the basket about six rows up. I guess the little boy in me wanted some reassurance, so I cast a glance out of the corner of my eye toward them.

And there stood my mother, waving her arms at me in disgust over the call—my own mom. She was yelling at me, too. That's when I realized that my new life—living in the fishbowl better known as a basketball court—is filled with emotional responses and passionate allegiances that can even outweigh family ties. Everyone's a critic. But in the end, the only voice that matters is your own.

CHAPTER FOURTEEN

I'VE ALWAYS BEEN A NUMBER

His "own" voice guided Bob Delaney in times of danger and duress while infiltrating the Mob. It continues to shape him on the basketball court, fueling a confident, steady presence and his growing reputation as a top NBA referee in the 1990s. But now, following one of the country's darkest days, his voice is extending far beyond the confines of a basketball court.

It is late February 1996, and Delaney is in another hotel room somewhere on the road, watching CNN and waiting to work a game that night, when he sees a news report that disturbs him. The judge in the trial of Timothy McVeigh, charged in the bombing of the Alfred P. Murrah Federal Building in Oklahoma City ten months earlier, has moved the case to Denver, ruling that McVeigh and co-conspirator Terry Nichols cannot receive a fair trial in Oklahoma.

The development makes him recall his days as a young New Jersey state trooper and the empathy he felt for victims of crimes he investigated. He thinks about the family of Debbie Margolis, the sixteen-year-old farm girl tortured and murdered by Frankie Miller. He thinks about the wife and children of the man killed by a drunk driver—then victimized again when thieves read the obituary and robbed the house when they were at the funeral. He thinks of the pain and sadness etched into their faces.

And now he thinks about the family members of the 169 people killed by the blast that ripped apart the federal building on April 19, 1995. With the McVeigh trial moved five hundred miles west, he wonders how families will be able to attend the daily court sessions and experience any sense of closure from the tragedy. Closure is a word he knows well. The dilemma stirs him to action.

Reaching out to law enforcement is second nature for Delaney. Even though he has been gone from that realm for nearly a decade by now, he's never stopped being a part of it, never stopped thinking like a trooper or detective, never losing touch with his many old friends and contacts. He calls the Oklahoma City attorney general's office, and is transferred to an official coordinating efforts to help the families of the victims.

"I'm a former detective with the New Jersey State Police, and I now referee in the NBA," Delaney says. He knows it is a unique combination that opens doors. "Is there some way we can help?"

The moment represents a convergence of two significant numbers in his life—2853, the digits on his faded gold State Police badge, and No. 26, which he sports on the back of his NBA referee uniform.

The first taps a time in his life when he developed an understanding for people whose worlds were shattered by crime.

The second is tied to a profession recognized around the world, giving Delaney a new way to make a difference.

Being sensitive to the victimology of crime is an intrinsic part of who I am. When you see firsthand the kind of pain and suffering I saw as a state trooper, it changes how you view the world around you. Criminal investigations focus on the person charged with committing the crime, hardly ever on the victims or their families.

For the past fifteen years, I've been giving leadership and teamwork presentations to corporations around the country, and on occasion have been asked to make appearances at state and federal prisons. But I've always declined to go behind those walls and share time with inmates. My reason: I've seen the victims of criminals. For every hundred prisoners I might meet on the inside, there are probably five hundred victims whose lives have been ended or devastated. My empathy, loyalty, and support is—and always will be—with those victims. I will go to youth facilities to make presentations, because I believe there's still time to help get younger criminals to choose the right path. But I won't go to an adult prison. That's what happens when you've seen as many victims as I have.

Think about it this way: If you ask people who was responsible for the Oklahoma City bombings, most could tell you the names of Timothy McVeigh and Terry Nichols. But very few will know who any of the victims were, unless they were personally connected to them. If you talk about the attack on the Twin Towers on 9/11, people will say Osama bin Laden. But as with Oklahoma City, unless you were personally tied in some way to the tragedy, the names of those who perished are not in your memory. Even historically, people know Bonnie and Clyde and Al Capone—but not the names of the people they killed and robbed. We publicize and sometimes even romanticize the criminal; but, though our hearts grieve at the news of terrible loss, we tend to allow the suffering of the victims and their stricken families to fade from our minds.

We rarely think about the pain they continue to deal with, the ongoing personal penalties they pay through no fault of their own. It isn't their choice to become victims; the burden of that role has been thrust upon them. Most feel a deep need for closure, for the chance to move forward with their lives, knowing that justice has been done. That's why, when I heard that the Oklahoma City bombing trial had been moved to Denver, there was never a question in my mind that I would try to lend a hand.

The governor of Oklahoma, Frank Keating, was working with the United Way to set up the Victims and Survivors Travel Fund. And when I made that call to the Oklahoma City attorney general's office, I learned that United Airlines had offered $100 round-trip tickets to family members of victims, designed to make it easier for them to attend the trial.

I knew that the families of those killed or seriously injured in that bombing would feel a deep compulsion to be in the courtroom, to be part of those proceedings, to hear testimony, simply to be present. But how were they going to get there? For many, even $100 might be more than they could afford. And once they got there—with the strong likelihood that the testimony would drag on—the cost of accommodations would make the trip unfairly expensive. I told the attorney general's office that our union, the NBRA—the National Basketball Referees Association—might be able to help.

That got the wheels in motion. At the end of the 1995–96 season, with the trial date still far from being set, I proposed the idea at the NBRA meeting held between the end of the regular season and the start of the playoffs. Everybody agreed that we'd donate one airline ticket each: Fifty-five referees equaled fifty-five tickets. We were well aware that we couldn't solve the entire problem of transportation costs. But I was sure that our donation would generate media coverage, and could be a catalyst—raising awareness and attracting public support.

In August, I flew to Oklahoma City and presented the check to Dr. H. C. "Mac" McClure, chairman of the Victims and Survivors Travel Fund. I also brought an NBA referee game jacket, to hang on what had become known as "The Fence"—a permanent chain-link memorial with hundreds upon hundreds of mementos left behind by mourners, including flowers, teddy bears, photographs, prayers, and messages of sorrow and tribute. It was a stunning and poignant sight.

The plan worked. We held a press conference, and word of our donation spread. Within a few weeks, the United Way reported that an additional $280,000 for the travel fund had been raised from donors around the country.

I'm constantly amazed at how sports connect us in society, even in times of tragedy. Sports are a diversion from everyday stress, with some power to soothe heartbreak and suffering, to express our hopes, and our wish to see ourselves triumphant. Sports figures become stand-ins for our dreams. We in the world of sports have a special calling—to use our position to help others, to be a positive force in our country in times of need. There never was a more urgent time to help than in the aftermath of the terrorist attacks in New York and Washington, and the crash of Flight 93 in Pennsylvania on September 11, 2001.

On 9/11 and the days that followed, like most Americans, I barely left the TV set. We all have personality flaws, and one of mine is thinking I can fix everything for everybody. My inner voice was saying, "How can I help?" The more I watched the coverage unfold, the more I tried to find a way to contribute. I understood that the horror could never be wiped away or the lives brought back. But if there was some small, healing act we could perform, I knew that the National Basketball Referees Association would want to reach out and do it.

What happened that day shook us to our core as Americans—and also hit many of us on a personal level. For me, it wasn't only the attachment I felt to the New Jersey–New York area. The tragedy hit close to home in other ways. Fred Morrone was a trooper I had worked with in the State Police Intelligence Bureau. He retired in 1993 as a lieutenant colonel to become Director of the Port Authority Police. The agency's office was on the 67th floor of Tower One. Soon after the first plane struck that tower, Port Authority chairman Lewis Eisenberg called Fred, who was already hurrying to the scene. He didn't have to go inside, but he led a small group of officers into Tower One, and they made their way up to the Port Authority office, assisting people as they went. Fred was last seen on the 67th floor, doing his best to reassure and help terrified victims attempt to escape the carnage. He was unselfish and brave—one helluva cop, and he perished that day.

The devastation also touched our NBA officiating family. Veteran referee Lee Jones, who now works as a league supervisor, lost his son Brian, who was also working in one of the towers. As friends and colleagues of Lee, I knew all of us had to do something.

My vision was to have a goodwill mission, with the referee staff bringing NBA hats, T-shirts, socks—anything we could to the firemen, cops, and rescue workers in and around Ground Zero. We would shake hands, talk, and let them all know that we cared about them.

That was the idea; next, it had to be implemented. Because of my contacts in New Jersey and New York law enforcement, I was able to make calls to the right people and cut through the red tape that existed due to heightened security. The city was locked down, and very few people were getting in unless they were essential to the ongoing emergency operations. But the top guys at the State Police had been my classmates in 1973. They were all guys I'd worked with.

My first call went to Joe Canatella, Badge No. 2852. If you remember my badge number, 2853, you can gather that Joe and I knew each other pretty well, being side by side the whole way through the Academy. Joe slept one bunk over from me. We marched together, we sparred in the boxing ring together, we studied together, did everything together—all because Delaney followed Canatella alphabetically, and thus numerically too. Now, three decades later, he was a major, one of the top five guys in the State Police. Talking to Joe set the wheels in motion, and I followed with calls to other contacts within the State Police, FBI, and NYPD.

Once I had the clearance from the law-enforcement side, I called Stu Jackson, the NBA's vice president of operations, and ran the idea by him. A few hours later, he called back with the go-ahead and an offer to provide the buses, hats, T-shirts, all the give-away merchandise we'd need.

That's how fast it fell into place. On September 29, we arrived at the Woodcliff Lake Hilton in Bergen County, New Jersey, for our preseason meetings, which only ten days earlier had been in doubt, like everything else in the country. That night, we held an NBRA meeting and agreed to make a donation to the 9/11 Fund to help the firemen and policemen. Early the following evening, two troop cars met us at our hotel, just a few miles from the New York state line, where a pair of buses arranged by the NBA awaited us. I climbed in one of the troop cars, while the rest of the officials boarded the buses bound for Manhattan—uncertain of what we would find there, or how it would feel to view scenes of destruction we had only seen on TV.

If you grew up in that area, as I did, you knew there was never a time when you could get into the city without sitting in traffic. During my undercover days, I had often gone to Little Italy, and even at 4:00 a.m., there was traffic going in and out crossing the Hudson River. Now, we were driving south on the Garden State Parkway, and picking up the New Jersey Turnpike during the early evening—with one State Police car in front and one in back, lights flashing—with both highways nearly empty. I was struck by how stark and eerie it was as we drove across the Bay Extension.

As I looked down from the elevated highway, in an odd intersection of worlds, I could see Communipaw Avenue and the boxlike building that had once housed Alamo Trucking. Strangely enough, it just looked like any other concrete building to me now. There were no ghosts from my past swirling in the shadows, no emotional responses triggered as the structure faded from view. I had literally and figuratively moved past it—my mind fully focused on the present.

After about thirty minutes—ten or fifteen minutes faster than usual, since we were the only ones on the road—we arrived at the entrance to the Holland Tunnel. It was completely desolate.

The tunnel had no activity other than military and law-enforcement vehicles—and the two sanitation trucks stationed at the mouth of the tunnel, blocking the way. The trucks were parked staggered in relation to each other, like the gates to a prison. One moved—permitting us to drive through the small opening—and then returned to its "closed" position. The next truck did the same, and we squeezed past, continuing through the tunnel to Manhattan.

At the other end, members of the NYPD were waiting. I got out and told them who I was. It was like any law-enforcement job I'd ever been on, when cops from different agencies joined together and became a single united team, no matter what branch we represented. That's what happened here. We became one on this mission.

Now that we were in New York City, the NYPD, not the New Jersey State Police, was in charge of the operation. The troop cars went to the back of the escort, and I jumped in one of the city police cars that led us the rest of the way.

The cop driving me in the lead car was adamant about one thing. "Make sure you take care of the firemen. They got hit hard." I was struck by his concern, his empathy for his FDNY peers. The cops looked at the firefighters as the ones who had suffered the most.

In a matter of minutes, our Ground Zero mission began to unravel. We pulled up on a street near the smoldering wreckage that had been the Twin Towers, and sixty NBA referees gathered on the sidewalk— staring at a city in shock, with the smell of ash lingering in the air, shreds of papers stuck to rooftops. We lined up on the sidewalk two by two, ready to be escorted into the Ground Zero rescue zone. But just then, an NYPD captain coordinating our visit got a radio call. She pulled me aside to tell me that six bodies of firefighters had just been found and were being brought out.

Of course, that changed our plans instantly. The fallen firefighters were being honored with a flag draped over their bodies. And it would have been inappropriate for us to be traipsing around, handing out NBA hats and shirts at a time like that. But then a secondary plan fell into place, thanks to the NYPD cop who'd been leading us around. I only remember his first name, Tom. He salvaged our mission with quick thinking. "I'll take 'em over to the firehouses, Cap," he said to his commander.

The referees reboarded the buses, and I shared the new plan with them. Minutes later, we began our revamped itinerary to a couple of firehouses. And if you've never been to a firehouse, that is what it truly is, a house. It's a home where a family lives, a family that happens to fight fires, and it's a place with its own sense of pride and history.

At each house, we shook hands, offering condolences and words of support. These guys had been going through hell for more than two weeks. At the front of each firehouse was some kind of makeshift memorial to fellow firefighters who perished at the World Trade Center. We talked. We listened. We handed out hats and T-shirts. We answered questions about the NBA—whatever helped get their minds off their troubles for a while.

As the night wore on, we arrived at the last firehouse we would visit near Ground Zero—Engine Company 4, Ladder Company 15.

Forming a line that stretched out onto the sidewalk, one by one, we approached Company No. 4's memorial—poster boards with photographs of the lost firemen—and simply stared at the pictures. Some of us offered prayers and made the sign of the cross. Everyone was speechless, feeling empty inside.

I went to the deskman on duty, and he explained that the firemen were upstairs sleeping. I told him that we wanted to leave some NBA gear for everyone, and he got up from behind the desk and shook my hand. And he insisted on waking his men and having them come downstairs. "They'll kick my ass if I let you guys go without having them say thanks," he told me.

How about that? The desk officer was saying that *we* deserved a thank-you. These were true heroes—guys who deserved cheers and admiration—and they were the ones coming down to say thanks. After a short time watching the refs and firemen together, I understood what the deskman knew all along. They had had nobody to talk to all this time, and they just wanted to mingle with us—people who weren't connected to the horrific sights and incomprehensible pain they'd been grappling with. They needed to vent their frustration, their sadness. For example, one firefighter I was talking to told me they had been working two-day shifts, followed by twelve hours off so they could see their families. He explained to me that while they were at work, they had many concerns: doing their job, trying to maintain their sanity while making sure that their fellow firefighters were holding up, worrying about the families of the guys who had died.

"From the minute I get in my car and leave to go home, I cry the whole way," he said. "And when I get out of that car, I have to stop crying 'cause I don't want my family to be more scared than they need to be or listen to all the shit that I've been living through. Because they've seen enough of it on TV, and they're just happy I'm alive."

He told me that he felt good getting some of this off his chest. I think they all were happy to speak to outsiders, because they didn't need to keep their guard up. They didn't have to act a certain way with us. What other outlet did they have? Were they going to talk to the fireman working next to them? That guy was living through the same nightmarish experience. Our job was to help them release their pent-up emotions.

Sometimes, all you could say was "Hang in there," "Thank you," or "God bless." But it meant something, both to them and to us.

To this day, in fact, there are referees who have maintained relationships with firefighters they met that night, not just keeping in touch, but taking them to Knicks or Nets games.

Several memories will always stand out in my mind in the years since our visit to the men and women of the FDNY and NYPD.

A New York City ferry connecting Manhattan and Jersey City has been dedicated to the memory of my late trooper colleague, Fred Marrone, Badge No. 1858. No matter how many times I'm in New Jersey for preseason meetings, it seems like I always end up on that ferry. There's a dedication plaque and a photo of him, detailing his law-enforcement career and heroism. And it gives me the opportunity to share with anyone within listening distance the pride I had that he was my friend.

I also represented the NBRA, offering words at the service for Lee and Pat Jones's son a few weeks after our visit to the firehouses. My closing comments: "Every step we took, every hand we shook, every hug we shared, every dollar we donated was in memory and honor of Brian Jones. God bless you, Brian. Rest in peace."

And then there was our final farewell that night at Engine Company No. 4, Ladder Company 15.

It was about 1:00 a.m., and we were getting ready to end the visit. I was busy making sure that everyone was on the buses. When I was confident that everyone was accounted for, I made one last stop to shake hands with the four or five firemen standing in front of the station. It reminded me of the way your parents stand in front of their house when you're leaving at the end of a visit. The final good-bye was offered, and I had started to jog across the street to the bus, when I heard, "Hey, ref!" I stopped and turned back to see one of the firemen pointing a finger at me as he barked, "Now remember—don't *fuck* our Knicks this year." They were looking at me with expressions of utter seriousness— holding their stern gazes for a few seconds as if to put me on notice, and then all of them burst out laughing. They got me.

Even with everything that was going on, they couldn't miss the chance to take a shot at the ref. But that brief moment shows the magic of sports—and the responsibility we carry as its representatives. Games may be powered by numbers—the stats, the trends, the dollars—but the real power of sports comes from the people involved. The same holds true for our entire society. In some ways, we're just a number in the latest Census Bureau report. But we all have a chance—a responsibility—to transcend that number, especially in difficult times, and make ourselves truly count.

CHAPTER FIFTEEN

A FINAL CALL

It is nearly 1:00 a.m. on that April night in 1999, and the two old part-ners have said their good-byes outside the Mountain Shadows Marriott lounge in Phoenix. Pat Kelly has his busy relocated life to attend to. And Bob Delaney has to catch a flight out of Sky Harbor International in less than six hours.

"Now remember, call me next time you're in town—I know a great little Italian restaurant," Kelly says with his familiar grin. "I don't wanna have to keep yellin' 'Alamo Trucking' to get your attention."

Then he disappears into the early-morning darkness, and Delaney heads to his room, his head swimming with so many memories that he can't sleep until he reclines in the cushy leather seat in 2B on the four-hour flight to Florida.

Seeing Kelly again has reconnected Delaney to a past that defined the person he would become—a past that ultimately put him on a path to this new life, keeping order on the court rather than courting danger.

It is as if the unplanned reunion had flipped a switch in his head, illu-minating memories that had dimmed with the passage of time.

Now that their paths have crossed again, two thousand miles away in the Arizona desert, Delaney vows that he'll stay in touch. The redis-covered friendship has linked two men in radically different worlds— one living in the spotlight to pursue a dream, the other living in secrecy just to stay alive.

Seeing Pat that night gave me a chance to relive our duty on the front lines of Mob life from a new perspective. It was the first time he and I had ever had the chance to reminisce and rehash what we'd accomplished—

and we could do it through the eyes of two older, wiser men twenty-two years removed from the fear, pressure, and peril that had followed us everywhere.

I started making it a habit to call Pat whenever I had a game in Phoenix. He and his girlfriend Maureen would sit near courtside, and I'd hear him yell things like "Good call, ref!" and "Good job, Bobby!" Pat and I would usually stop for a drink or get a bite to eat before I left town, and we never ran out of subjects to talk about. Now I was able to laugh about the things he had done that had pissed me off at the time.

"I really wanted to smack you," I told him.

"Yeah, and all I was tryin' to do was teach you how to dress and talk like a freakin' wiseguy," Pat fired back.

But somewhere along the way in 2001, we fell out of touch as unexpectedly as we'd re-established contact. I was busy as ever flying from city to city, and planned to call Pat the next time I got to Phoenix and give him a hard time for not returning my last call.

One night in early April of that year, I received a voicemail in my Philly hotel room. It was from a fellow official, Jason Phillips, who had recently worked a game in Phoenix. The bottom line to the message was this: A woman seated near courtside had managed to get his attention and told him that it was important that I get in touch with her. Her name was Maureen, and she'd left a telephone number for me. It didn't sound good—it had the same feel as a middle-of-the-night call that shakes you up with grim possibilities.

I dialed the number immediately. A female voice picked up. "Maureen? Bob Delaney. I got a message to call you," I said, doing my best to disguise my concern.

"Bob," she said softly, her voice breaking. "Pat died. He had a heart attack. I was holding him and I did all I could, but then he was gone."

The news left me momentarily speechless. "I'm so sorry, Maureen," I said after a few seconds. "When?"

She told me it had been more than a month before, but that she didn't have a way to get in touch with me—that's when she got the idea of giving a message to a referee. I barely knew Maureen, and she had no clue of the undercover life Pat and I had shared inside the Mob. So after a few more moments of respectful conversation about our mutual friend, I thanked her for contacting me and started to wrap things up.

"I have to ask you something," she interjected.

There was a pause, and I realized she was searching for words—trying to ask a question, a question she wasn't sure she wanted the answer to.

"The other day I was in the attic, you know, just going through some of Pat's things. And I found some old newspaper clippings and police reports. They mention New Jersey State Trooper Bob Delaney. I know that's you. And they mention a man named Pat Kelly."

She added slowly, "Is that *my* Pat?"

Suddenly I felt immersed in the kind of daily conflict I had lived undercover. Should I lie? Should I just tell part of the story and keep her at bay? I knew it wouldn't be good to tell her the whole story, or even part of it, over the phone. I guess I was trying to avoid the inevitable. So I said, "Maureen, when I get to Phoenix, we'll talk."

"*Bobby,* you just answered my question," she said in a tone that made clear she was no longer going to be fooled.

I knew she knew, but how could I explain nearly five intense years of life with Pat Kelly in one phone conversation? So I reiterated that we'd talk in Phoenix, and we said good-bye. I'd steeled myself to the news of Pat's death while talking to Maureen—that was something I was good at from years of police work—but now a sadness struck me as I hung up the phone.

I lay down on the bed as the TV droned on with the evening news—background noise to the thoughts swirling in my mind. One notion made me smile. Pat had lived in a world where informants die if they're caught. But to die of natural causes—to live the life he did with the Mob, and then start a new life in Witness Protection—I've got to tell you, Pat continued to impress me, right to the end.

It was the best scenario that could possibly have played out for Pat Kelly. The thought made me happy as I lay there, looking at the white stucco ceiling. The fact that our lives had once again intersected also made me feel good. I had been able to share my feelings with Pat— words of appreciation for a job well done—that I hadn't known how to convey at age twenty-seven or twenty-eight when the final Project Alpha trials were over. At forty-eight, my perspective on life, my awareness of our achievements, had deepened. Having the opportunity to reflect on our experiences together after all these years was something I'd never expected. It was a real bonus—something I would always hold on to.

That was the final call—the final call about Pat, the final call about Project Alpha, the final call about my life infiltrating the Mob.

But in the world I lived in now, there were other calls still to be made, with twenty thousand people watching me in person and countless more viewers on TV.

And of all the calls in my basketball life, I'd have to say the single most meaningful to date was made in a nationally televised game on Christmas Day 2004, with the Detroit Pistons visiting the Indiana Pacers.

It was a call I made before the game even started—a contest I knew the entire nation would be watching, given what had transpired between these two teams only a month earlier.

November 19, 2004, wasn't the best night in NBA history. The Pacers were less than a minute away from a double-digit victory in Auburn Hills, Michigan, when mayhem erupted—a few minutes of absolute chaos, later replayed on TV again and again. There's a good chance you saw the video clips and the stinging commentary about it on the national news in the weeks that followed. The game was stopped with 45.9 seconds left on the clock, giving the Pacers a 97–82 victory. But nobody won anything that night. It was a loss all the way around— resulting in suspensions, arrests, and a sad day for the league.

Inevitably, the next game between those two teams received a great deal of advance attention in the worlds of sports and national news. The contest was set for December 25, and I was scheduled to officiate. I had been given the assignment back in early November, a couple of weeks before the controversial game took place. But as the rematch neared, I was fully aware of the spotlight that would be shining on every move the Pistons and Pacers would make inside Conseco Fieldhouse.

Detroit–Indianapolis was set as the early offering on ESPN, followed by a much-anticipated contest, Miami–Los Angeles, with Shaquille O'Neal vs. former teammate Kobe Bryant. Because of the brawl, however, the early game I was working took on the feel of an NBA Finals clash. National media poured in to see what would happen when these two teams faced each other, with guys still on suspension and emotions still raw.

I didn't want to ignore the elephant in the living room and knew, as crew chief, that I had to address the underlying tension in some way at the captains' meeting before the game. In the days leading up to Christmas, I thought a lot about what I would say. I kept coming back to one of my favorite quotes by Dr. Martin Luther King, Jr.—words I learned from an African-American basketball teammate in college, John Scott. He was 6-foot-4, a good ballplayer, fantastic at the piano, and a tremendous student. John and I would often get into serious conversations about racial tensions in America. I'd read Eldridge Cleaver's *Soul On Ice* as a senior in high school, along with the writings of Malcolm X and Dr. King, and I wanted to know more. At Jersey City State, we weren't flying anywhere to games, so there was plenty of time for John and me to talk on our long bus rides. I'll never forget when he shared Dr. King's words with me. The quotation stayed with me as a profound and inspiring message that applies to every aspect of life.

A couple of days before the Christmas game, I decided that if the atmosphere seemed right—and you always have to play these things by ear—I would make Dr. King the centerpiece of my comments during the captains' meeting.

When the moment arrived, we brought the captains together—Ben Wallace and Chauncey Billups for the Pistons, Reggie Miller and Austin Croshere for the Pacers. "No lectures, guys. I don't have to tell you how many people are watching. I want to share my favorite quote—Dr. Martin Luther King said it best years ago and it rings true right here, right now."

Reggie was leaning forward to concentrate on the words. Chauncey and the other captains were looking directly at me. And as I spoke, I could see my fellow referees Courtney Kirkland and Jess Kersey nodding in approval.

"'The ultimate measure of a man is not where he stands in moments of comfort and convenience, but rather where he stands at times of challenge and controversy.'"

And I ended with: "Let's show the world the kind of competitive basketball we've got."

"You got it," Reggie said. I think all of us were conscious of the magnitude of the moment, and the captains broke the huddle ready to make a clean break with a bad memory. It was a good game, won by Detroit 98–93. It turned out that ESPN SportsCenter aired a clip of the captain's meeting. In the following days, mentions of the meeting appeared in sports sections around the country. And eventually ESPN's NBA columnist Scoop Jackson named the captains' meeting as the top NBA moment that season.

Even on a basketball court, Dr. King's message about the human spirit had an impact, inspiring others to rise above adversity and tap their true power. Long before then, at a different period of my life, his words had had personal meaning for me. I'd repeat them to myself often. They helped me through the adversity posed by the challenges and turmoil of my undercover life.

As I watched the reaction to those words in Conseco Fieldhouse that Christmas Day, I knew I had made the right call in saying them again. And they have become a part of me, a source of strength—with so many calls in life still left to make.

EPILOGUE

*"There are three groups of people you don't mess with in this world—
the FBI, the Mafia, and NBA referees."*

—*Mike Schuler, NBA head coach*

These words spoken by the former coach of the Portland Trail Blazers always make me smile. He wasn't referring to *me* when he made the remark years back. But he was right on the money, and I should know—I've been part of all three worlds.

It has been an amazing journey for me, but one that has come with a price.

The day my undercover life ended, I thought my new world would be free from the fear and tension that had shadowed me during the nearly three years I infiltrated the Mob. But the death threat that I faced after Project Alpha forever changed how I would approach life.

Situations that others might consider ordinary are never ordinary for me. I've gained some insights into how people who lived in England during the World War II Blitz must have felt. When the air-raid sirens sounded, they found shelter. When the raid was over, they came out and continued their lives. That became a lesson for me.

Since 1977, my personal security alert level has been at the equivalent of "orange"—the second-highest rung on the Homeland Security ladder. For the past thirty years, I've experienced what we've all gone through since September 11, 2001. It's been that way since the day I surfaced from undercover work, and it only became more pronounced when I made the decision to live life on my own terms in the public eye.

People ask me why I choose to go to work in the spotlight, inside sold-out basketball arenas, calling attention to myself through interviews—and now a book about my life. The implication is that I'd be better off keeping a low profile, finding a line of work that keeps my name and face out of public view.

But here's how I see it: Changing how I want to live *my* life, or hiding from the bad guys, would be giving them a power over me that they certainly don't deserve. It would be the same as saying to the Mob: You won. And that has never been, and never will be, an option for me.

As Americans, all of us face a similar choice today. We can choose to go on with our lives in spite of the potential unknown risks. Or we can allow the cloud of terrorism to dictate our choices—decide not to shop at the mall or refuse to fly on an airplane. In other words, live in a Homeland Security state of yellow alert—severe risk. But what's the result? We'd not be living, just existing. And that's precisely what the bad guys want to happen.

My duty as an undercover operative took place thirty years ago, and some of the wiseguys I put away have since died, but some have done their time and are back out in society. But I can't let the possibility of retribution, no matter how remote, deter me from pursuing my dreams. I still remain aware of my surroundings. I'm aware of who's in a room or on the street. I'm not going to go into all the measures my family and I take to ensure our safety; as I said, I have a strong post-9/11 mindset. That's the same as it should be for anybody else in this country. Be alert to suspicious behavior, exercise common sense, and don't let fear dictate your decisions.

Through the years, I have maintained strong, active ties to law enforcement at the state and federal level, giving me a link to useful information regarding my security. I not only rely on law enforcement—I'm still on that team. And it's a great team to be on.

Several times a year, I speak at the Federal Law Enforcement Training Center in Glynco, Georgia, addressing law-enforcement agents from the United States, Canada, and Europe. I open by asking the class for their definition of organized crime. And after the discussion, I offer mine: "Organized crime is an ongoing conspiracy, which uses fear and corruption in an attempt to make money and/or gain power in a community or society."

If you notice, that definition does not include the word "Italian" or the word "Mafia." We're socialized to immediately think *The Godfather* when we hear the term "organized crime." But if you look at that definition, it applies to the Irish Republican Army, an outlaw motorcycle gang, a domestic or international terrorist network—any group engaged in organized criminal activity.

I use the term "bad guys" to describe the people involved in those types of pursuits. The point is, whether you're talking about the Mob or Osama bin Laden, they're all *bad* guys—flat-out criminals. Sometimes they're right in your own midst and you never have a clue.

Unfortunately, at least in the United States, there's a growing trend that makes it easier for perpetrators to get away with their crimes. The "stop-snitching" movement has begun to take root in cities across the country, making witnesses to crimes fear for their safety and lives if they provide assistance to law enforcement. There are "Stop Snitching" T-shirts, DVDs, and Web sites. One of them—I won't bother giving their Web address—goes so far as posting photos and information taken from court documents of witnesses who have helped the government in prosecutions. I understand not wanting to give somebody up. I've lived it. I became friends with criminals, got close to them, and turned them in. I experienced feelings of guilt. But I also know that I did the right thing. The ones who are wrong are the criminals, not the people helping law enforcement.

As I said, we've been conditioned not to tell on our friends. If you grow up in an environment where you're leery of law-enforcement authority, I understand that as well. But to make a statement that you wouldn't turn somebody in who has committed murder illustrates the danger of this trend. Witnesses have to realize that criminals are not your friends. In fact, *they* will turn on you in a New York minute.

And we're not talking about telling on somebody for some minor infraction. We're talking about crimes against people. Crimes where innocent bystanders get shot, like a nine-year-old boy in Florida who was killed when two gang members chose to settle their disagreement with a shoot-out on a street corner. The sad thing is, it happens almost daily all over the country. I'm realistic. I'm not looking for it to be changed overnight. But if we move the bar a little each day, in a few years we'll have made progress.

In addition to discussing criminal issues at Glynco, I share insights with undercover agents. The self-awareness I gained from my informal therapy sessions with Dr. Hank Campbell broke new ground in understanding the personal stress caused by taking on that new identity. For the past twenty-five years, I've taught operatives how to cope with the change in lifestyle and the unique psychological and emotional pressures they will encounter.

I never stop learning, either. In the summer of 2007, I gained new insights about the physical effects undercover work had had on me. The fact was, I'd been feeling a little more run-down than usual, which I had attributed, in part, to the demands of another long NBA season and the many other projects that occupy my life. I was hitting the gym hard, but not making the gains I wanted. I had heard about the DaSilva Institute and the work Dr. Guy DaSilva has been doing in pathology, internal medicine, hematology, and anti-aging medicine, which is really *preventive* medicine. I wanted his opinion.

Dr. DaSilva knows about my NBA career, but had no idea about my past life undercover. He got right to work, taking more blood samples than I think I'd given in my entire life—about thirty vials—to do a thorough lab investigation. He measures biochemical parameters in the body and then comes up with a diagnosis, rather than eliciting information from the patient on the front end. It's an objective way of identifying a problem.

During my follow-up appointment, I was amazed as Dr. DaSilva started accurately describing things about me before we'd even finished our conversation. What really sparked his interest was that two hormones produced in the adrenal gland—part of the stress-hormone category—were abnormally low. At first he thought the labs had made a mistake. A person my age, in their mid-fifties, with a stressful job, should have a high level of those hormones. But what I had was adrenal burnout, adrenal fatigue—having depleted hormones that are supposed to be on the *rise* as you get older. And then he asked me point-blank: "Have you been through a prolonged, traumatic experience of some kind in your life?"

I was stunned. There was actually a long-term *physiological* impact of the Post-Traumatic Stress disorder. I had lived through so much stress that hormones governing the basic human fight-or-flight instinct were barely functioning—making me less effective at handling stress than I once had been. Some of the symptoms of that condition may include lack of sleep and pre-diabetic blood-sugar issues, both of which I had. Listening to Dr. DaSilva gave me a sense of relief—big-time. Dr. DaSilva explained that my strong willpower had been sustaining me, but that he had a medical remedy. Soon afterward, I started on a regimen restoring my hormonal levels to normal. I now have new information to share with undercover agents who have gone through the stresses of living a double life, immersed in danger.

One fact remains: When you surface from dangerous and prolonged undercover work, your world will never be the same. To some extent, you'll always be looking over your shoulder. And that can lead to some scary moments. A simple act like going to church can cause your heart rate to soar.

In the mid-1990s, I was in Manhattan just after New Year's Day to officiate a Sunday afternoon game at Madison Square Garden between the Knicks and the Milwaukee Bucks. We always arrive the day before our next scheduled contest, so I had the night free and decided to attend the 5:00 p.m. Mass at St. Patrick's Cathedral on Fifth Avenue, across from the NBA office. It was beautiful in the city, as it always is around the holidays. The Christmas lights and displays were still in place, a fresh layer of snow was on the sidewalks, and there was a real *Miracle on 34th Street* feel in the air. Attending Mass in St. Patrick's—an ornate, massive church with a lot of history—is something I savor. It gives me a sense of peace, a strong connection with my Catholic upbringing and faith.

After the homily and the consecration, I stood up in my row and moved into a long line of people waiting to receive communion from one of several priests in the front of the cathedral. This is a sacred time, when I pray for God's blessings on my family, my friends, and myself, and clear my head of the details of everyday life.

For those of you who are Catholic, you'll understand. And for those of you who aren't, let me explain. When you're in line going to communion, there's a respectful space people give each other. If you're with a family member, you tend to stand closer, but I wasn't in line with anybody from my family—and I could sense the person behind me invading my space. I could feel breath on the back of my neck, hear the sound of breathing getting uncomfortably close to my left ear. My pulse quickened. And I was aware, from having lived through so many similar situations, that the fight-or-flight syndrome was kicking in.

Just then, I felt a hand from behind grab my left elbow and squeeze tightly. In a matter of milliseconds, I evaluated my options: Do I wheel around and break the grip with a hand-to-hand combat maneuver I was taught as a young trooper? In the same instant, I felt a rush of fear as the thought ran through my head: "Is this it? Am I about to get clipped in St. Patrick's Cathedral?"

It was all crashing together in my brain like a torrent of flash-flood waters, when I heard a voice with a raspy Brooklyn accent whisper over my shoulder: "I don't know what the hell *you're* prayin' for, but I'm prayin' you get some calls right tomorrow."

I used my peripheral vision, and turned my head slightly to find out who had just caused my blood pressure to hit the cathedral ceiling. The rough-edged voice belonged to a man who couldn't pass up a chance to mess with a ref, a guy who looked like a physically fit version of Tony Soprano—Milwaukee head coach Mike Dunleavy. I'd known Mike from the time I came into the league and he was an NBA player. But I only gave him a quick, half-hearted smile and continued to move forward in line silently, my heart still pounding from the surprise greeting. Moments later, the calmness returned. But that's how it is for me. A sudden, unexpected flash of fear can jettison my equilibrium—*boom*—but the sense of calm returns as quickly as it had been disrupted. Those flashes have become part of my life, and that was the case inside St. Pat's that day.

After Mass let out, I met Mike outside the doors on the snowy cathedral steps. We talked about our families, the weather, just general conversation. I never let on to him how he'd unintentionally scared the hell out of me.

But that's my world: the result of having been a Jersey state trooper who infiltrated—and then infuriated—the Mob. Whether it's in a restaurant, on a flight, or in the middle of a crowded church, there are times the past jumps up and grabs me.

Those anxious feelings arise every once in a while: not every day, not every week, sometimes not for months on end. But I realize they'll never be gone from my life altogether. It's part of having been *Covert*.

It is what it is.

FOR THE RECORD

"Project Alpha bore fruit in and of itself. It had significant spillover effects. Intelligence gathered through Alpha resulted in dozens of indictments by federal and state grand juries well beyond the scope of Alpha."

Those words were spoken by Colonel Clinton Pagano, Superintendent of the New Jersey State Police and the chief architect of Project Alpha, when he testified before the United States Senate in 1981.

These are his words twenty-seven years later:

"Project Alpha was a primer into organized crime. We learned things that were never previously known about the inner workings of the Mafia. It was the biggest investigation of organized crime to that point—we were the leaders in that area. The idea that you're going to eradicate the Mob isn't realistic. As long as there's avarice and greed and violence in the minds of people, you're going to have some semblance of organized crime. But I am certain that Project Alpha set the Mafia back a long, long way.

"I knew the mission that we wanted to accomplish. I knew the dangers that would come—both physical and psychological. But I also knew the people involved. And guys like Jack Liddy and Bill Baum were very stable individuals, very strong personalities—people who also knew the mission and the dangers to the undercover operatives. The bottom line is that Bob went into something that was completely contrary to his nature and unfamiliar as far as his daily routine was concerned. We built, with great care, an entirely new life for him, a whole new identity. And I really have to credit Bob—what he did was very, very difficult.

"Throughout his undercover mission, Bob was very skillful in managing situations that could have easily gotten out of control and led to someone getting injured or killed—meaning we would have had to immediately end the operation. And if the mobsters he was around had

thought he was an informant, they'd have done him in a hundred times. No doubt about it.

"All along, we were very clear about what we were doing and very carefully documenting what we were doing, so we could step up and say we obeyed the law and we established these cases. We adopted a role, but we were not part of this kind of criminal world. Our mission was put in place by the legislature to take whatever steps were necessary to stop this unlawful conduct. And one of the unique steps we took was to cross-deputize state and federal prosecutors so that each would have access to the other's grand juries and courtrooms.

"When there was a threat on Bob's life after Project Alpha ended, we went right out there and laid it on the line to the Mob; we made it clear than any kind of retaliation would be met with similar retaliation.

"I'm proud of what we did and the kind of people we had doing it, especially Bob Delaney. That took a lot of courage. You couldn't easily find many people who had the physical and emotional stamina that Bob had. It had a negative impact on him for a time. But he came through and he went into an entirely new role in life."

The first wave of thirty-four arrests was made the day of Project Alpha's raid; many others were arrested in the days, weeks, and months that followed. They were arrested for crimes including possession of stolen property, loan sharking, unlawful sale of handguns, bookmaking, possession of counterfeit checks, possession of counterfeit New Jersey driver's licenses, interstate transportation of stolen property, possession of counterfeit New Jersey certificates of titles for trucks and cars, interstate conspiracy for possession of stolen property, illegal toxic dumping, and cases involving RICO—the Racketeer Influenced Corrupt Organizations Act. As I said before, by making use of the intelligence we obtained, additional cases and arrests were made for years after the culmination of Project Alpha. Many of the criminals we arrested in the September 28, 1977 raid, along with their ages and affiliations, are listed here:

William Brown, 24, Bruno Crime Family

Charles Cannizzo, 55, Gambino Crime Family

Anthony Cimmino, 22, associate of John DiGilio

Anthony Costanzo, 40, associate of Ralph DiNorscio

Spedito DeLuca Jr., 35, associate of John DiGilio

John DiGilio, 45, Genovese Crime Family

Ralph DiNorscio, 43, Bruno Crime Family

Joseph Insabella, 50, Gambino Crime Family

Richard Kohler, 40, associate of DiNorscio crew

David Kossakowsi, 23, street criminal

Joseph LaMorte, 47, Bruno Crime Family

Jack Lederman, 57, associate of John DiGilio

David MacQuirk, street criminal

Frank Massaro Jr., associate of John DiGilio

Lawrence Maturo, 35, associate of DiNorscio crew

George Mavrodes, 42, Gambino Crime Family

Charles Nuara, 56, DeCavalvante Crime Family

Anthony Pacilio, 34, Genovese Crime Family

Nicky Paterno, 56, Gambino Crime Family

Victor Pizzolato, 66, Lucchese Crime Family

Dennis Platt, 34, street criminal

Sylvester Reino, 47, street criminal

Daniel Roche, 49, bookmaker asssociated with Genovese Crime Family

Thomas Ruzzano, 32, associate of DiNorscio crew

Ronald Sardella, 33, associate of DiNorscio crew

William Schmidt, 38, street criminal

Joseph Stabile, 37, associate of Genovese Crime Family

Mary Szeztaye, street criminal

William Szeztaye (Mary's husband), street criminal

The impact of Project Alpha continued long after the raid was over. I provided countless hours of support testimony throughout the United States in other cases—such as *U.S. vs. Michael Clemente et al.* in New

York City, and the UNIRAC trial, which led to another conviction of Tino Fiumara and Michael Coppola. Many other arrests were made from spillover cases, and some of my old mob "friends" became new friends as confidential sources. I had more people wanting to talk than I had hours in the day. It took a few years, but my testimony finally helped put away Ray Suarez in a federal case in Harrisburg, Pennsylvania.

When I testified before the Senate, I was asked by Senator Don Nickles whether I thought the conviction ratio was sufficient and if we had enough success in the courts, in the end, to justify our efforts.

"I thought it was very successful along those lines," I replied. "We had a lot of people who pled guilty, and I think that was because of the overpowering evidence that was gained though the electronic surveillance. It was damaging to the defendant when we had the person's voice talking about the actual crime that was charged, along with the testimony of the undercover trooper or special agent."

Senator Nickles continued: "Were the terms given to those convicted sufficient or satisfactory to you? I notice that you had anywhere from three- to ten- or fifteen-year sentences, and some longer."

My response was: "I would think that they were sufficient. Of course, I would be prejudiced in that area and want the criminal to serve all those years, if not longer."

Then again, the judgment against many mobsters I investigated involved the harshest of fates.

"This is the business we have chosen."
The Godfather, Part II

John DiGilio: Shot five times in the head in 1988 while being driven in a car by fellow mobsters. DiGilio's body was found in a mortician's bag three weeks later in the Hackensack River, and George Weingartner was later indicted for the crime.

George Weingartner: Committed suicide in July 1998 during his trial for the murder of DiGilio.

Larry Ricci: Prior to being acquitted on November 8, 2005, on a charge of steering a waterfront union contract to the Mob, he disappeared. His corpse was found in the trunk of a car at the Huck Finn diner in Union, New Jersey, three weeks later.

William "Woody" Brown: Shot and killed on November 12, 1980, in front of Anthony's Pub in Newark, New Jersey.

Patty Mack: Found dead in the trunk of his 1977 Lincoln in May 1978.

Angelo Bruno: Shot to death March 12, 1980, while sitting in his car.

Johnny Simone, a.k.a. Johnny Keyes: Shot to death in Staten Island, New York, in September 1980, after Bruno's murder.

John McCullough: Shot to death on December 16, 1980, moments after being handed flowers by a hitman posing as a florist.

Jackie DiNorscio: Died of cancer on November 14, 2004, during filming of the movie based on his landmark trial, *Find Me Guilty*, starring Vin Diesel.

Raymond Suarez: Convicted on February 24, 1982, of conspiracy to defraud in the case of *The United States vs. Raymond Suarez, Albert Grasso, and Joseph Passanisi*.

Ralph DiNorscio: Died of natural causes.

Dominick DiNorscio: Died of natural causes in 1999.

Michael Coppola: Arrested and convicted for the Project Alpha/Bella Vita and New York UNIRAC cases. After serving years in federal prison, was released, only to be arrested again on March 12, 2007. He was found on New York City's Upper West Side (UPPER WEST HIDE, proclaimed the headline in the *New York Post*) after a ten-year manhunt; now facing charges for the 1977 murder of Johnny "Coca Cola" Lardiere, who was then on furlough from prison.

Tino Fiumara: Served 15 years of a 25-year sentence for convictions in the Project Alpha/Bella Vita and the New York UNIRAC cases. Upon release from federal prison, was arrested in 2003 for violating parole by failing to report contact with an organized crime fugitive (Coppola); served an additional eight months. Now under federally supervised release, he has relocated from New Jersey to Long Island, New York.

COURTSIDE

I've been courtside in both my professions. Portions of letters, reports, and notes you will find here are from my days testifying in courts, years before I started running the NBA courts. This section will offer a look into where some of my criminal cases ended up—before a judge and jury. What follows is a sampling of records from Project Alpha and spin-off cases, taking you through the final stages of an investigation that disrupted the Mob.

DEPARTMENT OF LAW AND PUBLIC SAFETY
DIVISION OF STATE POLICE

Date June 3, 1976

MEMORANDUM TO: Colonel C. L. Pagano, Superintendent, New Jersey
State Police, Division Headquarters, W. Trenton

SUBJECT   Project Alpha

It is requested that undercover Troopers

Ralph Buono #2819 and
Robert Delaney #2853

presently assigned to Project Alpha, be given
permission to carry PPK automatic handguns.

These men are in close contact with known
organized crime figures and large amounts of
money are involved in various exchanges with
the organized crime figures.

The request is made in view of the fact that
these two men have been involved in intense
situations that could seriously have jeopardized
their personal safety.

If permission is granted the men will be instructed that the carrying of the weapons is to
be authorized only in situations that warrant the
possession of the weapons and the weapons are not
to be carried in the normal daily activities.

Signature William J. Baum, Major
Title   Investigations Officer

WJB/ek

State Police 286

(x)	Type	(x)	Evaluation Code For Reporting	(x)		Reporting Date	
	Background		Of Source		Of Information		
	Surveillance		A— Completely Reliable		A— Confirmed by Other Source	Case Record / File Number	
	Interrogation		B— Fairly Reliable		B— Possibly True	D-0181	
	Interview		C— Unreliable		C— Improbable	Last Reference Number	
	Other		D— Reliability Unknown		D— Cannot Be Judged		
	Subject Or Title Of Incident			Assigned		Unit	Bureau
				Date June 16, 1977		Municipality Number	
				Assignment Number		County	

Details of Report

I received from Det. Weisert, a tape designated 0114.

At approximately 11:30 PM I arrived at the Bella Vita Restaurant located on Route 46,
Parsippany, New Jersey, where I made contact with Patrick Kelly and Lou Crescenzi. I was
then invited to the corner table located to the right side of the restaurant where I made
contact with Tino Fiumara, Joey Adonis, Michael Coppolla,   Larry Pappolla,
Ray Tango, Jerry Coppolla and Pat (LNU), another individual who was introduced to me as
Lukey (LNU). Also introduced to me at this table were Jimmy Higgins Palmieri, Joe "The
Indian" Polverino and Tony (LNU). A seating chart of the table will be attached to this
report.

A tape recording was made of most of the conversation held this date at this meeting and
this tape has been designated 0-115. Tape recorder was concealed on Patrick Kelly.

During the evening general conversation was had with those at the table and at approximatel
1 PM Jimmy Higgins Palmieri, Joe The Indian Polverino and Tony (LNU) departed the restauran

File Page Number	Reporting Officer Tpr. R. Delaney	Badge Number 2853	Page 1	Unit	Bureau	Section
			— of — Pages			

NJSP 382 (9-76)

*Since wiseguys rarely introduce each other by last name, law enforcement has developed
a lingo that identifies individuals early in an investigation when their full name is not known;
hence the shorthand "LNU" in my report above: "Last Name Unknown."

	(2) CODE	(3) CASE NUMBER	(4) REFERENCE NUMBER
ATION / UNIT			

During the early morning hours Tino Fiumara called Lou Crescenzi to his side and spoke to him briefly for a few minutes. Approximately half an hour after this took place Jerry Coppolla, Lou Crescenzi and Pat Kelly went to another table in the restaurant and had a conversation.

During the evening I spoke to Larry Poppolla and Michael Coppolla in reference to Alamo Transportation Company and Airport Landfill. Coppolla explained to me that it would be to my best interest to have the trucks which are at Alamo Transportation converted to have we lines placed in them for the dual purpose of port work and work that could be done for Airport Development and Landfill Corporations.

I departed the restaurant approximately 3:45 AM and returned to the apartment in Edgewater, New Jersey.

(34) REPORTING DATE	(35) NAME	(36) BADGE NUMBER	(37)	(38) STATION	(39) TROOP	(40) DIVISION
6/16/77	Tpr. R. Delaney	2853	PAGE 2 OF 2 PAGES			

S.P. 418A

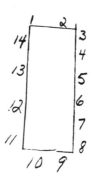

6-16-77
BELLA VITA RISTORANTE

1. TINO FIUMARA
2. JOEY ADONIS
3. JIMMY "HIGGINS"
4. MICHAEL COPPOLLA
5. LUKE (L.N.U.) SUPPA
6. PAT (L.N.U.) CERGUA

7. TPR. R.J. DELANEY
8. ████████████
9. LARRY PAPPOLLA (RICCI)
10. PAT KELLY
11 RAY TANGO
12 JERRY Coppolla
13 TONY (L.N.U.)
14 JOE "THE INDIAN" POLVERINO

PROFESSIONAL AUDIO LABORATORIES

7 SKYLARK DRIVE • SPRING VALLEY, NEW YORK 10977 • (914) 354-2229

17 April 1978

Captain Harold Spedding
Organized Crime Bureau
New Jersey State Police
Box 7068
West Trenton, New Jersey 08625

Dear Captain Spedding,

This letter is being written to inform you of the quantity and quality
of work performed by two New Jersey State Detectives, namely Robert J.
Delaney and Robert J. Weisert, in connection with Project Alpha.

These two men have exhibited a willingness to sit down and hack their
way through hundreds of hours of tape in a seemingly unending task so
as to provide the most accurate transcripts possible as input for our
processing.

These two gentlemen, who, from the subject matter of the tapes are
obviously among the best undercover operatives, are also tops when it
comes to following through on a project and seeing it progress to its
conclusion, even if it means weeks (or more) of sitting with pen, paper,
and headphones on their own time to get the best product out.

Finally, because of the efforts of these gentlemen, you can be sure
that thousands of dollars have been saved in time that we would have
had to spend in clarifying and correcting the transcripts.

I am proud to have worked with these men, and I hope to continue to
work with agents of their calibre in the future. It is obvious to me
why the New Jersey State Police has such a fine reputation.

Sincerely,

Paul Ginsberg, President
PROFESSIONAL AUDIO LABORATORIES, INC.

State of New Jersey

DEPARTMENT OF LAW AND PUBLIC SAFETY
DIVISION OF CRIMINAL JUSTICE

JOHN J. DEGNAN
ATTORNEY GENERAL

TRIAL SECTION
13 ROSZEL ROAD
CN 14
PRINCETON, NEW JERSEY 08540
TELEPHONE 609-452-9500

EDWIN H. STIER
DIRECTOR

G. MICHAEL BROWN
CHIEF, TRIAL SECTION

June 18, 1979

Capt. Harold Spedding
Commanding Officer
Organized Crime Bureau
West Trenton, New Jersey

Re: State v. Insabella
SGJ 43-77-3 (76-26)
(Possession of Stolen Property)

Dear Capt. Spedding:

During the successful prosecution of this matter, it was necessary to call a member of your command, Detective Robert Delaney, as a witness. Detective Delaney, as you know, was one of the undercover men assigned to the Project Alpha investigation. During the investigation of this case he met on numerous occasions with the defendants and was responsible for recording many of the conversations held with them. He possessed a detailed knowledge of the events and participants which gave rise to this prosecution. His testimony was critical to the conviction of the remaining defendant in this case.

Detective Delaney cooperated with this office during all stages of the prosecution and trial of this matter. He was extremely well prepared and displayed a keen awareness of the need for his testimony and the importance of being totally familiar with all facets of it. Detective Delaney remained with the case during the entire trial which was very helpful, and indicated to the jury that he as a police officer was interested in its outcome.

Too often, police officers have a tendency to feel that their responsibility and obligation ends at the time of arrest or indictment. Detective Delaney, however, demonstrated by his conduct and interest an acute understanding that the assistance and cooperation of the police officer is essential all the way through the trial of the matter if convictions are to be obtained. His performance and professional attitude reflected great credit upon himself and the organization of which he is a member.

I wish to take this opportunity to extend my appreciation and that of my office and to commend the excellent cooperation and conduct of Detective Delaney. It is only through the support, cooperation and professional dedication exemplified by Detective Delaney that prosecutions can be successful and convictions obtained.

Very truly yours,

Charles J. Hanlon, Jr.
Deputy Attorney General

CJH/dk

cc: Det. Robert Delaney

UNITED STATES DEPARTMENT OF JUSTICE

FEDERAL BUREAU OF INVESTIGATION

In Reply, Please Refer to
File No.

26 Federal Plaza
New York, New York 10007
May 14, 1980

Colonel Clinton L. Pagano, Superintendent
State of New Jersey
Department of Law and Public Safety
Division of State Police
Post Office Box 7068
West Trenton, New Jersey 08625

Dear Colonel Pagano:

This letter is to commend to you New Jersey State Police Detective Robert J. Delaney, who furnished this office with outstanding and sustained assistance in the recent investigation and prosecution of United States of America versus Michael Clemente, Et Al, which was successfully concluded on May 2, 1980, at United States District Court for the Southern District of New York.

Although several State Police officers provided valuable help regarding Clemente, I have been advised that Detective Delaney's contributions over a ten month period, commencing in July of 1979, are deserving of special mention and appreciation.

Besides investigative assistance, Detective Delaney made himself available for literally hundreds of hours, including numerous weekends and evenings, wherein he transcribed tape recordings, reviewed documents and records, and assisted in preparation of interviews and witness testimony. Throughout these many hours, Detective Delaney continued to give invaluable investigative aid to the Assistant United States Attorneys and several Special Agents assigned to Clemente. Moreover, he did so in a completely productive, courteous and selfless manner.

In several important instances, he provided critical insight and imagination in the interpretation and presentation of evidence. In one instance, it was Detective Delaney who deciphered a series of "code" names used by the defendants, Tino Fiumara, Carol Gardner, Thomas Buzzanca and Vincent Colucci, on recorded conversations which he also transcribed. The identification of these defendants by "code" name was of great significance in proving the theory of the Government's case.

As another example of this fine Officer's investigative ability, he was able to make a photographic identification of the defendant Gardner after having observed him with Fiumara for approximately one hour on just one occasion over two years before his identification.

Also, the outstanding integrity of Detective Delaney before the jury which heard his testimony in Clemente was singularly impressive. Although other witnesses in the case had identified a tape recorded voice as one of the defendants, Detective Delaney testified that he was unable to so identify that particular defendant, notwithstanding the fact that he had known said defendant personally while working in an undercover capacity in 1977.

The Special Agents who worked with Detective Delaney in Clemente have requested that I communicate their sincere personal appreciation, as well as their professional respect, for the truly outstanding assistance which this able Officer so enthusiastically rendered. Let me also add my personal good wishes.

This dedicated Officer is a credit to your organization and its highest professional reputation.

Very truly yours,

NEIL J. WELCH
Assistant Director in Charge

cc: New Jersey State Police
    Detective Robert J. Delaney
    State of New Jersey
    Department of Law and Public Safety
    Division of State Police
    Post Office Box 7068
    West Trenton, New Jersey 08625

-2-

United States Attorney
Southern District of New York

DHB:mb

One St. Andrew's Plaza
New York, New York 10007

June 16, 1980

Lieutenant John J. Liddy
New Jersey State Police
146 Rt. 17
Hackensack, New Jersey   07601

Dear Lieutenant Liddy:

         I write this letter to commend Detective Robert J.
Delaney. I worked with Detective Delaney during the past
year in connection with United States v. Clemente an
organized crime/labor racketeering trial in the United
States District Court for the Southern District of New York.
I can say without hesitation that Detective Delaney's work
was superb.

         In March, 1979, our office indicted twelve defend-
ants in a 245-count indictment which charged racketeering,
conspiracy, extortion, illegal labor payments, perjury and
tax offenses. The crux of the case was an illegal enterprise
which controlled the Ports of New York and New Jersey through
a pattern of racketeering activity including extortion and
illegal labor payments. The defendants included Michael
Clemente and Tino Fiumara who are powerful members of the
Genovese crime family and Thomas Buzzanca, Vincent Colucci
and Carol "Junior" Gardner who are presidents of locals of
the International Longshoremen's Association. After four
months of trial at which the Government proved over
$1,500,000 in payoffs, all defendants on trial were con-
victed.

         Detective Delaney provided invaluable assistance
to our office and was crucial to the success of our case.
Detective Delaney's undercover work in Operation Alpha
resulted in devastating evidence against a number of our
defendants including Fiumara. Because of Delaney's work we
not only were able to prove Fiumara controlled the waterfront in New Jersey, but were able to introduce a tape on
which Fiumara admitted that he controlled shipping lines.

Detective Delaney's testimony was totally responsible for convicting Michael Copolla, Fiumara's right hand
man. The jury hung as to all counts against Copolla except
the ones to which Detective Delaney testified. Thanks to
Detective Delaney, Copolla was convicted on conspiracy to
commit racketeering, which carries a 20 year maximum
sentence. I am convinced that without Detective Delaney's
testimony Copolla would not have been convicted at all.

I do not need to reiterate the outstanding work
Detective Delaney did while working undercover; you are well
aware of the diligence, ingenuity and skill he exhibited
during the investigative stage of Operation Alpha. I would,
however, like to bring to your attention - from an attorney's
point of view - the exemplary job Detective Delaney did in
helping the Government prepare for trial and in testifying
at trial. Our office did not become aware of the connection
of Operation Alpha with the facts of our case until well
after our indictment. At that time, we faced tremendous
pressure to assimilate a vast amount of evidence in a very
short time. Detective Delaney was invaluable in helping us
to prepare for trial. He worked countless hours - including
nights and weekends - to acquaint us with the details of
your investigation and to extract pertinent evidence from
thousands of pages of reports and hundreds of hours of
tapes. He also spent scores of hours working with me in my
office to prepare to testify. Detective Delaney coordinated
our efforts with the State Police, pulled together information from numerous divergent sources and provided invaluable
assistance to the FBI in its investigation. Over and above
Detective Delaney's substantive contributions to our case, I
was most impressed by his attitude. Detective Delaney never
gave the slightest indication that he was giving less than
100% because our trial was "somebody elses' case." From the
beginning Detective Delaney became a full member of our team
and acted with the singleminded purpose that our defendants
were criminals who should be brought to justice regardless
of the forum. Such selfless dedication to law enforcement
is all too rare.

Perhaps even more impressive than Detective Delaney's
pretrial work was his conduct as a witness. His demeanor
was perfect and he acted professionally in every respect.
He listened carefully to questions both on direct and cross
examination and his answers were always succinct yet fully
responsive. Although Detective Delaney was subjected to
vitriolic and abusive cross-examination he maintained his
composure at all times. Just as importantly, Detective

Delaney was extremely conscientious about being completely accurate and honest in his testimony. He was scrupulous in testifying only to that which he remembered and in always avoiding the ever-present temptation to color ones testimony to make the case just a little stronger. In short, the jury was extremely impressed by Detective Delaney's testimony, as was everyone else in the courtroom. I can say without hesitation that Detective Delaney was as good a witness as I have ever put on the stand.

Detective Delaney should be highly commended - not just for his valor in the field, but for his thoroughness, dedication and skill in helping the Government to successfully prosecute its case. After all, no matter how much a law enforcement officer accomplishes in his investigation, it all goes for naught if the criminal is not eventually convicted. Detective Delaney is a credit to the New Jersey State Police and to the law enforcement profession generally.

Very truly yours,

JOHN S. MARTIN, JR.
United States Attorney

By: _____

DANIEL H. BOOKIN
Assistant United States Attorney
Telephone: (212) 791-1156

U.S. Department of Justice

United States Attorney
Middle District of Pennsylvania

CMO:JAS:sks

Federal Building, 228 Walnut Street   *717/782-4482*
Post Office Box 793   *FTS/590-4482*
Harrisburg, Pennsylvania 17108
March 8, 1982

Mr. Robert J. Delaney
1200 Plymouth Drive
Brick, New Jersey   08723

Dear Mr. Delaney:

On February 24, 1982, the jury in United States of America vs. Raymond Suarez, Albert Grasso, and Joseph Passanisi returned a verdict of guilty as to all the defendants upon the Indictment charging conspiracy to defraud.

The Government presented the testimony of some fifteen witnesses in the trial of this case; and you, of course, were one of these. Each witness' testimony in this case contributed to the presentation of an accurate and complete picture of this criminal episode for the jury and contributed to a just and proper verdict.

On behalf of the United States, we thank you for your cooperation in this matter.

Very truly yours,

CARLON M. O'MALLEY, JR.
United States Attorney

J. ANDREW SMYSER
Assistant U. S. Attorney

AFTERWORD

"I knew there was a way out. I knew there was another kind of life because I had read about it. I knew there were other places, and there was another way of being."

—*Oprah Winfrey*

When you're on the road as much as I am, watching TV becomes a way of life. My main staples of entertainment are ESPN, CNN, and MSNBC. But you might be surprised to know that one show I watch without fail is *Oprah*. As a guy whose life so often revolves around games, I find myself drawn to a program about the game of life. Oprah's words, quoted above from a 1991 interview, remind me of my search for "a new way of being"—as I gained a greater sense of self-awareness in the tumultuous years after Project Alpha.

So many folks over the years have said "you should write a book" when hearing my undercover story. Segments on ABC, ESPN, and HBO brought attention to the story of Bobby Covert, as did an array of newspaper and magazine articles, but deciding when and why to tell this tale took years. This story, like our lives, grows each day. Had this book been written shortly after my undercover years infiltrating the Mob, it would not have told the full story.

This book is not about one person. It is about the thousands of men and women who ensure that order is maintained in society—law enforcement, military, and government—who serve us on a daily basis. Some have made the ultimate sacrifice. All are being saluted here.

Project Alpha was a success because of the personal sacrifice, dedication, courage, and teamwork of all involved. Those qualities are what people who uphold the law and maintain our security have done since long before Project Alpha; they continue to do so to this day.

I had various authors who were available and interested in my story. I got lucky again—Dave Scheiber wrote a two-part article on my life for the *St. Petersburg Times* in 2006. Simply put—we clicked. My wife Billie says it best: "Dave tells your story, not his version of your story."

I coined a saying years back.

"Some people *go* through experiences, while other people *grow* through experiences."

My hope is that *Covert* did that for you.

I know it did for me.

Stay safe.

A NOTE FROM THE AUTHORS

"The greater the obstacle, the more glory in overcoming it."

—Moliere

People have asked me, "How long did it take you to write this book?" My usual response? "Over forty years."

As with most joking remarks, there's an element of truth in the answer. *Covert: My Years Infiltrating the Mob* tells my life story from about age seven to the present. We have not listed footnotes or any other traditional types of source citations and references. That's because I lived this story, and have told it over and over—before numerous government committees in the months after we surfaced, and for years before law-enforcement training academies and seminars throughout the United States and Canada, including the FBI Academy. I have also met with members of European law-enforcement agencies and shared the effects of living undercover.

During my fourteen-year career, I was assigned to the New Jersey State Police Academy and told the Project Alpha story weekly. To this day, I make regular presentations at the Federal Law Enforcement Training Center/Homeland Security ICE (Immigration and Customs Enforcement) Undercover Operations School. I also have reviewed my "daily reports" made during the Project Alpha investigation, as well as my testimony before the 1981 United States Senate Hearings on Organized Crime and Waterfront Corruption.

I have constantly relived my experience through the numerous newspaper articles and TV interviews about my undercover days. It may help you to understand my ability to recall life episodes by thinking of a traumatic experience that *you* lived through—national or personal. Focus on the details you remember concerning the assassinations of President

Kennedy, Dr. Martin Luther King, Jr., or Bobby Kennedy, or September 11, 2001. You will remember more than you care to recall. That is why the stories you have read in *Covert* are still fresh in my mind after all these years. This is not a unique talent I have; it is what most of us are capable of doing after experiencing a life-changing event.

My co-author Dave Scheiber joined me for days at a time visiting my old family neighborhoods, my schools and college, as well as the hangouts of Bobby Covert. We spent time at the buildings that once housed the Mid-Atlantic and Alamo trucking companies, and we walked the streets from my undercover life—seeing the apartments where I lived, the clubs, restaurants, and diners I frequented, and the northern Jersey enclaves in which the Mob flourished. Dave took photos, and his video camera and tape recorder were constantly running, documenting my words and providing an invaluable visual aid when we wrote *Covert*.

In addition, the NBA Operations Department, in particular Matt Winick, Vice President–Director of Scheduling, was instrumental in providing information regarding my NBA career.

Some names and identifying details have been changed or omitted in the writing of this book.

The practice of keeping the "daily reports" is something that I carry with me to this day. I continue to maintain a journal. I document conversations, events, and situations—notes that will be helpful when the time comes for the next book. I look forward to sharing those stories with you as well.

—Bob Delaney
February 2008

Throughout the research and writing of *Covert*, I have never ceased to be amazed by Bob's recall of details and stories from his life—from his childhood days growing up in Paterson, New Jersey, to his tension-filled years infiltrating the Mob, and later building a new life in basketball. One thing happened repeatedly during our countless hours of interviews between December 2006 and June 2007: Whenever Bob related details of his life experiences, the process would trigger other vivid memories. He has a natural gift for conveying both the content of what happened and the event's context and nuances. His meticulous daily reports from Project Alpha also proved invaluable to me, as did the voluminous testimony he and other officials provided to the U.S. Senate. Interviews with many of his family members, friends, and former colleagues rounded out the picture, along with our visits to the places of Bob's past. But in the end, it was Bob's memory—and his constant determination to dig deep for significant details—that was the best source of all.

—Dave Scheiber
February 2008

Some names and identifying details have been changed in the writing of this book. Where a name has been changed, any similarity to any person with that or a similar name is purely coincidental.

—B.D. and D.S.

ACKNOWLEDGMENTS

"We cannot hold a torch to light another's path without brightening our own."

—*Ben Sweetland*

My co-author and I have had many who have "brightened" our paths, and we want to thank and acknowledge everyone who has helped *Covert* along the way.

So many people played a part in one way or another—and as the old saying goes, we apologize if we've left anyone off the list.

We've been fortunate to be part of a great team. Uwe Stender, our literary agent, opened a door to an amazing organization that we became part of—Union Square Press, Sterling Publishing. Philip Turner, editorial director, has guided us with his expertise and enthusiasm. His colleagues Charles Nurnberg, Iris Blasi, Kate Rados, Jason Prince, Marilynn Kretzer, Leigh Ann Ambrosi, Toula Ballas, and so many others, have been outstanding. Copyeditor Phil Gaskill gives new meaning to the words "attention to detail."

I would like to thank the National Basketball Association— Commissioner David Stern, Russ Granik, Adam Silver, Joel Litvin, Stu Jackson, Matt Winick, Jeff Mishkin, Ed T. Rush, Ronnie Nunn, Brian McIntyre, Tim Frank, Peter Lagiovane, Rosi Garcia, Cassandra Thompson, Mary Kate Shea, Teresa Sanzari, Paul Brazeau, Lee Jones, Joe Borgia, Tom Carelli, Todd Harris, Dana Jones, Joe Amati, and everyone at the NBA's New York and New Jersey offices.

Terry Lyons became a member of the *Covert* team shortly after retiring as NBA's Vice President of International Communications, and his experience and expertise have been a tremendous asset.

I also want to express my appreciation to past and present NBA officials Joey Crawford, Steve Javie, Ron Garretson, Mike Callahan, Danny Crawford, Bennett Salvatore, Bernie Fryer, Mark Wunderlich, Violet Palmer, Wally Rooney, Jess Kersey, Dick Bavetta, Bill Oakes, Hugh Evans, and Darrell Garretson for their friendship and help along the way; and to *all* the officials of the NBA, the Continental Basketball Association, and the summer pro and high school leagues who helped me get to where I am today, especially the IAABO Shore Board No. 194—with helping hands from Tom Lopes, Dave Vivino, and the late Mickey Hart.

In addition, I extend special thanks to:

The New Jersey State Police for the training that I carry with me to this day: Colonels David Kelly, Clinton Pagano, and Rick Fuentes, all my classmates from the NJSP 88th Class, and all the fine men and women I served with during my career.

Bob Scott for taking me under his wing and teaching me how to be a trooper and a leader; Gary Rinker, my trooper-coach; Captain Joe Rogalski, my first troop commander; Jack Liddy, one hell of a boss and an even better friend; the Project Alpha undercover team: State Troopers Ralph Buono, Bob Weisert, Bill Baum, Dirk Ottens, Bob Mackin, Charlie Hanlon, Al Duranik, Gary McWhorter, Baron Lardiere, Joe Saia, Bob Hopkins, and so many others behind the scenes to ensure my safety and support to get the job done.

Former Trooper Sam Cunninghame, whose guidance and support continues to this day.

The Former Troopers Association, especially Gail Carrigan for her help and research.

The FBI Special Agents assigned to Project Alpha—Al Koehler, Rich Blake, Len Perreira, and all the support agents; Special Agents P. J. Jumonville and Chuck Avakian.

My good friend and fellow Patersonian, Joe Pistone, a.k.a. Donnie Brasco, and Louie Freeh. Thanks for caring and helping in more ways than you guys realize.

John Schroth, fellow trooper, who knew something was troubling me and had the courage to address it. Thank you for your friendship and guidance.

Dr. Hank Campbell, my college psychology professor, who helped me years later learn the difference between Covert and Delaney.

My dear lifelong friends Jim and Laura DiLella.

My family—grandparents, aunts, uncles, cousins, and friends. I was truly raised by a "village," and so many members of it influenced my life, including my nephews Mark and Taylor, and my niece Siobhan.

Father Vince Malloy and Father John Sullivan, high school teachers who became lifelong friends.

All the pilots, flight attendants, mechanics, airline support folks, cab and limo drivers, and hotel personnel who get me safely from one town to the next in this vagabond lifestyle I lead.

Joyce Aschenbrenner, Nick Valvano, and Dick Vitale, for giving me the opportunity to be part of the Jimmy V Cancer Research team.

Ron and Laurie Coleman, Dana and Ken Miklos, Mark and Kathy Tudyk, and Sue and Richard Ellis—thanks for giving of your time reading and rereading our chapters.

Ryan Henderson, for taking care of the day-to-day operations of Delaney Consultants and keeping me on track.

Eddie and Andrew Silverman and everyone at SOS Security for doing what you do so well.

Ian Solomon, for his skillful graphics touch with our proposal.

Perennial Sports and Entertainment—Lamell McMorris and Brian Lam for representing me in this project and so many others.

The *Star-Ledger* library for providing us with the paper's account of the Project Alpha raid.

Production teams at HBO, ESPN, and ABC for conveying my story in television profiles so well; and the writers who shared my story over the years in award-winning style: Neal Hirschfeld for the *New York Daily News,* Jackie MacMullan for the *Boston Globe,* Chris Anderson for the *Sarasota Herald-Tribune,* and, most recently, my co-author Dave

Scheiber of the *St. Petersburg Times*, a true professional and a pleasure to work with.

—Bob Delaney

February 2008

For me, the ball started rolling toward *Covert* on a golf course. One of Bob's golfing friends, Tom Jewell, passed on a story idea about a certain NBA referee to my colleague, golf writer Bob Harig, who promptly alerted me. So, thank you, guys, for a great tip, and my further appreciation to the sports staff at the *St. Petersburg Times*, where an array of talented people contributed to the top-notch presentation of the series, including photographer Dirk Shadd and designer Chris Kozlowski.

I'm also indebted to longtime friend Jim Melvin, a former *Times* sports design director/writer and now an author (*The Death Wizard Chronicles*) living in South Carolina. Jim graciously steered us to his literary agent at TriadaUS, the aforementioned Uwe Stender, whose enthusiasm and efforts ultimately led to the perfect home with Philip Turner at Union Square Press/Sterling Publishing.

In addition, I'd like to thank my daughter Mollie for her diligent assistance in transcribing interviews; all my family members for their ongoing support and excitement; Mary Evertz for her consistently excellent advice; co-worker Roger Fischer, always ready as a sounding board; and *Times* sports editor Jack Sheppard and executive editor Neil Brown for "working a trade" to bring me back to sports from news features in 2004.

And lastly, I offer my gratitude to Bob Delaney—a man who has reached the top of everything he has undertaken with an unparalleled work ethic and energy to match. Thanks for the opportunity to help bring your remarkable story to life in the pages of *Covert*.

—Dave Scheiber

February 2008

INDEX

DiNorscio, Dominick (a.k.a.
    Tommy Adams), 120
  Bruno Crime Family and, 36
  death of, 235
  Kelly and, 58–60
  on New Jersey waterfront, 36
  in prison, 59, 77
  as young thug, 132
DiNorscio, Jackie (a.k.a. Jackie
    Adams), 36, 112
  death of, 235
  demands from, 83
  extortion by, 100–103
  fake hit by, 127–128
  favors demanded by, 98–99
  girlfriend of, 100
  Kelly and, 58–59
  in prison, 131–132
  recordings, 178
  threats from, 131–132
  trial of, 100
  trooper beaten by, 57
  wife of, 100
DiNorscio, Ralph (a.k.a. Ralph
    Adams; Ralph DeVita), 36,
    132, *Photo Insert*
  arrest of, 233
  auto theft by, 62–63
  death of, 235
  Kelly and, 58–59
Disorganized crime, 172, 180
Doby, Larry, 24
Docks, 143. *See also* Senate
    Waterfront Corruption hear-
    ings; waterfront corruption;
    International Longshoremen's
    Association (ILA)
  Mafia and, 127
  Mob and, 14
Donaghy, Tim, 200

Donaldson, James, 194–195
Donnie Brasco, 173
Douglas, Kirk, 1
Drucker, Jimmy, 190
Drug cartels, 182
Dunleavy, Mike, 228
Duranik, Al, 72, 258
Durham, Terry, 3, 7
Duvall, Robert, 6

E
Eisenberg, Lewis, 209
Erving, Julius, 190
ESPN SportsCenter, 198, 222
ESU. *See* State Police Electronic
    Surveillance Unit (ESU)
Evans, Hugh, 197, 258
Ewing, Patrick, 188, 203, *Photo
    Insert*
Extortion
  of Crescenzi, 107, 149, 177
  by DiNorscio, Dominick, 59
  by DiNorscio, Jackie, 100–103
  by Fiumara, 102, 105–107
  impact of, 178
  by Mob, 175
  testimony about, 178

F
FBI. *See* Federal Bureau of
    Investigation (FBI)
FDNY. *See* New York Fire
    Department (FDNY)
Fear
  author's battle with, 228–229
  "footsteps of," 169
Federal Bureau of Investigation
    (FBI), 14, 38, 39, 40, 171
  electronic surveillance unit,
    42–43
  Koehler as agent, 39, 113